THE PRIME OF YOUR LIFE

Miriam Stoppard, MD MRCP, practised clinical medicine for seven years, specializing in dermatology for the last three, before joining a major drug company working in clinical research. She was Medical Director, then Managing Director, before leaving in 1980 to devote herself full-time to writing, broadcasting and medical education.

Miriam Stoppard was Radio London's resident phone-in doctor from 1970 to 1972 and presented the BBC radio series *Well Woman*, devoted to problems of women's health. Dr Stoppard was medical presenter on television's *Don't Ask Me*, *Don't Just Sit There*, *The Health Show*, *So You Want to Stop Smoking*, *Where There's Life*, and *Baby & Co*. She has contributed articles to many leading magazines and writes a regular column on medical matters for *Woman*. Her books include *Miriam Stoppard's Book of Health Care*, the best-selling *Every Woman's Lifeguide* and *The Pregnancy and Birth Book*.

Miriam Stoppard is married to the playwright Tom Stoppard and has two sons and two stepsons.

THE
PRIME OF
YOUR LIFE

Dr Miriam Stoppard

PENGUIN BOOKS

Penguin Books Ltd, Harmondsworth, Middlesex, England
Viking Penguin Inc., 40 West 23rd Street, New York, New York 10010, U.S.A.
Penguin Books Australia Ltd, Ringwood, Victoria, Australia
Penguin Books Canada Limited, 2801 John Street, Markham, Ontario, Canada L3R 1B4
Penguin Books (N.Z.) Ltd, 182–190 Wairau Road, Auckland 10, New Zealand

First published in hardback by Dorling Kindersley Ltd under the title *50 plus Lifeguide* 1983
Published in Penguin Books 1986
Copyright © Dorling Kindersley Ltd, London, 1983
Text copyright © Miriam Stoppard, 1983
All rights reserved

Printed and bound in Great Britain by
William Clowes Limited, Beccles and London
Typeset in Sabon

Preface

Up until recent times very little attention was paid to our special needs as we got older and our mature years were quite wrongly regarded as a time of increasing decrepitude and frustration. Today, however, we certainly expect to live longer and we are in a position to benefit from modern scientific discoveries with regard to prolonging good health and the current re-thinking of life choices. As a result, for most of us this period is the most important in our lives. It has become increasingly necessary, therefore, to provide products and philosophies which will sustain people throughout this very important period – a fact borne out by the increasing attention paid to this age group by all areas of society. It is my hope that this book, with its practical, positive outlook and wealth of useful information should add years to a reader's life, or at the least, make it a healthier and happy one.

Contents

Retirement 185

This is the time in our lives when we are required to make abrupt changes in our standards of living, daily activities and social contacts. Here, the sociological, ethnic, psychological and financial issues of retirement are discussed as well as pre-retirement plans and preparation.

Specialist help 199

It can be useful to consider help from various other health specialists as long as you bear in mind that you can't necessarily expect outstanding results. Your doctor will advise you of the benefits or disadvantages.

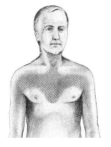
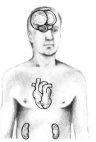

Special medical problems 211

The special conditions which show as we get older occur because our bodies' machinery is changing down a gear and this alters the way they work. This chapter considers the warning signs which may represent something dangerous so that you are aware of them and can seek appropriate medical help in good time without feeling alarm.

Living with long-term ailments 265

Fifty onwards is a significant stage in our lives when we may not be as fit and healthy as we would like, or we may have a partner or parent who needs our special attention. Here are suggestions for various aids to overcome any lack of full mobility or any other long-term ailment.

Adapting your environment 297

This chapter illustrates the best methods to "age-proof" the house in order to make it more comfortable and safe, and it introduces some of the numerous labour-saving devices available.

Growing through life

Today, we expect to live a good deal longer than our ancestors did. The average life expectancy of men is seventy-five and women eighty, this means that the majority of us live one-third of our lives beyond fifty. It is not surprising then that there is a clamour for products and philosophies to enable us to get the most out of this important period in our lives.

Research has shown, irrespective of gender, that people with the greatest feeling of well-being are the older ones – at last we have arrived. Our satisfaction with life, however, depends on success in the spheres of work and social relations. Through these we may find mature love, true friendship, the freedom to make independent choices, self-respect, and a fulfilling lifestyle.

Throughout our mature years we constantly search for some meaning of life and by middle age we are in a better position to confront this question. Now is the time for us to step back from the rat race and consider those dormant skills that hitherto we have not had the time and courage to develop. The tendency is to think that we have stopped growing. The truth is that growth in the latter one third of life can bring ultimate happiness.

Fifty plus

It's time to have confidence and pride in celebrating our fiftieth, sixtieth and seventieth birthdays. No longer need we worry so much about what other people think or say, and we needn't be as concerned with saying the right thing at the right time to the right people.

Women and middle age

Many women find their greatest happiness in middle age. They have passed the menopause, their grown-up children have left home and they are friends with them, but not confined by them, they have a firm feeling of their own identities for the first time. They feel less lonely, less bored and more in tune with their inner needs and the outside world.

Women in middle age are more likely to report no major fears for the future. Generally, women thirty-five to fifty feel better about themselves than they did when they were younger, and they may even reach a new level of sexual pleasure. This is a very different view of the life-cycle held by younger women. For many women a sense of accomplishment influences how smoothly they enter middle age. For most, a satisfactory job can help this transition as the mothering role diminishes. Paid employment seems to contribute most to self-esteem.

Adjustment can be difficult for women who have interrupted their careers for family life. Such women were obviously independent and achievers with many intellectual interests when they were younger. During the long years of marriage they suppressed their ambition to become conscientious wives and mothers. As they enter middle life many of these women report that their energy levels seem to be going down, their weights going up and their spirits, especially as the youngest child leaves home, are sinking into despondency.

The intelligent "doers" manage to pull out of this as they disengage from their mothering roles and are stimulated to revive their more assertive goal-orientated skills.

Many women feel excited as they move into their fifties. They start to be themselves, they no longer repress their anger or carry on trying to be perfect in order to make everyone love them. It could even be the time when women realize they could be better off without the men who have kept them in unsatisfactory, bad marriages.

Women often feel increasingly satisfied with life in their fifties until they reach fifty-seven and then from this point their satisfaction just seems to soar.

Men and middle age

The picture is not quite the same for men at this age. They are likely to feel distinctly dissatisfied at fifty: worried about health, career and missed opportunities and ageing. However, research has proven that satisfaction follows the same path as with women – satisfaction rises.

Men, like women, quite mistakenly feel that getting older is synonymous with things getting worse. The pattern of milestones within a man's life is more volatile than a woman's, men's ups and downs occur more frequently and usually at different times from women's. Nonetheless, it seems probable that older men are happier and more satisfied with life than younger men.

Men who are more satisfied with life and happiest are those who have expanded their interests well beyond those provided by their careers. By the age of fifty if not before, they are involved in art, music, gardening, dancing, cooking and community service – all things which lead to self-esteem and the discovery of leadership qualities they didn't know they had. They walk or jog, play strenuous sports and get involved in outdoor activities with their children and friends. They feel more relaxed, laugh more, and get more aesthetic enjoyment out of their environment! Many men in their fifties and sixties

SATISFACTION WITH LIFE

Gail Sheehy in her book *Pathfinders* describes a questionnaire relating to members of the American Bar Association. Those lawyers who were judged to be most happy and contented were almost all older than forty-seven. Those who were older than fifty-five thought life was wonderful and were loving it, but the most contented age group of all consisted of lawyers over the age of sixty-five.

Ages 37 to 45

"Not enough time for anything but work."
"Obsessed with money and material success."
"Feel this is my last chance to pull away from the pack."
"Worry about becoming trapped by others finding out I am not as good as they thought I was. About messing up my personal life."
"Uncertain about my objectives. Ambivalent about my values."
"Envy the spirituality of others."

Ages 46 to 55

"Finally feel I have it all together."
"Secure enough to stop running or struggling."
"Easy to relax, open myself to new feelings, take vacations."
"Not so concerned about what others think of me."
"More willing to help others, not so competitive and compulsive."
"Feel that time is running out."
"Suddenly notice my friends are looking old and unhealthy."
"Was over-monitoring my own health."

Ages 56 to 65

"Delighted to see vigour of life is continuing."
"Pay more attention to my body and I am in better physical condition than I was five years ago."
"Sex is still important."
"Feel a new tolerance. Formed companionship with my mate."
"More focus on the spiritual dimension."
"Vacations are essential."
"Less concerned with money, more concerned with comfort."

feel an opening up of their expressive, artistic and intuitive lives, the "feminine" sides of their characters which they repressed as part of their younger "macho" image.

Opportunities for the future

One of the most reassuring thoughts of all is that we have special strengths and new potentials in middle age that we don't have at any other time of life and which usually find their expression between forty-five and sixty. Here are some of them:

- Relaxation of stereotyped roles.
- Greater assertiveness in women.
- Greater expressiveness in men.
- Being free to say what we think.
- Being free to pick up past interests.
- More time and money for ourselves.
- More tolerance towards others.
- Greater opportunites for companionship with our partners.

- A chance to make new friendships with our children.
- The possibility of contributing to the community, and having time for hobbies.

By the time we are in middle and later age we know ourselves better than at any other stage in our lives. We know who we are, what we need, and how to get it. All we have to do now is make the effort in the best way we know how.

One of the mistakes that all of us make at every age is believing we'll be doing the same things, having the same interests, same aims, same friends, the same preoccupations. If we imagine having a brisk game of tennis now and imagine trying to do that in twenty years time of course it's depressing. But the chances are we won't be doing that or wanting to. If we're still playing tennis, the game will depend more on finesse than speed, and be just as pleasurable for that. But luckily tennis could be replaced by leisurely and sociable bowls, golf and other relaxing sports which open up new interests and friends for us.

Most of us are quite rightly stubborn about resisting any pressures that may be put on us to reduce our daily commitments because removal of anything prominent in our lives may we think lead to a vacuum. This need not necessarily be so. Research has shown conclusively that release from demanding, lengthy work means more enjoyable leisure time, closer family ties and better physical health. Our fifty plus years are increasingly being looked upon by everyone as a normal and expected phase of the life path which we look forward to, prepare for, and enjoy.

What we forget is that each age has its own pleasures and its own excitements. No one I've talked to who is contented with their life as they grow older will admit that life is any less thrilling or less challenging. This is because our view of life and what makes it satisfying and fulfilling changes, if we let it and don't fight against it. It's as though the prescription for our spectacles changes as we get older so that we see the same things in a different way. Different enough so that what we desire and what we can achieve are not disparate. And this is as you'd expect. We'd be a sadly adapted race if we hadn't learned how to make each of our ages successful and happy. The truth about our mature years is that we've learned most of the lessons and consolidated them, so if we allow ourselves to grow we stand a greater chance of achieving happiness than at any other time in our life.

The rewards are marvellous to enjoy. Remember those words by Ezra Pound: "One of the pleasures of middle age is to find out that one *was* right and that one was much righter than one knew at say seventeen or twenty-three."

Society and the older generation

Why should the number of years we have lived be considered so important? Physical, mental and social ages are far more important than chronological age. We have to resist the relationship which society tries to create between chronological age and human value. Ten years older does not mean ten years worse. It means ten years more valuable. Many of us overlook the important fact that society *needs* us as we get older. Of course, society has need for "junior" and "senior" people but there is no need to press people into premature responsibility or premature retirement or, for that matter, to hold them back from opportunities they wish to pursue regardless of age. We would all be helped if we bore in mind the difference between ageing and being old. As ageing is a continuous process over the years, it should be looked on more as a dynamic change or set of changes, rather than a cliff we jump off at a certain time.

Turning the clock back

We will probably see "old age" rolled back for quite a time to come. Very recently, statisticians would define "old" as sixty-five. More and more, this definition is moving towards seventy-five. This makes more sense in terms of life span and the activity older people can enjoy if they are encouraged to. In the USA the mandatory retirement age is now in the process of being moved back to the age of seventy – a sign that a government recognized the retirement age of sixty-five was an increasingly inappropriate policy. Renaldo Madure, the anthropologist, found a colony of artists in northern India where the oldest members were encouraged to be at their most creative and to advance themselves and their art on into old age. In the West, people reach an early peak and then face years of doing little. At last this is changing.

There is a move to stop pushing older people aside. More of us are realizing that people and society take leave of each other whenever they want to with mutual consent. There is a lessening in the extent to which society steers people to the sideline. Of course, there is a natural tendency for older people to remove themselves from the mainstream of society. What we have to guard against is discrimination and segregation of the older members of society as a matter of political expedience.

Most of us nowadays accept that we are older, this is "successful ageing" (see *Keeping a tranquil mind*), which means that we have the inner calmness, confidence, experience and maturity to be of great benefit to society for many years to come. Of course, in order to be able to do this we must keep as physically active as we possibly can.

In the past, old and young alike worked together as best they could on whatever tasks had to be done to keep the family and the community in a healthy state. Older people worked as long as they were able and the young worked as early as they were able. It was the way a person functioned that determined when he or she entered and departed from the work force.

In today's world the young and old are increasingly excluded from this role. The basis for this is not biological, because children and older people are generally healthier and stronger than their ancestors, it is cultural. People are defined as too young or too old for much longer periods of their lives than they ever were before. We have to guard against this sociological type-casting. We must begin to see ageing as it was seen not so very long ago, as a ritualistic progression from having one's worth measured in terms of productivity through experience to wisdom and seniority.

Keeping physically fit

Good health is not the prerogative of the young. Researchers in the USA have recorded that many people remain active and fit until well after their late seventies. However, as our bodies begin to age from our early twenties onwards, they require special attention if we are to keep them as fit as possible. This chapter therefore concentrates on the initiation and maintenance of good health habits at as early an age as possible, and the adaptation of routines to meet changing lifestyles. Feeling physically well, rather than just being not ill, involves adjusting our health habits to accommodate natural changes.

Knowing what and why changes occur as we get older means that we can make sensible decisions about changes in diet, exercise programmes, skin care, smoking and drinking habits, choice of clothing, sleeping patterns, even about where we live and work. Most important, we can put these changes into practice early enough to offset some of the undesirable aspects of ageing.

Nutrition, diet and ageing

"We are what we eat," is a well-accepted adage. "How we eat is how we age," also has a good deal of truth in it. There are several theories which relate ageing to dietary intake. Some researchers believe that cell death and regeneration have a dietary component, and most people accept that diet plays an important part in the development of some of the diseases which accompany ageing.

In the UK at least, the medical world is convinced that adequate dietary intake of fibre can prevent such conditions as diverticulosis, cancer of the large bowel and possible heart disease. Too much sodium in a diet leads to high blood pressure, congestive heart disease, cirrhosis of the liver and fluid retention. Arterial disease seems to be related to the amount of fat and cholesterol in our diet. Refined sugars have been implicated by some researchers as major components in the development of heart disease, besides playing a role in dental caries and diabetes (see *Special medical problems*).

Changing calorie needs

Although the number of calories we need to take each day almost certainly decreases with age, there is no evidence to show that we need less foodstuffs. The quality of the food, if anything, should be higher than when we were younger.

Minimal requirements will keep away actual disease but they are not satisfactory; older people living at minimum nutritional levels will not be able to get through a period of increased stress such as injury, surgery or infection.

The great bulk, 65 to 80 percent, of our daily calorie needs comes from *carbohydrates* . Carbohydrates which are not used are converted to fat. Refined carbohydrates should be eaten in only small quantities. Natural, unrefined, whole food carbohydrates such as fruit, vegetables, grains and cereals are fine, providing energy plus minerals, vitamins and roughage.

Naturally, our calorie needs depend very much on our age and the amount and type of activity we undertake and this should be reflected in our daily diet. Below, I have set out a complete diet which, with added snacks and drinks throughout the day, will provide approximately 2000 calories daily.

SAMPLE BALANCED DIET

Our bodies need energy to perform two functions: firstly, to keep all our basic body functions in good order; secondly, to provide the extra energy which is burnt up when we do active exercise. Some of us are *fast burners* and manage to use up more energy than we consume, thus staying slim no matter how much we eat, while others are *sleepers* using less calories than they take in and so getting fat. As we get older our metabolisms do slow down gradually so we need to adjust our daily calorie requirement accordingly. In order to maintain our ideal weight we need to balance the calories we take in against those we expend each day.

Breakfast
tea or coffee (6)
2 fl oz (57ml) milk (36)
½ oz (14g) sugar (56)
2 oz (55g) muesli (210)
2 oz (55g) slice of wholemeal toast (136)
½ oz (14g) butter (105)
2 oz (55g) boiled egg (80)

Lunch
6 fl oz (168) tomato soup (120)
2 oz (55g) cheddar cheese (190)
1 oz (28g) lettuce (30)
1½ oz (42g) beetroot (18)
2½ oz (69g) tomato (10)
1 tbs french dressing (60)
2 oz (55g) slice of wholemeal bread (136)
½ oz (14g) butter (105)
5 fl oz (124g) fruit yoghurt (110)
coffee or tea (0); 2 fl oz (57ml) milk (36); ¼ oz (7g) sugar (28)

Dinner
¼ melon (30)
4 oz (112g) roast beef (320)
4 oz (112g) green beans (8)
4 oz (112g) roast potatoes (120)
4 oz (112g) stewed apples (76)
1 glass of red wine (22)

Protein needs   These provide 8-10 percent of total daily calories. There is no great change in our protein needs as we get older. There is some evidence to show, however, that if we are stressed by infection, gastro-intestinal problems, surgery and other illnesses, we lose more protein from our bodies than we did when we were younger, and this leads to a relative increase in our protein needs during illness. This is particularly important information for those of us taking a marginal protein diet. A low protein content is often caused by the high cost of protein-rich foods or the inability to chew properly.

Fat needs   These provide 5-10 percent of total daily calories. Our bodies' need for fat doesn't change with age at all, and in a balanced diet, fat should never account for more than 20 percent of our total calorie intake. The American Heart Association has said that we would all be fitter if this ratio were nearer 10 percent.

Mineral needs   Iron, calcium and potassium are the three minerals which may present problems as we get older. Iron deficiency is fairly common at any age, but it is a difficult mineral to absorb. The tendency to develop an iron deficiency anaemia is worsened as we get older because of poor diet and because blood may be lost from the gastro-intestinal tract by such things as a peptic ulcer, hiatus hernia and diverticular disease (see *Special medical problems*). An interesting study in Scandinavia has shown that the haemoglobin level of a person – a good measure of iron deficiency – is often associated with the inability to chew foods which are rich in iron.

Meat improves the absorption of iron from other foods, and if we are unable to chew meat as we get older we may develop iron deficiency anaemia. Potassium deficiency is nearly always caused by bouts of diarrhoea, kidney disease, or treatment with diuretic agents, though physicians are usually careful in the latter case to give potassium supplements. To a certain extent, calcium deficiency in older people remains a mystery. There is no evidence to suggest that our calcium needs increase as we get older, but the use of calcium by the body is certainly related to sex hormones and to a sufficient amount of vitamin D in the diet. Over the age of sixty-five calcium supplements may be necessary to counteract osteoporosis (see page 232).

Vitamin needs   **Vitamin C**
Our vitamin needs do not alter as we get older. Foods rich in vitamin C may not only be expensive but also heavy to carry and this makes them difficult to handle. A relatively cheap

source of vitamin C, the potato, is often mistakenly eliminated from diets in attempts to lose or maintain weight. It is important for us as we get older to take some foods containing vitamin C every day, as it is believed that our ability to retain vitamin C in our bodies decreases.

Vitamin B

Although the incidence of vitamin B deficiency seems to become more common as we get older it is not related to an insufficiency in our diets. Our gastro-intestinal tracts are less able to absorb vitamin B12 as we get older and so a deficiency is not correctible through taking supplements by mouth. Injections are always needed. A person who takes diuretics over a long period of time may become *thiamine deficient*. This can be worsened because many older people prefer a high carbohydrate diet, a diet which requires more thiamine for proper metabolism.

Deficiencies of the vitamin *riboflavin* are rare; soreness at the corner of the mouth, or greasy skin around the curve of the nostril, suggest a problem. Green vegetables, eggs, milk and liver are good sources of riboflavin. This vitamin is resistant to heat but not sunlight – so milk should not be left in the sun.

Vitamin A

This is found in all dairy products, liver, fish and in green, yellow and red vegetables. As we grow older we may become faddy about milk, butter and cheese and we may find vegetables hard to chew and digest, leading in some cases to a vitamin A deficiency. However, this is not very common.

Vitamin D

As we get older we tend to stay indoors more often and therefore we have less opportunity to get outdoors to expose our skin to the sun. If this happens, lack of vitamin D may occasionally become a problem, especially if we reduce our intake of milk. Milk is not always very popular because it can lead to constipation; the best sources of vitamin D are fortified milk and fish liver oils.

Unbalanced diet

One of the effects of not eating the right vitamins is that we begin to take an unbalanced diet, even though our intake of calories may be adequate. This results in obesity. We may selectively reject the most nutritious foods, along with meat, and balance our calories by taking in foods containing hardly any nutrients at all, for example, refined flour, refined sugar, fat and alcohol. An excessive intake of empty calories, along with the rejection of high-quality foods, results in obesity.

FACTORS AFFECTING WHAT WE EAT

At all ages we are affected by psychological, social and domestic factors which determine the sort of food we eat and its quality and quantity. So too is food influenced by our lifestyles. Some studies have shown that as we get older we attach more importance to the social reasons for eating foods than to nutrition. Other factors can contribute:

Teeth

If we have lost teeth or have problems with our dentures, then we are likely to avoid foods which are hard, sticky and difficult to chew, opting for those which are softer and easier to chew. This can lead to a lessening in the amount of fibre in the diet with bowel complications. Chewing problems are all too real.

If we wear dentures we have to chew food four times as long as a person who has teeth to masticate our food. The more teeth we lose, the less efficient we become at chewing. Any chewing problem is made worse by our producing less saliva and having dry mouths. This makes mastication difficult and swallowing hard.

Smell and taste

As we get older our senses of smell and taste become less acute. This doesn't just make food less savoury; it may also actually supress our appetites, so that we tend to eat less good food as we get older. As our senses of taste go we may begin to overseason foods. This can irritate our mouths and other sensitive parts of our digestive tracts. Adding too much salt can contribute to high blood pressure, heart disease and malfunction of our kidneys.

Certain medical conditions such as a stroke or Parkinson's disease, arthritis and certain sight disorders can mean that we suffer a decline in the very fine co-ordination needed for cutting food, lifting it to our mouths and chewing. All our fine co-ordination declines to a certain degree as we get older, but difficulties with handling utensils, appliances and foods, make eating less pleasant.

Diet

Many of us claim to feel discomfort after eating certain foods. This becomes more and more common as we get older. What's more we tend to become somewhat entrenched in these attitudes and feel recalcitrant about changing dietary habits to the extent that they become fads. This kind of inflexibility can sometimes lead to dietary deficiency and certainly to an unbalanced diet.

Income

If our incomes become reduced, we have to buy smaller quantities of food. Sales or quantity discounts are no longer available, and many of the packaging and marketing ideas in stores are geared towards younger, wealthier consumers.

Psychological reasons

For all of us food is a comforter. As we get older we may seek solace in eating to help us over the loss of a loved one. It is not uncommon for the loss of a mate or a friend to cause great dietary upset. The loss of companionship can affect our desire to shop, cook, eat and our ability to remain interested in food. Widowers in particular suffer. Having been taken care of most of their lives by loving spouses, they find themselves unable to make the same effort when they are alone. The worst nutritional problems occur amongst elderly widowers. Women, however, when they find themselves bereft of a partner, may very well retain their ability to look after themselves, but will often no longer have the financial resources to do so.

Obesity is prevalent as we get older and it is considered to be the most important single medical problem of today. There are many statistics to show that obesity shortens life and increases the severity of certain diseases.

However, as we get older, a bad diet has an ever-increasing, negative effect on how we cope with life. It reduces our potential to become rehabilitated after having any disease and it means that major fractures and strokes are all the worse for being overweight. There are absolutely no physical benefits to be derived from being overweight. Over-eating, over-drinking, and over-smoking are never good, but as we get older they not only can ruin our enjoyment of life, they increase ageing and may make serious illness fatal.

Dietary fat and health

There is an association between diets rich in saturated fats and coronary heart disease. This means that the more saturated fats we eat, the more likely we are to die of heart attacks. In Europe, the Scandinavians are the people who eat the most animal fat and as a result they suffer most heart attacks. The Italians, who eat the least animal fat, though a lot of vegetable fat, suffer least from heart attacks. In certain primitive cultures, with diets of mainly maize and beans, with very little meat or eggs, heart disease is virtually unknown. There is a tribe living in northern Mexico whose members have never suffered from cardiac or circulatory disease. These people are thin and small and weigh on average less than 9½ stones (60 kg). Their daily calorie intake is well below the level recommended by nutritional experts in developed countries who say that these tribesmen are undernourished. However, these people can run races lasting a continuous 48 hours, maintaining a steady pace of 6 miles an hour for over 150 miles. They can chase a deer until the animal has dropped from exhaustion! Could it be that the Western nutritionalists are wrong; that these Mexicans are ideally undernourished and we are overnourished?

Almost all animal fats are saturated, and almost all vegetable fats are unsaturated. Saturated fats are "saturated" with hydrogen atoms and this gives them a high melting point. They are, therefore, solid at room temperature – like lard, for instance. Unsaturated fats have empty spaces in their molecules instead of hydrogen atoms, and this lowers their melting point, thus they are liquid at room temperatures – like vegetable oil. It is thought that very unsaturated fats (polyunsaturated) may even remove some of the fatty deposits from the coronary arteries, though this is still a controversial point.

Most authorities would agree that it's a good rule to keep the amount of fat in your diet low, be it animal or vegetable – no more than one ounce (28g) per day. It is better to substitute vegetable oil for lard, and soft margarine for butter.

Foods vary in the amount of saturated and unsaturated fats they contain, though their calorific values are identical. We still do not know how cholesterol causes heart disease, but a statistical association between high blood cholesterol and heart disease has been proven. It is, therefore, a wise step if we avoid foods which contain large quantities of cholesterol. The yolks of eggs and salmon are particularly rich, so as a preventative measure we should eat these foods sparingly and indeed avoid them altogether if we have heart trouble.

Research undertaken nearly forty years ago shows that the incidence of heart disease varies between districts where the drinking water is either hard or soft. Heart disease is lower in the areas where the drinking water is hard. So if you are going to install a water softener in your domestic water supply, make sure it leaves the drinking water untouched. Dietary guidelines from the Royal College of Physicians in London will promote a healthy heart. Though you may have to change your lifestyle to follow them, you may well live a little longer as a result.

TIPS FOR A HEALTHY HEART

- Reduce the fat in your diet. Replace most of the animal fat with unsaturated vegetable fat such as soft margarine, corn oil, soya bean oil, or sunflower oil. Do not have more than ½ ounce (14g) of butter a day, and never use lard for cooking.
- Eat lean rather than fatty meat, for example beef not pork. Always cut the fat off meat if possible.
- Grill food when you can; never fry it.

- Try to eat less red and more white meat such as poultry and fish.
- Make sure that you eat some fruit every day, and some green or root vegetables to provide roughage. If you cannot, take two tablespoonfuls of fibre supplement or bran every day.
- Do not eat more than one egg per day, or more than three eggs per week.
- Avoid cream whenever you can.

The Royal College of Physicians recommends a very strict diet for people who suffer from heart disease, which aims to reverse the existing condition. It recommends that meat is restricted to 8 ounces (226g) a week; that soft margarine and poly-unsaturated fats are always used; that milk must always be skimmed; that no more than three eggs a week are eaten; that cheese be kept to a minimum with cottage cheese as a substitute; the intake of cakes, pastry and biscuits should be restricted. In fact, a vegetarian diet seems to be particularly suitable for people who have suffered from heart disease, and certain communities whose diet is mainly vegetarian with very few dairy products, have reduced incidence of heart disease.

A balanced diet The rational approach to good nutrition as we get older is exactly the same as when we were younger. We need to aim at an intake of natural foods in the amounts needed to provide the essential nutrients, including high quality protein – to at least a minimal level, and to take in only sufficient calories which approach our desirable weight. To meet this aim, the table of core foods (below) can be used as a general guideline for our minimal requirements. In general, the core food plan allows a variation of items within each basic food group. It doesn't allow changes in the food groups which provide the minimal amounts that we need. Because there are differences in the amounts of nutrition we get from different foods, no one food group can be substituted for another – though calorie value seems the same.

CORE FOOD LIST

Food Group		Amount to Use Daily	Approx. Kilocalories	Approx. No. of A.D.A. Exchanges
Breads (4 servings per day):	Bread or toast (whole grain or enriched)	2 slices	140	2
Cereal (whole grain or enriched)	Cooked *OR* Ready-to-eat	1/2 cup 3/4 cup	70	1
Potatoes or substitute (white)	Baked or boiled *OR* Mashed potato *OR* Rice, pasta	1 medium 1/2 cup 1/2 cup	90	1
Fruits (2 servings per day):	Citrus juice or fruit Other fruits Whole fresh fruit (peach, apple, etc.) *OR* Cut or sliced fruit, berries, grapes, etc.	3/4 cup 1 medium 1/2 cup	80 70	11/2 1
Meat and meat substitutes (6 ounces (170g) per day):	Lean meat, fish, fowl (flesh only) (1 egg or 2 tablespoons peanut butter may be substituted for 1 ounce (28g) meat)	6 ounces	300	6
Milk and milk substitutes (2 cups per day):	2% Low fat milk (1 cup yoghurt, 1 ounce cheese or 1/2 cup cottage cheese may be substituted for each cup of milk)	2 cups	300	2
Vegetable (1 serving per day):	"A" Vegetable (spinach, snap beans, cabbage, tomatoes, summer squashes, cucumber) *OR* "B" Vegetable (peas, lima beans, winter squash, carrots)	1 cup 1/2 cup	50	1
TOTAL CALORIFIC VALUE (per day)			1100	

The core food list alone is hardly palatable as an everyday diet. It lacks those certain items which make food tasty (butter and other fats, and sugar) and 1100 calories a day is quite often not sufficient to maintain or approach a desirable weight. Most of us will want and require more than 1100 calories a day, and it is important that we should know which additional foods can be allowed. It might be argued that as long as we are approaching, or are at our desirable weights, we can eat anything else that we want, such as butter, margarine, sugar, sweets, pastries, fried foods of any kind, and alcohol, but it is better to pursue a middle course. It is better for us if we try to eat larger amounts of natural foods but you may find some of the optional foods listed below useful.

ESTIMATING MEAT PORTIONS

All portions of fish, poultry and meat are two to three ounces (60-80g) cooked weight without bone, skin and visible fat

2-3 Ounces (60-80g) of Fish
1/3 cup canned tuna or salmon
1/2 cup cooked lobster, crab
5 medium clams, oysters
3 medium scallops
8 medium sardines
1 medium fish fillet

2-3 Ounces (60-80g) of Poultry
1 medium chicken leg
1 medium chicken thigh
1 slice chicken, turkey
1/2 medium chicken breast

2-3 Ounces (60-80g) of Meat or Substitutes
2 slices beef, veal, lamb, pork
1 x 3 inch (7.5cm) diameter beef patty
1 lamb or pork chop
1 slice Canadian bacon
4 tablespoons peanut butter

OPTIONAL FOODS

	Amount	Approx. Kilocalories
Fats:		
Butter or margarine	1 teaspoonful	34
Cream, 18 percent, Coffee	1 tablespoonful	32
cream, 36 percent, whipping	1 tablespoonful	55
Salad Dressing, French or Italian Mayonnaise	1 tablespoonful	72
	1 tablespoonful	93
Thousand Island Dressing	1 tablespoonful	90
Cooking or salad oil	1 tablespoonful	124
Sweets		
Sugar, granulated	1 teaspoonful	15
Jelly, jam	1 tablespoonful	55
Candy bar, plain chocolate	1 ounce	148
Desserts		
Apple pie	1/8 of 9-inch (22cm) pie	302
Cupcake, chocolate, iced	1 medium	203
Ice cream, vanilla	1/2 cup	147
Snacks		
Nuts, mixed	1/2 cup	438
Peanuts, shelled	1/2 cup	421
Popcorn	1 cup	64
Potato chips	1 cup	91
Pretzel	Medium size	78
Corn chips	1/2 cup	112
Cheese tidbits, nips	1/2 cup	110
Alcoholic Beverages		
Whiskey – bourbon, Irish, rye	1 ounce (28g) fluid	83
Scotch whiskey, gin, rum	1 ounce (28g) fluid	75
Wine	1 ounce (28g) fluid	33
Beer	12 ounces (340g) fluid	151

Standard measuring spoons are to be used and are to be filled level, not heaped.

It is never easy to change the habits of a lifetime, and changing our eating habits is notoriously difficult. They are no less difficult as we get older, but here are a few hints which might help you to change your thinking and your lifestyle with regard to what you eat and on page 27 are some myths exploded.

TIPS TO ACHIEVE A BALANCED AND HEALTHY DIET

• Some of the most basic factors have to be tackled first. It is important that you face up to the fact that you may have some kind of chronic ailment which requires a special diet, that there may be social problems, that you may have difficulty in chewing, or that money might be short. If these difficulties are ignored, nothing else can be put right. So you should seek help from your doctor, social worker and therapists to help you to correct these factors as far as you possibly can.

• Go for as simple a diet as you possibly can. One that hasn't unneccessary restrictions, which caters for your likes and dislikes as much as possible, and one which allows you good food to look forward to with at least one or two treats a day. You are going to have to impose some kind of discipline on yourself, so decide that you are going to have yourself regularly weighed so that you can report your progress to your family and doctor.

• No goal can be achieved quickly, and you have all the time in the world, so set yourself realistic goals which can be reached in months or perhaps even a year. By this time, you will have achieved the additional goal of modifying your inadequate diet, into a balanced and healthy one.

Our attitudes to food The majority of people go into middle age eating an unhealthy diet, and most continue to eat the same diet until they die. Such a diet consists of many highly-refined processed foods from which much of the goodness has been removed, where the flavour is artificially boosted with too much salt, too much sugar and, often, saturated fats. Snack foods are readily available and fast food restaurants encourage fast, often stressful, eating of junk foods.

Many of us are misinformed about our diets, and in the belief that we are following sensible guidelines we may be doing the opposite by eating too much protein and too many dairy products. We are conditioned to consume far more fat, sugar, calories and cholesterol than we need. If we haven't done so before, now is the time to call a halt. It's one of the simplest and most important ways we can help shape our futures for good health. This entails making adjustments to our diets, not sweeping changes but fine tuning, and none of the changes need mean deprivation. However, we can't expect to make many changes to life-long habits without feeling a certain amount of resistance. It is important that we take things easy at first, recognizing those areas which may act as stumbling blocks to our efforts.

The new foods I'm supposed to eat will be too expensive
In the first place you could cut your meat bills in half. Fresh food is much cheaper than processed food.

I enjoy my food a lot and don't want to give it up
You've learned your food preferences. It's not too difficult to unlearn them and learn new, possibly more enjoyable ones and you don't have to give up any food altogether.

I don't think I could change my eating habits, it would be difficult for me
It's easier if you make gradual changes. Tell your family what you're doing and they will support you.

I think I'm healthy as I am '
If you're eating a typical Western diet you could be still healthier if you cut down on salt and sugar and become more vigilant about the amount of fat you eat for the long term.

Sticking to a chosen diet

Most people who reach middle age with a weight problem have tried, perhaps several times, to lose weight. Some people may have tried every diet available and still have not been able to lose as much as they would like. Others may have been able to take off weight only to put it back on, and so have had difficulty in maintaining a good weight. It's not the aim of this book to lay out examples of the many diets which have been popularized in the past; their plethora suggests that none has the answer.

The answer lies within ourselves. In our willpower and our determination to reach a good weight and stay there. The way to achieve this is not through intermittent dieting, certainly not

27

through crash dieting (not advisable at any age but it does become more dangerous as we grow older) but through changing our eating patterns. We may feel demoralized at the prospect of having to try again to do something which we've failed to do earlier in life. I hope that some of the following suggestions on *how* to change your eating habits will help you more successfully than those diet sheets and books which told you *what* to change.

One of the reasons why you stand a better chance of success this time is that any changes you make to your food patterns will affect your life, and its length, more than any change you tried to make previously. Losing weight will lower your blood pressure, your blood cholesterol, and so lower your risk of a heart attack. Just by losing weight you will feel more physically active. Your heart risk will drop again as you abandon your inactive lifestyle. Some of the relaxation techniques that are used for weight control will help you counteract stress in everyday life, and unburden your cardiovascular system accordingly. You may have been through all this before and feel that you can't try it again. However, it's never too late to start again. It has been shown many times that small attentions to our lifestyle will benefit us immediately.

Coping with 'problem' foods
Nearly all of us can manage to give up most of the high-calorie foods, but there are always one or two favourites which cause us problems. We may be convinced intellectually that we shouldn't eat these foods, but unfortunately this doesn't automatically cancel out our craving. Imagery training helps.

IMAGERY TRAINING

In the USA at Stanford University researchers believe overcoming a craving can be helped by this drill – conjuring up images which make the craved-for food seem less attractive. Let's say that what you crave most is a nice, big fat steak and chips. First get a basin of dripping or a block of lard from the refrigerator and look at it. Spoon some of it on to a plate. Feel it with your fingers. Now you are ready to start the drill.

1. Find a quiet place and sit or lie down.
2. Get as physically and as mentally relaxed as you can.
3. Think of your steak and chips, the look, the smell, the overall picture.
4. Now think of the appearance and texture of the dripping which comes from the steak and chips.
5. Imagine that this thick fat is slowly working through your arteries.
6. Link the image of the food with the sludge in your arteries.
7. Now think of a less fatty but delicious food – turkey.
8. Link this image with clean, healthy arteries throughout your body.

HOW TO CHANGE TO A HEALTHY DIET

CONTROL FAT AND CHOLESTEROL INTAKE

Reduce weekly servings of whole milk, cheese (other than low-fat cottage cheese), fatty meats (beef, lamb, bacon, spareribs, sausages, and luncheon meats) and ice cream by one-half. (Do not eat chicken skin.)

Change from ice cream to ice milk and from whole milk to non-fat milk

Reduce meat fat by trimming and by broiling or roasting instead of frying

Eliminate, except for rare use, intake of organ meats such as liver, sweetbreads and brains

Change from butter or hard margarine to soft margarine

Change from lard or shortening to unhydrogenated vegetable oil including olive oil if desired. Avoid use of large amounts of vegetable oils as you want to lower your total fat intake

Reduce consumption of egg yolk to no more than four a week. Use egg whites liberally

Reduce consumption of fast foods, processed and convenience foods

LOWER THE SALT IN YOUR DIET

Eliminate, except for rare use, high-salt items such as bacon, ham, sausage, frankfurters, luncheon meats, salted nuts, sauerkraut, pickles, canned soups, canned vegetables, potato chips and other salted snack foods

Switch from regular table salt to a light salt (one-half sodium chloride, one-half potassium chloride)

Gradually decrease salt use in cooking to about one-third previous levels; simultaneously decrease, and eventually eliminate salt use at the table

Explore the use of other flavours in your cooking – spices, herbs, lemon, wine, vinegar, are all tasty substitutes

WATCH THE AMOUNT OF SUGAR YOU EAT

Reduce consumption of soft drinks by half. Limit intake to two or three a week

Gradually eliminate use of sugar in coffee or tea and on fruit

Substitute fruit for pastry, cake, pie, or other sweets in one-third of all desserts

ADD FIBRE TO YOUR FOOD

Increase intake of complex-carbohydrate foods – including legumes (e.g. beans, peas, lentils), starchy root vegetables such as potatoes, as well as other vegetables and fruits

Gradually introduce lightly milled or whole-grained cereals into your food plan (e.g. whole-wheat bread and flour, bulgur, couscous, cracked wheat, rolled oats, brown rice, etc.)

Increase intake of whole fruits (fruit juices lack much of the fibre contained in whole fruits)

Increase intake of whole vegetables (vegetable juices lack much of the fibre contained in whole vegetables and often contain significant amounts of added salts)

LIMIT THE EMPTY HIGH-CALORIE FOODS

Reduce intake by one-third

Partially or fully replace such foods with complex carbohydrates

Because alcohol may add to weight control problems and may displace valuable nutrients, limit alcohol consumption so that no more than 10 percent of your total calorie intake is derived from alcohol, e.g. approximately two bottles of beer or three glasses of wine or two cocktails per day

"Don't foods"
It is very important that we avoid as many rich foods and their sources as we possibly can. There is a great deal of cholesterol in eggs, meat and milk and hidden salt in cake mixes and savoury snacks.

Conquering the urge to eat Sometimes our eating urges can be almost too difficult for us to control. Don't wait for them to overtake you out of the blue. Instead practise a suppression drill which has been devised by American behavioural scientists to prepare us for coping with an urge when it strikes. It can be made equally useful when trying to give up smoking.

SUPPRESSION DRILL

Try to practise the drill every day for a couple of weeks or so. It's different from the usual method of dealing with cravings because it makes you face the craving. It can be practised at any time of the day or night.

1. Sit or lie down in a quiet room.
2. Think of the food you really want.
3. Concentrate on the food until you really want to eat it.
4. Imagine an unpleasant sensation connected with food – a bitter taste – and if this doesn't reduce your desire for the food go on to think of feeling sick, being fat, having dirt mixed with your food.
5. When the urge to eat is under control, relax as deeply as you can.
6. Reward yourself (not with food).

Maintaining our ideal weight For all of us up to now, the major difficulty in our lives has been maintaining control of our weight and we all need help against relapsing. Some of the major pitfalls to be on the lookout for are considered on page 31.

WEIGHT IN PROPORTION TO HEIGHT

Height			Women		Men	
ft	ins	m	lbs	kg	lbs	kg
5	0	1.52	104–116	47.2–52.7	118–131	53.6–56.2
5	1	1.55	107–119	48.6–54.5	118–131	53.6–56.2
5	2	1.57	110–122	50.0–55.2	121–135	55.0–61.3
5	3	1.60	113–126	51.3–57.2	124–138	56.3–62.7
5	4	1.62	117–130	53.2–59.0	127–141	61.2–64.0
5	5	1.65	120–133	54.5–60.4	130–145	59.0–65.8
5	6	1.68	123–137	55.9–62.2	133–148	60.4–67.2
5	7	1.70	127–141	61.2–64.0	137–152	62.2–69.0
5	8	1.73	132–145	60.0–62.1	140–156	63.6–70.9
5	9	1.76	135–150	61.3–64.2	144–160	65.4–72.7
5	10	1.78	139–155	63.1–70.5	148–164	67.2–75.6
5	11	1.80	139–155	63.1–70.5	152–169	69.0–76.7
6	0	1.81	139–155	63.1–70.5	157–174	71.3–79.2

Eating socially

We mustn't fall into the trap of feeling that we owe it to our host or hostess, or ourselves, that we must reciprocate their hospitality by eating heartily. If the choice is open to us we must avoid rich, high, empty calorie foods. However, there's no need to reject them altogether if we don't have this choice; we might emulate one famous film star who dines out a great deal – she leaves half of everything on her plate, even if she likes it. I have a mental list of my favourite, healthy foods which are real treats and I choose these whenever I see them on the menu.

Losing enthusiasm

As with any "contract" made with our families and friends to help us make a change of habit, their enthusiasm starts to wear off after a while. Envy at our success may even creep in. We must attempt to keep them interested by making new goals.

Changing our personal lives

Our enthusiasm and morale may flag if our lives are abruptly interrupted by accident, illness, domestic problems, difficulties at work, extensive travel, etc. One of the best ways to protect ourselves against relapse is to be flexible, resetting our goals more realistically in the face of upset.

Sudden cues to eat

Just seeing a box of chocolates or smelling the aroma of cooking will stimulate our desire to eat. We can either decide it's not time for a treat and overcome our urge with suppression drill or, as long as we're realistic and truthful with ourselves, we can allow ourselvs a treat.

Rewarding our achievements

Most of us are stingy with ourselves over rewards. If we're attempting to change our basic habits we should reward ourselves for every step of progress we make, with positive, encouraging statements, pleasurable activities, symbolic rewards and material rewards. They are important. They increase morale and renew enthusiasm.

Hazards of the Western diet

Research has shown quite conclusively that the majority of people living in Western countries are eating an unhealthy diet. In addition to eating too much fat, we also eat too much sugar and too little fibre. In the chart on pages 32-33 I have outlined those hazards in diet which we should attempt to avoid, where they occur, how best to go about avoiding them and the benefits which will follow.

HEALTH HAZARDS OF THE WESTERN DIET

Substance	Protein	Calcium & milk	Sugar
Average consumption	14-15% of total calories consumed	For many children 4 glasses a day. For many adults 2 glasses a day	102lbs of sugar per year per person in the USA and 24% of total calories are derived from sugar
Hazard to health	Animal protein contains animal fat, e.g. an untrimmed sirloin steak is 70% fat in terms of the number of calories it provides. Trimmed, it is still 45%. A near vegetarian diet provides more than an adequate amount of protein. All the rest we eat is possibly hazardous	It's important to reduce the amount of butterfat we eat (70% of the calories in cheese is from butterfat) see hazards to health of saturated fat	It speeds the development of late-onset adult diabetes. It may promote heart disease by increasing the levels of certain lipoproteins which are associated with atherosclerosis
Food	All animal proteins, but especially red meat and dairy products	Full-fat milk, butter, cheese, dairy products from full fat milk	All commercially-baked foods, cake mixes, ice cream, tinned fruit, puddings, sweets, chocolate, biscuits, pickles, sauces, tinned beans, drinks, squashes
Alternative food where possible	White meats, fish, low fat dairy products, vegetable proteins like legumes, nuts, the skins of fruit and vegetables (jacket potatoes)	Skimmed milk and skimmed milk products. Low fat cheese	Fresh fruit and vegetables, whole grain rice, potatoes, legumes (beans, peas and lentils), cereals, low calorie drinks, natural sugars like fructose and dextrose
Action	Reduce protein intake to 8-10% of total claories consumed. Not all of this need be in the form of meat, nor even animal protein. Start to take meat as a condiment	Reduce your daily intake of milk	Alter ratio of refined to unrefined carbohydrates so that emphasis is on unrefined food. Cut down on intake of sugar as a whole
Benefits & comments	Fewer problems with obesity. The benefits are the same as those when restricting cholesterol and saturated fats	The belief that milk is good is wrong. Indeed it's harmful. We would be no less well getting the calcium we need from vegetable sources; broccoli, artichokes, and greens are all high in calcium, so is non-fat milk, low fat cheese	There is no biological need for sugar as such. Sugar tends to be linked to the rest of the carbohydrates, including the complex ones which have fallen into disrepute because of "low carbohydrate diets"

Salt	Cholesterol & saturated fats	Rich foods
12g/day (1g/day is ample for health)	15% of total calories eaten	Western society has a fixation with rich food
It leads to elevated blood pressure. Some races consume 1g/day or less and their blood pressure is much lower and doesn't rise with age. Solomon Islanders who cook their food in sea water have high blood pressure	Animal fats in general are saturated. Vegetable fats except palm oil and coconut oil are unsaturated. The animal fat in shellfish, poultry and wild game is less saturated than in red meat. Cholesterol levels are closely associated with saturated fat intake and they influence the incidence of heart attacks and strokes	The hazards are the same as those when eating too much milk, meat, sugar and salt
Hidden salt in bacon, cake mixes, cheese, peanut butter, crackers, crisps, salted nuts, tinned fish, soups, tinned vegetables & vegetable juice, frozen vegetables, pickles, chips, biscuits, bread, sausages, diet bread, corn flakes	There are large amounts of cholesterol in egg yolks, shellfish, organ meats such as liver and kidney. There are significant amounts of cholesterol in all meats. Nearly all animal foods have some cholesterol as do cakes	All rich foods and sources
Wholegrain bread and cereals, fresh vegetables, fruit, fish, meat, untreated nuts, puffed rice, shredded wheat	Cholesterol is absent from all vegetable foods. Low fat milk, cheese, yoghurt, egg whites, chicken without skin, turkey, soft margarine	Natural and refined unprocessed raw or lightly cooked foods
Gradually reduce intake to wean your palate back to being salt sensitive	The American Heart Association suggests that less than 10% of total calories should be derived from saturated fat	Convert your diet so that it consists more of wholefoods
Blood pressure level drops. There is no biological need for a high salt intake. Salt tastes are learned, so they can be unlearned. Heavy salt users can tolerate loss of salt	Low cholesterol levels and low saturated fat diets can slow down and sometimes halt the development of atherosclerosis. There is no proof yet that they will prevent heart attacks (they have many causative agents) nor is there any to suggest they do any harm. My own opinion is that we should lower our intake of cholesterol	Presumably our fixation began in harder times tempered by two world wars when more food treats disappeared and for many an egg was hard to come by. Then rich food was a symbol of wealth

Exercise

A decrease in physical activity is directly related to ageing. Exercise greatly helps the metabolism of food by the body, and it will relieve tension and promote mental well-being as well. If for any reason our vigour decreases, our desire and ability to take part in physical activity is affected. Mental stress from depression and anxiety can further dampen down our desire to participate in any kind of physical activity. A chronic cycle of less activity and more stress, withdrawal and depression may follow, with results which are very worrying.

Inactivity–stress syndrome

The inactivity-stress syndrome becomes more common as we grow older. It adversely affects our energy and motivation no matter what we attempt to do. It is infectious, it pervades all aspects of our everyday living and it follows that we get less out of life. We are able to participate less, enjoy ourselves less, and we become less and less happy – no further argument is needed in favour of retaining our physical activity.

As we get older, however, we can no longer rely on having mobile joints, supple muscles and strong bones. Our insurance policy is exercise. Exercise promotes an agile, healthy body which will respond quickly. We need to have strong muscles which can maintain effort and give us stamina. Just as important, we need to have healthy minds which are eager to encourage our bodies. None of this will happen if we neglect our bodies. They have to be put through their paces regularly to bring them up to a level of physical fitness that has to be maintained. Exercise will keep us young.

How exercise keeps us young

Heart benefits
It decreases the risk of a heart attack. Much medical research has shown that there is a relationship between inactivity and coronary heart disease. Many years ago an experiment was made on bus drivers and conductors. Given that all other aspects of their lives were equal, it was found that bus drivers were much more prone to coronary heart disease than conductors. At the end of the experiment it was concluded that this was due to the fact that conductors were much more active, running up and down stairs collecting fares, than were the drivers whose lives were almost entirely sedentary.

Exercise is also important in the rehabilitation of heart attack patients, who usually undergo graded exercise programmes to get them back to full and active lives. It makes the heart stronger by widening the arteries, making a complete blockage, by, for instance, a blood clot, less likely.

Psychological benefits

Anyone who has exercised will tell you about the sense of euphoria felt after completing an exercise programme. This is not just due to the satisfaction of having done something well, it is an hormonal effect. If we exercise we will release many beneficial hormones throughout our bodies. One of them affects our state of mind. It counteracts depression and makes us feel tranquil and generally content with life.

Brain benefits

It is not fallacy that if we let our bodies slow down so will our brains. Regular exercise can speed up the rate at which they work and also speed up their rates of recall so that our memories improve. Exercise is also one of the best medicines for anxiety, nerves and panic. It has a calming effect throughout our bodies.

Muscle and joint benefits

There is no doubt that if we exercise regularly we will have healthier muscles, joints and tendons, resulting in fewer aches and pains such as fibrositis, lumbago, sciatica and even arthritis. The health of our joints and bones depends largely on the strength of our muscles, ligaments and tendons because these support and protect them. All of these are improved by exercise. Stiffening of the joints and limitation in the range of joint movement, unyielding muscles, inelastic ligaments, poor posture and softening of the bone can all be legacies of an inactive life and not easily put right.

Lung benefits

Through exercise the efficiency of our hearts and lungs is improved to the point where they can take care of any emergency. Their health is such that they can spring to action and cope with the demands of our bodies. We can walk, run and play for longer. In other words our bodies become more tolerant of exercise, and our physical working capacities increase. Our body metabolisms improve. If we exercise regularly, our bodies become lean and our muscle-to-fat ratios improve. These are the bodies which the best athletes have. During exercise cholesterol and triglyceride, both of which are associated with heart disease, drop markedly. Appetite is suppressed by exercise and carbohydrate metabolism and ability to cope with sugar is significantly better in those of us who exercise, no matter how moderately. One of the most significant benefits which will come as a result of exercise is that we will not feel so breathless.

We look better, younger

There is hardly one aspect of body function which is not affected by exercise, but most important, particularly as we get older, is posture. We cannot hold our bodies properly without strong back muscles; these keep our spines erect. In this respect, posture is not only important if we are to look better as we grow older, it is also a protection against developing backache. The bones of the spine tend to soften as we get older, particularly in women. We may lose height because the vertebral bones tend to become thinner.

However, with good, strong back muscles, even slight softening of the spine can be mitigated, preventing rounded shoulders and an ageing hump from developing. Just as important, an erect spine holds the chest at maximum capacity so that our lungs can work efficiently. Not only are our chests helped, so are our hearts and the muscles of our chests which help our breathing. Our digestion is helped by an erect spine. Strength and mobility exercises help to prevent a hesitant, shuffling walking pattern. Joints remain supple, the tendons don't tighten and weaken and this strength gives us confidence so that there is less likelihood of our falling and fracturing bones.

Guarding against back pain

Our spines take a tremendous amount of wear and tear in our everyday lives. The amount of movement which occurs in the neck as we move our heads from side to side and up and down causes a great deal of strain.

Because of its crucial position in the body, the spine is subjected to strain all day and most of the night, too, if we don't sleep on a mattress which supports the back. Think of the stresses on the lower part of the back because of bending, stooping, twisting and turning which we have to do in the course of a normal day. An artificial joint would wear out in a very short time given this amount of stress, so it is not surprising that the spinal joints tend to wear out, too. If we stand or sit, lift or bend wrongly, walk incorrectly, or drive in a bumpy car, we are overworking our spines and their muscles and ligaments. Even if we do not injure them we overtire them which can lead to backache and pain.

Because the lower back is pivotal in all the movements of the body, once it has been injured it rarely returns to normal. No matter how much care is taken to make sure that the injury has healed, there is always a certain weakness left. It is, therefore, very important to learn how to use your back properly, in order to strain it as little as possible to prevent injury from ever recurring. As a result of good posture, the spine is rested and the ligaments and muscles in the back do not suffer from any strain and the nerves are not compressed by the bones.

Good posture There are proper ways to stand, sit, bend, lift and walk which throw the strain of all these movements on to much stronger muscles and joints than the spine. These joints are more stable and less likely to be injured. The intervertebral discs between the spinal bones can be injured so very easily. They take so long to heal that it is worth protecting them; it makes common sense to use the stronger muscles and joints that do the work of the spine in order to protect it from being overstrained.

Standing
To assume good posture when you are standing, hold your shoulders firmly but not rigidly backwards and downwards with your head up and your stomach pulled in. There is nothing "sergeant-major-like"about it. If you fix your arms to your sides and your shoulders back too rigidly, you will find that your breathing is restricted. Just taking up this posture helps to accentuate the curvature of the spine and to keep it well supported by the muscles of the back and shoulders.

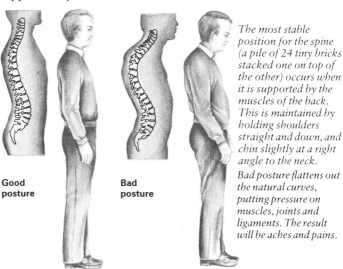

Good posture

Bad posture

The most stable position for the spine (a pile of 24 tiny bricks stacked one on top of the other) occurs when it is supported by the muscles of the back. This is maintained by holding shoulders straight and down, and chin slightly at a right angle to the neck.

Bad posture flattens out the natural curves, putting pressure on muscles, joints and ligaments. The result will be aches and pains.

TIPS FOR POSTURE

- Practice walking along in a straight line, so that you correct any tendency to walk with your feet too far apart or with your toes pointing out.

- When you walk, try to balance your head and upper and lower torso in line.
- Try to centre your body over the balls of your feet.
- Also, lead with your thigh, not your foot.

37

Sitting

At work and at home we spend much of our time sitting so we should make sure that we use well-designed chairs. A chair which is good for posture is one which keeps the angle of the spine to the hip at about 120 degrees, ensuring maximum comfort and minimum strain on spinal joints and spinal muscles. In addition, a well-designed chair should be convex where the back joins the seat so that the lower part of the spine is well supported. Look out for this feature when you are buying a new chair and when you are buying a car.

Sit back on the seat of the chair and make sure that you are comfortable and upright with your shoulders and head balanced over your hips. Whenever you reach forward from this position don't reach forward from the arms but bend from your hips. You can practice sitting correctly and stretching forward in the proper way so that it feels natural and comfortable.

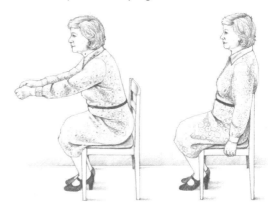

Driving

We spend a great deal of our time driving and it is essential both for driving comfort and safety that our car seats are designed to support the lower part of the spine. If you have a car in which the seats do not provide enough support, most car accessory shops can provide you with a cushion which can fit into the lower part of your seat to provide you with support.

Sleeping

Considering that we spend approximately one-third of our lives asleep it is worth paying some attention to the sort of mattresses we sleep on. While most of us love fluffy, downy, soft mattresses, they are extremely bad for our backs since they allow our spines to curve outwards. A firm mattress is much better than a soft one. Old-fashioned beds with a box which provide an inflexible base are better than those without. Most of us know someone who, having injured his or her back, has been told by a doctor that the best way of curing back pain is to put an old door underneath the mattress to support the back during the night. What is good when we are in pain is even better when we are not. It prevents an overworked spine from being strained more than is absolutely necessary.

Avoiding back injuries   Many back injuries occur when we attempt simple, everyday tasks in the wrong way or when we are doing something very strenuous when unfit. There are right and wrong ways for us to use our backs.

LIFTING, BENDING AND PUSHING

It's important to maintain good posture when lifting or carrying heavy weights or bending. Not only does it make life easier, it also save unnecessary wear and tear on muscles and joints. Here are some tips to help every day.

Kneel right down when doing a job at floor level, such as cutting a dress or weeding. Stooping is very tiring and a strain on the back.

To shift a big weight, such as a wardrobe, push with the back not your hands. It's always best to ask for help.

To lift a large or heavy object, bend down from the knees, not the waist. Carry a heavy package close to the body, not out in front. Again, bend when putting it down.

How fit are we?   Before we can aim for the right level of fitness for our ages we must know how unfit we really are. This can be assessed in a simple way by examining the response of our hearts to exercise. Strenuous exercise is that which increases the oxygen requirements of the body above normal. Incidentally, our hearts and lungs are only exercised when we increase our oxygen requirements above normal. This happens when exercise involves large muscle groups such as those of the legs, the hips, the pelvis, the arms and the shoulders; as it does in jogging, swimming, cycling and rowing. We measure the response of our hearts by taking our pulses.

If we have unfit hearts they will start to beat very fast when we exercise strenuously because this is the only way they can pump more blood around our bodies to keep up with our increased demand for oxygen.

A fit heart, however, will not beat as fast because it can pump out more blood with each beat than an unfit heart. It goes without saying that anyone who has any trouble at all, or who has been told by his or her doctor that he or she has had heart trouble, should not undertake any heart or lung exercises. If you are in doubt, you should consult your doctor first.

TAKING YOUR PULSE RATE

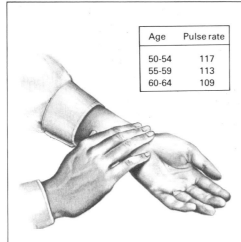

Age	Pulse rate
50-54	117
55-59	113
60-64	109

To see how fit you are, run on the spot for 30 seconds, then take your pulse (count beats for 15 seconds and then multiply by 4). This is your pulse rate for mild exertion.

When you exercise, your pulse rate should not go any higher than the rate you have just calculated. The aim of heart and lung exercise is to keep up this pulse rate for about 15 to 20 minutes. The pulse rate you should be aiming for is shown.

"Whole-body" exercises

The aim of "whole-body" exercises is to maintain a pulse rate for a period of ten minutes of continuous exercising. As a margin of safety, your pulse rate must go no higher than your personal pulse rating which you have calculated. If, after running on the spot for 30 seconds, your pulse rate is at your personal pulse rating, you can continue taking your pulse every minute or so to make sure that your heart is not being overstrained. If, after 30 seconds, your pulse rate is higher than your personal rating, then you must wait and rest until it falls. You should continue to do this every half minute or so if the exercise increases your pulse rate beyond your personal rating. When you are very unfit you have to stop and start your exercises frequently for rest periods. It is very important to do so to make certain that you do not overstrain your heart.

As we improve our fitness we will be able to go for longer periods without raising our pulse rates above our own personal ratings, and we will have to rest less often. We will achieve our goal when we are able to exercise continuously for ten minutes without our pulse rate going above our personal rating. To do these exercises properly we are going to have to become very familiar with taking our own pulses.

Clothing   We must pay some attention to our clothing and make sure that it looks and feels just as we want it: loose; comfortable; absorbent. Shoes should be light with plenty of room for our toes to move about and good support over the arches of our feet, say with laces. Track shoes are ideal.

Warm-up exercises   We should always start off with some warming-up movements to get our joints and muscles working. The following are ideal: arm circling, done standing with feet wide apart and arms hanging loosely; side bends standing with feet wide apart and hands on hips; and trunk and hip bends, standing about 18 inches (0.5m) behind the back of a chair with hands and arms outstretched, and alternate ankle reaching, standing with feet wide apart with both palms resting against the front of the upper left thigh (see page 42).

These warm-up exercises improve the mobility and flexibility of our bodies ensuring that they stay as supple as possible. They help to promote agility and good posture. When we are exercising we should start off with the warm-up exercises or mobility exercises. We should then go on to the strengthening exercises which help to increase our muscle power so that we can go through our daily tasks easily and prevent undue wear and tear and injury. Last of all come the heart and lung exercises which give us the stamina to make a sustained effort and give us endurance. These are sometimes called "aerobic" exercises and they have become very popular recently.

Mobility exercises   These are designed to take all our major muscles and joints through a complete range of movement. Once we have achieved mobility fitness we will be able to move, stretch, twist and turn in all directions with freedom and without feeling any discomfort or pain in our muscles or joints.

Strengthening exercises   These are designed to enable our bodies to cope with the extra effort we are sometimes called upon to make in special circumstances, so we build in a safety margin or extra strength over and above the normal requirements. It is important that we have this reserve because when it is not there, making a sudden and extreme effort can result in damaged muscles, ligaments and tendons and even a slipped disc. To build up those extra resources we need to increase the duration and force of the exercise we take, a little at a time.

Strength will not suddenly arrive when we start exercising, it will develop as we start doing things we know we are capable of on a regular basis. Walking up a nearby hill to the shops is better than going to the shop at the end of the road.

41

WARM-UP AND MOBILITY EXERCISES

Arm swings and shoulder rolls (5 times)
Stand with your feet slightly apart and swing forward with your right arm, then backwards. Repeat with your left arm. Now slowly roll each shoulder forward and then backwards in a full circle.

Body bends (3-5 times)
Stand with your feet slightly apart and place your hands on your hips. Bend slowly forward as far as you can manage and then backwards. Take this exercise gently at first.

Body turns and side stretches (5 times)
Again stand with your feet apart. Now turn your body to the right and back and then to the left and back. Next, place your left hand on your left hip and extend your right arm over your head. Now change hands.

TIPS FOR EXERCISE

- Always find out how fit you are before you start on an exercise programme, and if you are in any doubt about your fitness, check with your doctor.
- Always choose activities and exercises that you enjoy, or you will never stick to your exercise programme.
- Exercises shouldn't be a chore. If they are, you are doing the wrong ones.
- Exercises should never be physically punishing. If they are, you are pushing yourself too hard.
- The best form of exercise is one that fits in with your daily life. Like taking the dog for a walk, cycling to work or to the shops, climbing stairs rather than taking the lift, and doing the odd bit of exercise while you are working at the sink.
- There is no need to spend a lot of money on expensive equipment. You can do all your exercises effectively without buying anything.
- Never exercise on a full stomach. Always wait at least an hour. Spend a few minutes loosening up before beginning your strenuous exercises.
- Never be overzealous about increasing the length of your exercises too rapidly. Slowly and surely should be the motto. Always check your pulse rate so that you reach the level of fitness suitable for your age over a period of weeks, and this should never be less than six weeks.
- Try to exercise at least three or four times a week once you have reached your level of fitness to maintain it.

NECK, SHOULDER AND ARM EXERCISES

Shoulder swings (10 times)
Lean forward with your feet apart to as far as 90° as you can comfortably manage and swing each arm from side to side across your body. Next, swing both arms together.

Arm circling (3 times)
Stand erect with your feet slightly apart and your arms by your side. Bring one arm forward, upward and backward to make a large circle. Next reverse the direction of the swing.

Neck rolls (3-5 times)
Let your head fall forwards, then slowly pull it up. Let it fall to the side then pull it up again.

Arm lifts (3-5 times)
This is quite a vigorous exercise so do take it easy at first. It's not necessary to hold weights to gain strength and mobility, in this case books. Stand with your feet apart, your knuckles facing away from your body (far left). Now raise your arms horizontally, slowly turning your hands so that your palms face the ceiling (centre). Finally, raise your arms to meet above your head (left). Slowly reverse to the starting position.

43

BACK, HIP AND LEG EXERCISES

Single knee pull (5 times)
*Lie on your back on the floor and grasp
one leg with both arms so that you can pull
it back onto your chest. Then hold for the
count of 5 before repeating with your
other leg.*

Leg ranging (5-10 times)
*Lie on your side and raise
your leg to as near as 45° as
you can manage and hold
for the count of 2. Then
lower. Try to keep your
leg straight.*

Ankle circling
*Sit down and cross
your legs. Now, slowly
trace a circle with your
toe. Repeat this
motion with your
other foot.*

**Reaching and bending
(3-5 times)**
*Stand erect with your
feet slightly apart and
one hand in the air.
Breathe in and stretch
upward as far as
possible still keeping
your feet flat on the
ground. Now, breathe
out slowly, bend over
and touch the ground
between your feet. Do
bend your knees if you
feel the need because
this is quite a difficult
exercise to master.
Repeat the exercise
with your other arm.*

Groin stretch (3 times)
*Stand with your feet as
wide apart as possible
and your back straight.
Bend knee forward
and count 5. Then rise
onto your toes for the
count of 3.*

Thigh stretch (3 times)
*Stand at a right angle
to the wall, for
support. With your
free hand pull your
ankle up towards your
bottom and hold for
the count of 5.*

Calf stretch (3 times)
*Stand facing a wall.
Lean against it and let
your hips hang forward
for the count of 5.
Then rise onto your
legs for the count of 3.*

Fitness playing sports

Playing sport of any kind is a valuable way of looking after our health, keeping our bodies supple and agile. It also involves getting out of the house and a change of surroundings. Through sport we manage to meet other people and keep our social lives active and varied.

Many sports are played outdoors, which is a good deal better and more interesting for us than remaining indoors all day. Whether we win or lose they bring a great deal of physical and emotional satisfaction, because they involve perfecting quite complex, physical movements, which can bring the joy of achievement. If we play team games, team spirit can do wonders for our morale, and simply being a member of the team gives us a sense of being needed and a feeling of security in belonging to a group. The social aspects of sport also make a great plus.

Renewing our interest

If we gave up sport completely when we were young, or were never interested in them, it may be worth thinking about trying one again. We may always have had a desire to take up a particular sport but never had the time. Well now we do and we mustn't be put off by the fact that we are getting older. Many sports can be taken up for the first time quite successfully in our fifties and sixties. I know of a newspaper editor who took up skiing at the age of fifty-three, and now, as he approaches sixty, he manages the moguls and wedels like a young man. I have seen old couples on ski slopes. Not, of course, racing downhill rather taking things easily and gracefully on safer, shorter skis. As long as we prepare ourselves for skiing with several weeks of mobility and strengthening exercises before we go away, this is a wonderful sport to take up.

Knowing our limits

We mustn't rely on playing a sport to keep us fit. We may be fit enough to play most sports without being really physically fit. This is because most sports don't require use of the large muscles of legs, arms, pelvis and shoulder girdle for any length of time. They don't exercise the whole body to the point where the heart and lungs are being fully stretched. The only sports which do this are running or jogging, swimming, cycling and, possibly, tennis. To really exercise the body well at any of these sports, however, we need to do them briskly.

There is absolutely no need for us to play a sport flat out, either to enjoy it or to keep ourselves healthy. We should participate at our own speed, with people who want to play it at about the same speed and with the same force and enthusiasm.

45

Swimming

This is for almost all of us the perfect sport. Once we are immersed the water takes the weight off our bodies, so that our limbs become weightless and our joints are relieved of strain. Just floating in water is a treatment in itself for our muscles, joints and bones. The water supports all our movements through the full excursions of our joints and limbs, so that we can exercise with very little discomfort. As a result, our joints can gain in flexibility and our muscles can gain in movement and elasticity with us hardly being aware.

Swimming is good for the whole body, exercising all our muscles. If we do it for pleasure, even once a week, we can do an awful lot to keep our bodies flexible and strong. It is extremely good for relaxation and rehabilitation after an illness, especially for our backs and legs. Swimming can also be used as a method for keeping fit, though it would involve swimming fairly hard for twenty to thirty minutes, at least four times a week.

Tennis

This is an enjoyable, sociable sport which we can play at any age. It is particularly good for keeping our shoulders, arms, and legs supple and strong, and helping our co-ordination. Tennis is also very good for our posture and for keeping our youthful stride and it can be played at any pace.

It's a sport which enables us to socialize before and after playing. It's important to play tennis at a steady pace at first, with partners of similar ability.

Golf

Although golf is not a sport which will keep us fit, it's very good for improving our strength, flexibility and muscular co-ordination. Because golf is mainly walking, and slow walking at that, the calorie expenditure is quite low – about 1000 calories for eighteen holes. So it really can't be used as a means of shedding weight. The amount of energy which we expend during golf depends very much on whether or not we carry our golf clubs, or drive ourselves around in a golf buggy.

Obviously we will be fitter if we do the former, but as we get older it's very nice to take things more easily and slowly, with less strain and fuss. Carrying our clubs will certainly exercise our bodies and our hearts more than travelling around in a buggy. It has been shown that the heart rate will rise to an average of about 113 beats per minute if we carry our clubs, whereas it stays at a fairly steady 80 if we drive around in a cart. Thus we are asking our hearts and lungs to work about 50 percent faster if we opt for carrying our clubs. Remember that having a drink at the 19th hole may imbibe more calories than we used in playing the game.

Cycling

Here is an excellent way to exercise as it involves the whole body, and again it is one of those sports which we can regulate according to how much we want to work our bodies. If we cycle steadily and energetically for twenty minutes or more, it's an extremely good way of increasing the strength and endurance of the whole body, including our hearts and lungs.

It is one of those sports which can make us physically fit in tip-top condition as it's very good for strengthening the large muscles in our bodies and it is also efficient at strengthening our knees, ankles and hip joints.

It is also very good for the shoulders, though we don't often notice that we are using them. Because some roads are now very busy it might be worth considering an exercise bicycle – to practice on at any time, day or night.

Lawn bowls

This is a game which is growing in popularity in almost all parts of the world. It is not a sport which will help to make us fit, but it does help to ensure that our leg muscles are strong and also that our shoulders and arms are flexible and mobile with good co-ordination. One of the real benefits of this game, and others like it which involve social involvement, is that through its formalized activity of game rules, certain courtesies of playing, the stimulus of competition, the protocol of dress and the opportunity for renewing old friendships and possibly making new ones, there is help in maintaining personal esteem, good spirits and self-confidence.

Dancing

According to the sort of dancing which we choose to do, we can exercise our bodies gently or very actively. Many couples take up ballroom dancing which, besides its social pleasures, will help to keep the body and joints flexible and co-ordinated. Other types of dancing which involve running, jumping, stretching and swinging exercise our bodies as much as bicycle riding or running. We can get out of breath in a very short time and so the heart and lungs are fully exercised, too. This kind of dancing is called "aerobic dancing". We should never continue aerobic dancing if we get very out of breath, if any part of the body feels painful or if we develop a pain anywhere. We don't have to dance this hard in order to gain benefit from it, and this is particularly the case as we get older.

We can use aerobic dancing to become physically fit, as long as we approach the programme very gradually, increasing the amount of effort we make over a period of about six weeks. Remember that very vigorous aerobic dancing can equal the amount of energy which basketball players or top tennis players use when they are at full stretch.

Walking and jogging

We can walk for pleasure or we can walk to keep fit. Brisk, vigorous walking so that we sweat and pant for about 20 minutes, three or four times a week, is an excellent way of staying fit. It exercises all the muscles in our bodies and it also exercises our hearts and lungs. If we haven't been walking to keep fit before, however, it would be foolhardy to start taking long vigorous walks out of the blue. We need to make sure that we get ourselves fit first over several weeks.

TIPS FOR WALKING

- Always do your flexibility exercises before you go out to walk.
- To start with, walk on level ground and avoid hills.
- Always walk "within your breath". This will mean that your heart is beating at about 60 percent of its maximum rate.
- The level of intensity of exercise which you should be aiming at is one which allows you to have a limited conversation while you are moderately out of breath.
- Never push yourself further than you feel you want to go. Never try to strain.

- Don't try to increase the speed at which you walk. Try to increase the distance or the time you spend walking.
- At the beginning never walk into the wind. This will increase your workload by quite a lot. If you suffer with heart disease you can walk along quite comfortably for one or two miles when the wind is behind you but you can get severe angina if you turn and face the wind.
- Work at your walking until you can walk continuously for about three miles without stopping in about 45 to 55 minutes.

Walking is an enjoyable, relaxing exercise, but remember not to walk too far without taking a break.

Once we have reached this level of walking, we are ready to go into the jogging/walking programme. We need to start by doing mobility exercises (page 42), and then walking briskly for a while and jogging until we feed we need a rest, then back to walking until we feel ready to run again. We can repeat these cycles for 20 minutes or so. We should do this at least every other day but not more than five days a week. Once we can manage this quite comfortably we can start trying to jog at our own pace with a friend or alone.

You can perform a test to see whether or not you are healthy enough to start jogging straight away. Try and walk three miles in 45 minutes. If you can, you can probably start jogging without any risks, but if you cannot, you must stick to the brisk walking exercises already described until you can progress to jogging. Remember, do the mobility exercises before you start and, if possible, after you finish. Do check with your doctor before you take up jogging, he or she will tell you whether there is any danger in exerting yourself. It is most important to take things easy at first.

TIPS FOR JOGGING

- Jog at a comfortable rate for about 50 yards (45m) to start off.
- Slow down and walk 100 yards (90m).
- Keep repeating this cycle until you have been going for about 20 minutes.
- Never exercise to the point where you feel that you are completely out of breath, dizzy or sick.
- Never extend the time limit over 20 minutes, until you can jog for the whole of the 20 minutes.
- Very gradually increase your jogging up to half an hour.
- There is no particular benefit in extending your time beyond half an hour unless you are really seriously involved in exercising.

Make jogging comfortable
Most people jog for fitness and it is important that you try to develop a comfortable and economical style. Here are a few suggestions which may help.

- Run with your arms bent at the elbows and your wrists and fingers held loosely.

The forearm should be about parallel to the ground. Your hands should just about scratch your abdomen when you run.

- Try to run tall and upright but avoid leaning forward. Keep your back as straight as you can and your head up. Look about 15 to 20 feet (5-6m) in front of you, and try not to look at your feet.
- Keep your stride fairly short but don't force the pace by reaching out.
- If you are feeling a bit stiff, shake out your arms to ease your shoulders.
- As you land take your weight on the heel of the foot and then roll forward onto the ball before taking off again. If this is a bit difficult just run flat footed until you develop the heel-toe technique.
- Don't try to run on your toes as this will strain your calf muscles.
- Breathe fairly deeply and help yourself by pushing your abdomen outwards as you breathe in. It doesn't matter how much noise you make, in fact making quite a bit of noise often helps.

Jogging is somewhat different from other sports. Only ten years ago it was uncommon to see people jogging in the streets. Nowadays it is fairly common to see track-suited, middle-aged people jogging. Jogging has almost become a national addiction. To a jogger the reasons for this are pretty plain. Some people may start jogging for the fun of it, some do it to lose weight or to reduce tension, and others do it to just tone up their muscles. Some people do it for self-discipline.

For many people jogging is truly addictive but unlike other addictions it is helpful rather than harmful. Very often it helps to control other personal habits which are undesirable like smoking. People who start to run find it easier to reduce their consumption of cigarettes and may stop altogether. Jogging, of course, has all the benefits that regular exercise has on the whole of the body. It helps the body to use up oxygen; it lowers the heart rate, thereby saving us between ten and twenty thousand heart beats a day; it increases the efficiency of the heart and lungs; it lowers the blood pressure and it helps to burn up extra weight.

51

Medical check-ups

Doctors and patients may become dangerously polarized in their views about medical check-ups. Doctors, on the one hand, fear that too much knowledge is a dangerous thing, and an unqualified person in possession of medical information about him or herself may be pushed into being a hypochondriac. Patients, on the other hand, feel a desire to know, they even feel the right to know, every single bit of medical information about themselves and will take advantage of all the medical check-ups that are available. In my opinion both are wrong. I feel it necessary for everyone who wants to have information about

Your doctor will be quite willing to explain why he or she is performing various tests.

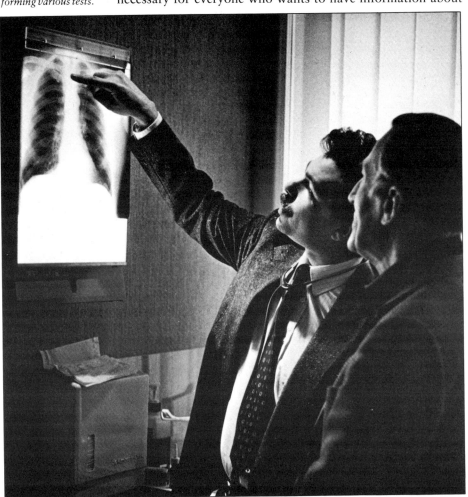

how their body functions and maintains itself should be able to have it, but they need not become a hypochondriac in the process. The obsessive patient who gathers medical data about his or her own body at every opportunity and becomes anxious and overworried if the slightest thing goes wrong is at fault and is in more danger from this than any ailment he or she may have.

The most important aim of medical check-ups is to prevent disease in the long term, and most of us should see the long term as stretching throughout our lives. Ideally we should start looking after our bodies at an early age, during our teens would be my recommendation, but certainly in our twenties and thirties. If we haven't started earlier, there is nothing to be lost in starting to look after our bodies now. We can make the greatest changes if we start early, but we can still make substantial changes if we start late, and it is never too late to make small changes.

You shouldn't rely on your doctor to suggest when a medical check-up is necessary, you should use your own initiative, but your doctor will give you sound advice as to how often your medical check-up should be done whether by yourself or by him or her. As a reminder, you can keep a medical check-up chart at home and show it to your doctor to get him or her involved. An understanding physician will reciprocate.

Whenever you are going to have a medical check-up you should ask your doctor if the tests will be useful, how they will be done, what they will examine, what results he or she expects and how these results will be interpreted. You should also ask how you will be given the results of what the test has shown, and what you should do.

As we get older, some of the medical check-ups which were important when we were young become less relevant and others achieve greater importance. There are certain tests which become increasingly more important as we grow older, their purpose, when they are recommended and where they are carried out, is explained in the chart on pages 54-55.

I should like to give you one piece of advice about the results of medical check-ups. Even though you think you know how often you need check-ups and how results should be interpreted, make sure that you heed the advice of your doctor. In all probability some of the tests will come back not quite normal, but let your doctor assess the importance of this. By all means question your doctor as to what steps you might take to improve the situation, but if your doctor reassures you that nothing further need be done try and take his or her advice. If it is impossible to do this ask for a referral to a specialist for a second opinion.

MEDICAL CHECK-UPS

Name of test and purpose	When recommended	Age to begin
Chest X-ray To detect recent, current, and sometimes past, disease of the lungs	To check that the lungs are clear after a chest infection; if you spit blood; if you have chest pains; if you smoke; if you work in dusty conditions	As early as possible
Blood pressure To check on the state of the heart and arteries	If you have a family history of high blood pressure, heart or kidney disease, stroke or diabetes; if you are overweight	As early as possible
Complete physical examination To check on the general health of heart, lungs, brain and major internal organs	After a serious illness or surgery; if you are worried by a non-specific symptom	As early as posible
Internal examination To examine the pelvic floor, perineum and pelvic organs. This is less important after the menopause	If you have a persistent complaint of the pelvis, vagina or perineum	Before you start any new contraceptive If you have a pelvic inflammation
Vaginal smear To detect pre-malignant changes in the vaginal cells. This is less important after the menopause	If you have a positive family history of risk factors	As early as possible
Mammography To detect small breast lumps	If you fall into a high risk group, or if you have a positive family history	Annually
Eye tests To detect defects in vision and glaucoma	If you have a pain in the eye and it is red	As early as possible
Dental check-ups To check on the general health of teeth and gums; to detect caries, and incorrect alignment	As early as possible. If your parents have poor teeth; if you have a rare dental disorder, like soft teeth	
Rectal examination To check on size and consistency of prostate and for presence of haemorrhoids	If any bowel or urinary symptoms appear	Rarely needed before the age of fifty

Frequency of follow-up	Who will arrange test and where	What the results will show	Who can interpret the results
Annually	Your doctor in a local hospital or mammography unit	Most diseases of lung tissue	A radiologist and your doctor
Annually	Your doctor in your doctor's consulting rooms	If taken correctly and frequently elevations in blood pressure may indicate a serious medical problem	Your doctor
	Your doctor in your doctor's consulting rooms	Gross disease of a major organ, and indications for further tests	Your doctor
According to your doctor or gynaecologist	Your doctor or gynaecologist in your doctor's consulting rooms or a hospital clinic	Gross disease of a pelvic organ, and indications of further tests	Your doctor or gynaecologist
As your doctor advises	Your doctor or gynaecologist in a hospital cytology clinic	Early changes in the vaginal cells before they become malignant, and indications of further tests	A cytologist
Every 6 months if you are in a high risk group	Your doctor or a surgeon in a hospital X-ray department	Tiny breast lumps	A radiologist
Annually	Your doctor, ophthalmologist, optometrist or optician. In your doctor's consulting rooms; in hospital	Visual defects; early signs of increasing pressure on the eyeball, and indications for further tests	Your doctor, an ophthalmologist or an optician
Every 6 months	Your dentist or dental hygienist in your dentist consulting rooms	Early gum diseases or tooth decay	Your dentist or hygienist
Annually unless symptoms develop	Your own doctor will perform the examination and may refer you to a specialist	Enlargement of the prostate or the presence of haemorrhoids	Your doctor or a proctologist

55

Sleep

Our need for sleep diminishes as we get older. Whereas a newborn baby needs anything up to fifteen or sixteen hours a day, a child of eight or so probably doesn't need any more sleep than an adult. In young adulthood most of us can function on six or seven hours of sleep a day. However, by the time we reach our seventies it is quite common for us to sleep for only about two hours and to doze intermittently for the rest of the night.

Sleep researchers believe that our need to sleep is not entirely physical. There is almost certainly a chemical and hormonal component, so it is not a tired body that drives us to sleep, it is a tired brain. Think of the brain as a battery: sixteen to eighteen hours of wakefulness runs the battery down and it needs to sleep to recharge. When we have had enough sleep, our brain cells are charged with granules containing chemicals necessary for efficient intellectual function. When we are tired, however, brain cells become depleted of these granules. During sleep the granules reappear.

Sleep patterns

An internal clock with a regular 24-hour rhythm governs all our body functions. For each individual, this rhythm is slightly different, but it does conform to a general pattern. It is largely determined by blood levels of cortisol, the life-giving hormone, which is secreted by the adrenal gland. By about midnight the blood level of cortisol is sinking rapidly to reach its lowest ebb between the hours of 2 and 4 a.m. Subsequently, the adrenals start to pick up and cortisol floods the body sufficiently to trigger off waking somewhere between the hours of 6 and 9 a.m. Early-morning people have an early cortisol peak. People who are slow to wake and don't really get going till midday, have a later peak.

Whether it is early or late in the morning, most of us enjoy a cortisol 'kick' which makes us alert, energetic and active. Then just after lunch there is a post-prandial dip in the plasma cortisol and this accounts for the drowsiness which many of us feel in the early afternoon. Towards evening, our cortisol levels begin to increase again which enables us to enjoy evening activities. Then as the clock moves towards midnight, the cortisol falls away, and this is one of the triggers which makes us feel sleepy.

Sleep mechanism

Sleep is controlled by two centres in the brain. One is sensitive to external factors like darkness, social and domestic cues, other people saying that they are tired and going to bed, habits, and internal cues like physical or mental tiredness and these *send* us to sleep. A second centre *keeps* us asleep; this is triggered off by chemical reactions in the body and brain cells which occur towards the end of the day.

When we are asleep our bodies enter a state of semi-hibernation. Our body temperatures drop 1°F (0.5°C) and our heart rates slow down. Our breathing becomes slow and shallow. Digestive processes and movement of the intestine virtually stop at night. By contrast, movements of the large muscle don't stop altogether. It seems that muscles have to contract now and then in order for them to recover completely and rest. During the night we move a good deal more than we think. Most of us turn approximately twenty times during our sleep. Some people, usually after fifty, can exist on cat naps. I like the Mediterranean habit of taking a siesta after lunch, a time when we are of little use to anyone, so that we are fresh for the late afternoon and evening. An hour of sleep between 2 and 4 p.m. is very energizing. Even smaller amount of sleep, maybe just fifteen minutes of deep sleep, a real cat nap, can be a lot more help to the body than several hours of light, fitful sleep. While many of us may learn the trick of cat napping during the day, the majority of us cannot cat nap during the night until we are approaching sixty.

The amount of sleep we need consists of the number of hours we remain asleep if left undisturbed. On those rare occasions when we indulge ourselves in this way we sleep a couple of hours longer than our normal working days allow us. Therefore, most of us are about two hours of sleep below par each day and so it is not surprising that we feel we are not functioning properly, physically or mentally and that we cannot cope with stress as well as we would like. As a general rule of thumb, our need for sleep runs parallel with our growth rate. Our sleep needs starts to tail off from around seven or eight hours a night by roughly an hour every decade, until we may need as little as only four hours per night in our sixties.

If you find yourself habitually lying awake at night next to a snoring partner, don't lie there fuming, allowing resentment to build up. It's better to be constructive about insomnia and take advantage of it. Get out of bed, go downstairs and make yourself a cup of tea. Find a book to read or do some job which you have been waiting to do for ages. It is never a good idea to lie in bed feeling resentful if you can't get to sleep. Try and think positively about the few hours you have gained and make the best of them. After all, this is the one time in your life when you may not have to get up to get to the office by a certain time. Take advantage of your freedom and relish the fact that you can sleep till 10.30 in the morning if you wish.

TIPS TO HELP YOU FALL ASLEEP

- Avoid coffee, tea, cola drinks and tobacco after 4 p.m. Don't eat any sweet snacks before bedtime, these all act as stimulants to the body.
- Try to arrange to do something quiet and relaxing before you go to bed. Going for a walk is a good idea, so take the dog. So is half an hour of yoga. You could watch television in bed or read a newspaper or a book. Whatever it is make sure it is not exciting.
- The temperature of your bedroom should be comfortable. It should be neither too hot nor too cold and you may have to open a window to allow the air to circulate to be comfortable.
- Dripping taps and squeaky doors can be very irritating if you wake in the middle of the night, so don't leave taps dripping and close all the doors. If you have radiators that "knock" then bleed them to get air out of the system.
- A lumpy, uncomfortable mattress, particularly if you have back trouble, is a bad idea and don't settle for it. Invest in the best mattress you can afford. This is a health as well as a comfort measure.
- You should always wear loose fitting night clothes but choose cotton or another natural fibre.
- Try to give yourself or have your companion give you a back and neck massage.
- Many people find that a hot bath last thing at night is soporific. The blood is diverted from the brain to the skin and this makes you feel sleepy.
- A warm drink will have the same effect.
- Certain herbs like camomile in tisane or a hot pillow or herb pillow to sleep on might help.
- Cut down on your hours of sleep, make their quality better.
- Here is an instant relaxation method that you might like to try when you are just dropping off to sleep. Starting at your toes, check your ankles, knees, hips, fingers, wrists, elbows, shoulders, torso, neck, face and head, and make sure all your muscles are relaxed. Now slow down your breathing to deep breaths taken at half speed. Try to make your mind a blank. My own tip is to think of black velvet.
- Remember, sex is the best hypnotic.

Smoking

Whilst I am a very keen advocate for giving up smoking, I am not out to persuade you. I only wish to offer help to people who want to stop. Indeed, research has shown that the only people who can be helped are those who want to stop. Even such alternative therapies like hypnosis and acupuncture will fail completely if you do not want to stop.

In a way I envy smokers, because the minute you give up smoking you enter lower risk groups for death from a heart attack, bronchitis, emphysema and lung cancer. There is no other single step which is likely to improve your chances of health so significantly and so immediately as giving up smoking. Even if you feel that you are quite healthy you are suffering without realizing it. Cigarette smoking interferes with the smooth movement of oxygen round the body.

Stopping smoking There are all sorts of ways to give up smoking, the best way is the one that suits you. Before you start on a programme to stop smoking, you should try to adapt any method to your own framework, but there are a few tips about the best way of giving up smoking which have resulted from research. Nearly all experts on smoking cessation agree that you improve your chances if you stop smoking in steps.

One of the best ways of preparing yourself to stop is to draw up a daily diary, noting every time you smoke a cigarette, what you were doing and how much you wanted it. At the end of each day you will find that even if you smoke more than forty cigarettes, there are only about seven or eight which are really crucial to you, and you need to concentrate on these. You can give up the others quite easily. The "tough" cigarettes have either to be avoided by breaking the situation in which you reach for a cigarette, or simply faced straight on. A good method of maintaining your will power is to sign a contract.

BENEFITS OF NOT SMOKING

● You will live longer, five minutes longer for every cigarette you don't smoke.

● You will lower your risk of getting bronchitis, emphysema, peptic ulceration, cancer of the lung and heart disease.

● From the moment you give up smoking your body will be healing itself every minute. Your lungs will no longer produce an excessive amount of phlegm to get rid of the smoke particles. Most important, the cells which have become flattened by irritation from chronic smoking will start growing normally again.

● You are likely to suffer from fewer colds and when you do they will clear up a lot more quickly. Colds are less likely to go down onto your chest or cause sinusitis.

● If you have angina pectoris you can keep the pain at bay for much longer if you stop smoking.

● If you have trouble with your circulation you will start feeling the cold less.

● You are going to be fitter and more active. You can go walking, hiking, swimming and play tennis with your family once more.

● You will no longer smell of stale smoke.

● Your breathing will become easier, you won't become breathless with minor exertion. Your smoker's cough will disappear. ·

● You can wear contact lenses for longer.

● You are more attractive.

● Your fingers and teeth will no longer be stained with nicotine.

● You will enjoy food more, partly because it tastes better, but also because you will have a real appetite for the first time in years, and this doesn't mean that you have to gain weight if you are careful about your diet.

● Your car, house and office will be free of messy ash trays, look more pleasant and clean, and smell sweeter.

● You are setting a good example to others, particularly younger people. You have made it much less likely that your children will smoke.

● It is a source of great pride to conquer your habits because it is a real achievement, and your self-esteem will improve.

● You will save money.

● If you are a singer or an actor, or just enjoy using your voice, you will notice that it has improved.

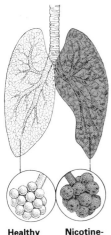

Healthy alveoli   **Nicotine-damaged alveoli**

Sign it with a friend so you feel bound to a programme of stopping. If you stop, you and your friend get an enormous treat like a holiday. If you fail, you and your friend give a large sum of money to a cause you both greatly dislike.

Some people like to follow rules and a method evolved in Germany will provide you with an endless set of guidelines. If you wish to you can write your own rules, of course, as long as you are not easy on yourself. Most people when they come to write the rules do the opposite, setting themselves fairly high standards and are strict in making sure that they are kept. In writing them you are making a contract with yourself to obey and never break them. One of the attractive things about his method is that you can start off with fairly manageable rules and then as you stick to them successfully you can make them more difficult.

Don't obey all the rules on the first day. You should choose three or four, never more than five to begin with. If you prefer, choose those which seem the easiest to achieve. Success breeds success, and once you have mastered them add one or two more rules each day. When you get to the point where you are obeying all the rules you will have stopped!

TIPS TO HELP YOU STOP SMOKING

1. Never smoke in the car.
2. Only start smoking when you are near your destination.
3. Refuse every cigarette offered.
4. Stop smoking before a meal.
5. Don't smoke before breakfast.
6. Buy one packet of cigarettes at a time.
7. Only buy ten cigarettes at a time.
8. Buy a different brand of cigarettes every time and not just your favourite.
9. Before you light a cigarette count ten.
10. Every time you take a cigarette put the pack away at a distance from where you are – in another room if possible.
11. If you run out of cigarettes, never take one from someone else.
12. After each puff put the cigarette down.
13. Never smoke out of doors.
14. Never smoke in bed or at work.
15. Don't carry your lighter or matches with you so that you need to ask for a light.
16. Stop smoking when you are using your hands for something else.
17. Stop smoking in the house.
18. Stop inhaling.
19. Stop smoking a cigarette more than half way down.
20. Stop smoking after a meal while you are sitting at the table.
21. Stop smoking while you are waiting (e.g. for a phone call or a bus).
22. When you are smoking, stop doing everything else. Don't drink coffee, watch television, or listen to music.
23. Stop smoking if someone lights up in your presence.
24. Don't smoke while you are relaxing after work with a drink.
25. Only smoke if you are sitting in an uncomfortable chair.
26. Keep a rubber band around your cigarette pack so that you are aware of opening it.
27. Time your smoking frequency. Have a cigarette on the hour, then try every alternative hour.

Alcoholism

Not everyone is aware that alcoholism and alcohol-related problems such as drunkenness, or development of cirrhosis of the liver, are rapidly increasing in society. Many people wonder how they will know if their drinking has reached the stage where it has become a problem, and, if it has, how best to go about finding expert counselling.

IS ALCOHOL A PROBLEM?

You only have to answer yes to one of the questions below to realize that alcohol is affecting your life in a major way and that you should seek help.

1. When faced with a problem do you turn to alcohol for relief?
2. Are you sometimes unable to meet home or work responsibilities because of your drinking?
3. Has someone close to you sometimes expressed concern about your drinking?
4. Have you ever required medical attention as a result of drinking?
5. Have you ever had distressing physical or psychological reactions when you have stopped drinking?
6. Have you ever experienced a blackout or total loss of memory while still awake when drinking?
7. Have you often failed to keep the promises you have made to yourself about controlling or stopping drinking?

Difficulties are really starting when you develop an increasing tolerance to alcohol, that is, when you need more and more to achieve a desired effect. Surreptitious drinking means that dependence has developed to an unacceptable level. This is the beginning of a critical phase where it becomes increasingly more difficult to stop drinking and as a result social responsibilities and diet are neglected. Alcoholism has terrible effects on the body. It damages the liver irreparably and affects the nervous system. Eventually, it becomes impossible to judge distances or make co-ordinated hand and eye movements, the memory goes and there may be permanent brain damage.

There are several reasons why alcoholism is on the increase, and they can be grouped under the following headings.

Economic causes At the simplest level, alcohol is becoming increasingly available to more people because of rising income levels, particularly amongst women, where alcoholism is rising more steeply than in any other group. Advertising exploits the fact that it is usually younger women who earn the most money. The fastest growing market in alcohol is wine, where women are the most frequent purchasers and consumers. Research in the USA has shown that the higher the income bracket, the more alcohol women drink.

Another reason is that alcohol is now sold in supermarkets and other large stores making it very easy for anyone to obtain it without provoking comment.

Social causes

Most drinking problems start at a social level, because drinking has become socially accepted, even fashionable. Many people work in occupations where free or cheap drink is readily available, in bars, or clubs, and where there exists a natural risk of increased alcohol consumption.

There also seems to be an increase in the number of professions where there is a high risk of contracting drinking problems as a result of stress, including journalism, publishing, advertising and marketing. It is also quite easy for an executive in middle management to increase his or her alcohol consumption two or three times in a very short period by indulging in business lunches and business dinners several times a week. This kind of increase is barely noticed until the wining and dining stops but the need for alcohol remains and the pattern of drinking is continued socially. If you don't take control of yourself and cut down on your drinking before this happens you could be on the slippery slope to chronic alcoholism, vitamin deficiencies, peptic ulceration, a severely damaged liver which will eventually fail and cause death and a disturbance of brain function.

Psychological causes

We are all vulnerable to those disturbing life events which have a profound psychological and social effect on us. Stress, reactions to specific life events and difficulties over self-image all become more prevalent as we get older.

Anyone who drinks alcohol knows that it is a mood changer and tranquillizer, and people therefore often drink to escape from problems. Many of us, as we get older, tend to increase our alcoholic consumption when we are faced with difficult life situations. For both sexes loss of any kind including children, divorce, separation, sex drive, empty nest syndrome, the female and male menopause, and an inability to enjoy sex are all heavily implicated in increased drinking, but do seem incontrovertibly part of modern life. Threats to a woman's feminine role of mother, wife, homemaker and lover are closely associated with alcoholism. The same applies to men. If their masculine roles seem to be questioned, if their roles as breadwinners, senior members of firms, heads of families and stereo-typically dominant lovers come into question. Feelings of inadequacy about performing these roles are often brought on by society's changing and occasionally conflicting views of what a person's role is and ought to be as they get older.

Treatment for alcoholism This is often complicated by the double standards in the various strata of society. While social drinking is accepted, heavy drinking, particularly if it affects work, is heavily frowned upon and this encourages people to be secret drinkers. Many alcoholics tend to drink alone frequently during the day but deny doing so. There are three main lines of treatment.

Detoxification and medical care

This is really only for the severely-affected alcoholic who must recover from the acute effects of drinking before he or she can change in other ways. It is usually undertaken in institutions where alcoholics are "dried out" by gradually reducing the amount of alcohol they drink under the umbrella and support of sedative drugs. Medication and diet are adjusted to the drinker's condition and after a period as an in-patient, treatment may continue on an out-patient basis.

Therapy

The most important step is for drinkers to come to terms with why they are drinking and the problems it causes. The next and crucial step is to consult a doctor about it, or at least to admit to a friend that a problem exists. This represents a leap forward. Individual, group and family therapy are all available through the National Health Service. Anyone with a partner must involve that partner. After the initial drying out period one of the most successful ways of continuing treatment is through psychotherapy (see page 207).

Alcoholics anonymous

This is a voluntary association which exists to help people who want to stop drinking. All members have been alcoholics and thus they are able to use their experiences to help other alcoholics stay sober and rebuild their lives.

Drugs

People have been taking drugs to alter their states of mind since time immemorial. As long ago as biblical times the problems of dependency and addiction were discussed.

Drug dependency There are two main ways in which dependencies start. one has more to do with the personality of the taker and the other has to do with the nature of the drug. Dependence develops because with certain drugs repeated use leads to a change in the way the

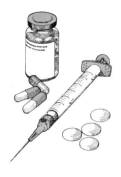

user reacts to the drug. The first change is a reduced ability of the user to choose when and where to take the drug, thus there is a loss of control over decision and a loss of autonomy. As control is gradually lost, the life of the user may be completely given up to securing a supply of the drug and the use of it. Even after a period of abstinence there is a tendency to start using the drug again, even if the addict has been undergoing treatment.

The word "addiction" derives from the Latin which means "to be given over to a master, to be enslaved". Nowadays, the term is used to describe any kind of dependence such as smoking, and in the last few years to describe any person's behaviour which stems from an almost uncontrollable desire, for instance addiction to gambling.

Initially, the user or potential addict seeks out a drug in order to escape from situations which he or she feels are too painful to contemplate, even though they may simply be the realities of life to another person. He or she may experiment with drugs in adolescence, or earlier, and they have been described as having an inadequate personality. This kind of behaviour can also affect people with relatively normal personalities who can "learn to use drugs".

Researchers believe that many factors contribute to the dependency and relapse after withdrawal: a psychopathic personality; adverse home background; poor socio-economic conditions. We must also recognize the fact that other forms of dependence, though without personality disturbance, can be seen with drugs like nicotine, tranquillizers or sleeping pills.

Drug factors Research has shown that biological changes occur with certain drugs such as the opiates and probably with alcohol and barbiturates as well. These lead to physical dependence. Nevertheless, many patients are given opiates several times a day to relieve pain following surgery and virtually none become psychologically dependent or addicted. Why do some people use drugs prohibited by society until they become addicted, while others are able to stop using them after they have been physically dependent? How much can you attribute to the drug, to the individual and to the circumstances in which people find themselves? In almost every consistent drug taker there is an escalated use of drug use and dependence. It is also known that different factors: psychological, sociological, biological and pharmacological, can all have different impacts at different stages. They affect the initial experimentation stage, the second stage of being a casual or recreational user and then to intensive or compulsive use, addiction. This is a downward spiral which involves withdrawal symptoms when the drug is not taken.

The reasons for relapse are complicated. It is possible that the addict becomes so used to treating the withdrawal symptoms which occur several hours after each dose of the drug with yet another dose that the craving is almost reflex, hardly real at all. So, drug, or narcotic, addicts who are cured and feel no craving in hospital may feel the need for a "fix" as soon as they return to their home environments where they are used to using drugs and where they had previously experienced withdrawal symptoms.

Men are much more likely to use illicit drugs than women. Only about 25 percent of cannabis smokers or takers of illegal drugs are women. However, women are the overwhelming consumers and misusers of legal drugs such as tranquillizers and sleeping tablets which not only result in dependency, but often addiction as well. The minor tranquillizers, *valium* and *librium*, are intended to relieve anxiety without producing the drowsiness so characteristic of barbiturates. However, the sensation of prolonged regular use can usually produce withdrawal symptoms comparable to those of barbiturates, such as abdominal and muscle cramps, insomnia, anxiety, depression, convulsions, vomiting and sweating, and there are certainly problems resulting from the excessive use of both of these drugs such as drowsiness, depression, altered sex drive, jaundice, constipation, skin problems and confusion. What's more, if they are taken in conjunction with alcohol they can be lethal. Cannabis, even though it is an illegal drug, is quite often smoked socially. It is a depressing drug which slows reaction time, impairs co-ordination, and may induce drowsiness. The desired effect of a high or euphoria, can either be good or bad for the user.

Tolerance builds up rapidly with these drugs, so users need steadily-increasing amounts to produce the desired effect. Prolonged use has been associated with damaged blood cells and severe psychological impairment. Recent research has also shown that it affects the production of sperm.

One mandatory component of treatment is emphasis on social and, if the patient is married, marital relationships. The greatest difficulty to overcome with the smoker, the alcoholic and the drug addict is avoiding relapse. Coming off the drug for a few days or weeks is usually not very difficult, but a relapse is frequently precipitated by crises such as depression, anger, failure and hopelessness. It is important for the addict to avoid such situations whenever possible and for us to support them through the stressful times when they occur. Doctors also know that the presence of the drug, regardless of what it is, can increase craving, so they should not be readily available.

Treatment for addicts Addicts have a tendency to abuse more than one drug, so it is important to give up all dependencies at the same time, otherwise slippage on one can lead to relapse on another. The average family doctor is generally not in a position to help addicts, but your family doctor will certainly be able to refer you to a hospital department which specializes in drug dependents, and may even know of a self-help group. Most addicts prefer the latter because it involves mutual support, identification and shared experience. It also helps with coping through involvement with others.

Other self-help groups concentrate on teaching self-control, social skills and relaxation (see *Keeping a tranquil mind*). Two methods are used in hospital for the drug dependence programme. The first involves a long period of stay in hospital, up to three months, and the second a briefer period of three weeks or less. Staff have all the necessary skills between them as doctors, psychiatrists and social workers. Medication is given to help cope with withdrawal symptoms and depression. There are group therapy sessions which help addicts to face up to their own problems and psychotherapy is usually available from a psychiatrist or psychologist. In a group of patients who were followed up for two years, there were found to be no differences between the two methods of treatment.

Drug addiction can be cured. Quite a number of former drug addicts attribute their success in kicking the habit to a radical change in their lives. It is usually something good happening. Often the formation of a new friendship. They nearly all point to the importance of the love for someone who is special and nearly all describe the turning point as the time when the reasons for changing were greater than were for continuing.

Maintaining mental agility

Most researchers who study ageing no longer believe that the brain stops developing at eighteen. Performance in verbal as well as other skills remains constant over the years. Intellect can easily be maintained up to seventy if we remain in good health. Thus I would dispute the attitude which suggests we are "over the hill" at fifty. With new ideas and new technology appearing every ten years or so, it is possible for us to have a "retread" with each decade. Bear in mind that new ideas and new technology need new learning and if we take advantage of the influences from outside we can continue to develop throughout our lives in any number of spheres we wish.

Mental exercise   Our minds have to be exercised to stay agile. As we grow older our short-term memories lose power. For most adults, the context of what we are trying to learn is very very important, so learning by rote is not very successful as we grow older. Important information which is meaningful to us, however, we remember, so we should try to make sure information is related to what makes sense to us.

All of us notice that intellectual faculties seem to become blunted or slowed down even as we reach early middle age, memory being one of them, and we are fearful that this deterioration will plummet as we get older. Research has come up with the very reassuring news that this is probably not the case, certainly not as far as intelligence is concerned. A study measured the intellectual functioning of men across a broad spectrum of age groups, in three ways, related to different tasks: firstly, the intelligent use of a telephone directory; secondly, understanding some common legal terms; and thirdly, finding a way through the bureaucracy of the social services. The triumphant results were that middle-aged and older adults scored higher marks as a group than younger participants.

There are certain factors which contribute to being a good learner but which we can't do anything about. The first is heredity which largely determines intellectual capacity and health, which we may be able to control. So just as we have to exercise regularly to maintain physical mobility, we also have to regularly exercise our brains to maintain mental agility. Our bodies' health is for anything we wish to do. The third thing which helps us to learn is time. As we get older we need a little more time for the organization which is necessary to allow us to become "wise". Certain general conditions enable us to learn more. If we haven't been learning or exercising for some time, we may feel a bit rusty, so we have to "chip off the rust". In the beginning this can be tough, but remember the adage "a rusty person is worse than a rusty piece of iron".

If you have not studied for a time, you should not take on demanding courses with lots of pressure. New horizons, new opportunites and courses lead you back in. Preparatory courses enable you to try yourself out and to get back into shape in a cossetted environment. Mature students can do well, but they often lose face when they take on difficult courses which are beyond their capabilities and don't do well at first.

Choosing a subject   It's best if we consider a subject from which we will get a lot of mileage – a continuing interest – not just a series of short courses, which will interest us all our lives. We should ask ourselves: "What subject will I be interested in five years from now?" A subject which enables us to cope with the technological changes taking place would be immensely useful, for instance learning about micro-computers. If possible, we should choose skills which enable us to keep up with society, perhaps even become an authority. This makes us worthwhile not only to ourselves, but also to society. At our age, choice should never be between learning for a job and learning for its own sake. All learning is for our own sake, so that we remain healthy and interesting to the people around us, and are able to continue learning we have to understand the problems which society puts on older people which discourage us from learning. Because it is closely linked to our social disposition, it is something we can change. Most people can't do full-time programmes, but there are full-time residential courses available for short-term work.

People who go back to work or take up new work are wide-ranging in age and work qualifications. They have the advantage of a mass of qualifications, skills, experience and knowledge. Family commitments and circumstances might seem to constrain us, but we should try to decide whether this is because we feel frightened and nervous. Some commitments are real and long-lasting. Others are just a waste of time. We must make a realistic assessment of the present situation and the information we have about job opportunities, so that we can get everything that is required for our work. It's important not to choose a job which is obviously unsuited to our age. Medicine and law are non-starters, as are dancing and physical education. Social services would certainly make a good place to start.

It's better if we do not stop working if this is possible. In most established professions such as accountancy, medicine and law, it's possible to continue work on an advisory basis. In business and commerce, however, this may be harder because they are areas which rely on team work a great deal. Japanese research has shown that businessmen who continue to take an interest in their work, even going into the office once or twice a week and really contributing mentally as advisors, counsellors and senior executives, manage to keep themselves more mentally alert and they live longer than businessmen who take retirement and cut themselves off from all mental activity. So in a way keeping the brain going keeps the body going.

Never forget that it is possible to reactivate skills by taking a refresher course. There are also some self-help programmes from manuals, television and specialist newspapers. There is outside help, for instance the paramedical profession provides retraining. However, government funds and private industry scholarships are more often than not restricted to youngsters.

Sometimes it is quite possible to move sideways, say from secretarial to accounting or buying, and it's always worth us adapting our work skills. For instance, if there are a lot of primary school teachers but few business teachers, it might be worth considering switching, and again old skills can be used in a new way. Managing and organizing at home can lead to doing exactly the same work in personnel or managing an office. Yoga, pottery, gardening and cooking are lively growth markets where it is easy to sell products. All that's needed is a knowledge of running a business and a professional approach.

Skill-centres offer courses about practical subjects that can back up any skills, because it's necessary to have counselling, which is nearly always available at the local job centre or Citizens' Advice Bureaux. Don't be put off by being told there are no vacancies. Get as much information as you can. Go and see career advisors, prowl around the job centres, and look for specialist advisory services.

Voluntary work Don't forget that if money isn't important it's possible to fulfil potential through unpaid, voluntary work. As unemployment is universal in advanced economic communities and it will continue, the greater the number of people who will not work at all for any form of salary. Volunteer work also creates paid work. The skills acquired in voluntary work can later attract some cash. Caring for the elderly is social work which begins at home, and 25 percent of all women between the ages of fifty and sixty-four are caring for a disabled person in the home. As we get older we are very good at jobs which require caring. Caring for the community. Jobs in the health field, social work, and looking after older people. An experienced, cultured person is attractive as a gallery guide, as an usher, for cleaning precious objects in museums, rescuing the sites of our environment, participating in archaeological projects and working to conserve the environment.

If these questions raise serious doubts, think twice before volunteering. If you decide that you want to do volunteer work, here are some of the questions you ought to ask yourself before you start.

- Does it require a skill I already have?
- Will my health allow me to do this kind of voluntary work?
- Do I have the time to give it what it needs?
- Is is something about which I care a great deal?
- Is it something which will hold my attention for a long period of time?
- Are the people involved the kind of people I like?
- Can I easily get to the place where I will work?

Keeping a tranquil mind

Tranquil young people will probably grow into tranquil old people; as a general rule our personalities don't change as we grow older. If we are placid and easy-going with a rather philosophical attitude towards life, this attitude will almost certainly extend to our middle and later years. If we are excitable, enthusiastic and precipitous, the likelihood is we will remain this way. If we have been anxious, nervous and inclined to worry, it will be similar later on. If we have had bouts of depression, moodiness and withdrawal from society, the chances are we won't change as we get older.

As we grow older our mental well-being is threatened by all kinds of environmental stresses as any doctor working in the field of psychiatry will testify. We suffer bouts of depression during and after disruptive life events such as retirement, breakdown of marriage and bereavement. As at any other time of life we are much better equipped to cope with setbacks, even such serious ones as mentioned, if we are well prepared for them and know where to turn for help and support. One of the aims of this chapter is to put you into that strong position so that mental traumas will be less distressing and enable you to face the future more calmly and confidently with the prospect of happiness.

Growing older gracefully

One of the most important aspects of mental well-being as we grow older is adapting to the fact that we *are* older, and accepting it. Gerontologists, people who study what happens as we grow older, call this "successful ageing". Quite a lot of research has been made into what makes ageing successful. The sort of people and personalities who age successfully are well documented and we can learn from them. From all this work it is possible to draw up some guidelines as to how we could maintain a tranquil mind in later life.

People who perceive themselves as elderly or old are significantly more maladjusted than those who perceive themselves to be only middle aged. "Identification of oneself as old" has a detrimental effect on happiness and can be very important when retirement comes; those people who are employed, yet identify themselves as old, are more likely to be maladjusted and discontented than those who are retired but continue to identify with middle age and an active life.

Another crucial ingredient for happiness and contentment seems to be a positive relationship between activity and satisfaction with life. The person who ages best is the person who stays active and who manages to resist the temptation to withdraw too much from the social world.

Our broadening perspective

Most of us don't pursue youthfulness but accept that our bodies are changing with a calm befitting our maturity. In a way chasing youth indicates a personal inadequacy. None of us can avoid the inevitable; it is important for us to accept and enjoy every part of life for its own special pleasure.

I wouldn't wish to turn the clock back one day. Each day is better than the last with a sense that I finally do know how to cope with life. I have a new way of savouring all life's pleasures even those which, in the past, I didn't find remotely interesting. Maturing gracefully to my mind is a happy blend of keeping up with things, reading, seeing people, following world events, continuing hobbies, being adventurous within our limits and maintaining interests as wide as possible. It's about knowing and liking ourselves for what we are, with our imperfections. It's about being as physically active as possible, especially if partner, friend or child will accompany us.

How women respond

Men and women in middle age hold different values. In women the physical and psychological attributes of sexual attractiveness in early adulthood are supplanted by the socially-valued attributes of being a wife and mother. In men the physical and psychological attributes of masculinity can be sustained almost indefinitely, not because there is no loss in virility, physique and appearance, but because those masculine virtues of vigour, strength, competence and courage can all find direct expression in sexual and parental activities. Furthermore they can find symbolic expression in work and leisure activities throughout life.

The middle age of a married woman is framed by her marital circumstances, her family, her job and where she lives. It starts with the release from responsibility, daytime care and control of her children. This process is gradual rather than abrupt, and it is affected by such factors as the number and ages of her children, their schooling and employment. It also roughly coincides with the onset of middle age for her husband. Much of a married woman's domestic life continues unchanged into middle age because social and family activities easily fill the time formerly occupied in looking after her own children. More married women are returning to paid employment after thirty, when their children start school. A woman's age at the marriage of her last child has decreased from fifty-five to forty-five since the end of the nineteenth century. Deterioration in a marriage usually starts to appear in early adult life to middle age. The currently-increasing presence of divorce, representing perhaps the tip of the iceberg of marital disharmony, supports this idea. As time goes on married partners may feel increasingly less satisfied with their relationships.

A few women are predisposed to physical and psychological disorders, precipitated by age changes and the emotional stresses of adult life. The incidence of emotional maladjustment is higher for women than for men, though the suicide rate is lower. High-risk disorders such as lung cancer and heart disease are commoner in men.

How men respond

In middle age, men become more concerned with their health and anxious to maintain their fitness at work and play. Women too, become more concerned with their husband's health. Men watch themselves carefully for the development of symptoms, so-called "body monitoring", whereas women engage in "rehearsal for widowhood", in the sense that they attempt to anticipate what they would do if their husbands fell ill, died or became mentally disturbed. Wives may even press for assurances that they will be provided for in the future.

Research shows (see page 195) that retired men were less active compared with those still in employment, but more active in domestic jobs, household maintenance, social visiting and the pursuit of productive hobbies. They showed as much if not more political interest, especially in relation to pensions and earnings. They stressed the disadvantages of retirement and the advantages of working for a living, whereas the individual still at work stressed the value of leisure in retirement and tended to underestimate the advantages of working and earning. Many unemployed men were anxious about their impending retirement, but few of those who were retired were upset at not working for a living. They complained only about their reduced financial circumstances. The normal, reasonably well-adjusted older man is fairly realistic in his appraisal of facts, accepts himself for what he is, tends to see his wife as an equal partner in a joint enterprise and is fairly tolerant in his assessment of the work of his close relatives.

There was no great difference in physical health between the retired and the working subjects. The older retired subjects are

73

more easily fatigued and physically weaker, though they claim to be in better health than when they were working. On the whole life seems to get better with increasing age, there is less anxiety than in the younger men and the older a man gets the prouder he seems to feel about his advanced age and achievements. They also felt less anxious about death. The retired group were less passive and less dependent on their relationships with other people, and more responsible. They were also less defensive, less officious and less erratic in social relationships. They gave the impression of being more open and trusting, more secure and stable, less hostile towards women and more sociable. The men nearing retirement appeared to be somewhat more inadequate, resentful, depressed, apathetic and contemptuous towards themselves (see page 195).

When very bright children grow into adult life they are likely to be physically healthier, richer and better adjusted than average, intelligent adults and are less likely to need psychiatric attention or to commit suicide. In the same way, healthier, brighter, older people have a number of characteristics indicative of better personal adjustment.

• An inclination to see the advantages of old age and retirement in terms of accumulated experience, skill, freedom from worries and responsibility.

• A better retention of the capacity for original thinking.

• More ingenuity when faced with practical problems.

• Greater involvement with other people when it came to matters of mutual interest.

These same older, brighter, healthier people are somewhat more obsessive, restless and inclined to complain about their work and their families. However, these negative traits may show because such people are still fully "engaged" with life. They are likely to experience disappointments and frustration which are avoided by more fully disengaged older people. The study showed that better adjusted men have certain characteristics.

• They were more often married and living with their wives.

• They were financially better off. They had taken the trouble to plan for an adequate income and good material assets to help bring security and confidence.

• They had constructive rather than defensive attitudes towards retirement.

• They undertook more useful activities and had a more realistic picture of themselves and older people in general. They travelled more and held more cultural interests.

• Their emotional relationships with other people were warmer and more stable.

Motivation and frustration

Our drive tends to decrease as we get older because we have less energy. As we get older we commonly have less enthusiasm and frequently need strong incentives, support and encouragement before starting on a new course of action. However, the way we handle the changes that come with age are very much a matter of continuity and development, depending on temperament and experience.

Long-term aims and established patterns of social behaviour at home and work form the framework for us in life. Thus a well-adjusted person gains strength from a stable personality and temperament and environmental influences such as home and domestic circumstances, relationships at work, money, material possessions and geographical position. After retirement, some of this external framework is removed and we may be forced to change our ways even though we have less outside support than formerly. If we are not prepared for retirement, adjustment is difficult. When goals and long range aims are thwarted, frustration and emotional stress often result.

Whatever age we are frustration and emotional stress focus our motivation on the immediate future; our main concern is protecting our interests and mobilizing our inner resources. In early adult life, we are motivated much of the time by self-interest. In middle age, equilibrium is established for most people, but in later life, motivation is towards withdrawal and avoidance because our physical and psychological resources cannot sustain the demands made upon them. This can make stress difficult to face. One of the worst kinds of frustration is created by any persistently stressful situation or insoluble problem which leads to a violent reaction such as anger or violence, leading to despair, resignation and apathy.

CAUSES OF FRUSTRATION

- Failure of occupational aspirations with a consequent limitation of long-maintained living standards.
- Failure to keep pace with cultural, social and scientific developments, leading to a feeling of being out-of-date and out of touch with what's happening in the world.
- Loss of youthful vigour and freedom, coupled with the uninviting prospect of growing old, usually reinforced by prevailing social attitudes.

- Restrictions on activity.
- Occupational redundancy.
- Loss of valued or stabilizing emotional relationships through bereavement.
- Loss of employment or the departure of children from the family home.
- The insoluble problem of being caught in a web of unsatisfactory circumstances from which escape seems impossible, such as family ties, physical disability or lack of sufficient funds.

A critical episode at any time in our lives can change our attitudes and demands that we make adjustments. Some events are traumatic such as bankruptcy, divorce, becoming deaf. Such experiences mark brief periods of conflict and frustration resulting in reorganization of our motives and actions. Although they leave a mental scar they need not undermine our confidence. Other experiences can be gratifying, for example, falling in love, coming into money, achieving success in cultural or scientific work. Being well-adjusted means as we get older being emotionally stable and resourceful in adapting to changed circumstances like bereavement, retirement, ill-health or loss of employment.

To accomplish this our basic personalities appear to be strengthened, perhaps even simplified, and more clearly delineated throughout late maturity and old age.

Successful and unsuccessful ageing

Many of us are likely to have evolved ways of making personal adjustment which help us to avoid disturbing situations, but there are still factors which can make adjustment difficult.

Anxiety increases steadily with age, especially amongst women. Anxiety arising from what psychologists call "cross pressures", which are typical of adolescence, probably diminishes with age because the older we get the more likely we are to have ironed out the difficulties and contradictions in our circumstances and relationships with others. We all differ as we get older but many of us become more cautious and less confident.

Rigidity is the inability to modify habits. Naturally habitual ways of thinking and behaving increase with age, partly because the long familiarity with a stable environment has "shaped" behaviour in this direction. Clinging to old ways will ultimately make ageing a difficult transition.

Intelligence, too, is an important determinant of personal adjustment, so that age changes in intelligence bring about changes in personality which make ageing more or less difficult.

Personal adjustment is considered to be high if a person can overcome frustrations, resolve conflict, and achieve socially-acceptable satisfactions and achievements. As you'd expect good adjustment expresses itself in happiness, confidence, sociability, self-esteem and productive activity.

Personal adjustment is felt to be low if the individual cannot overcome frustrations, resolve conflicts, or achieve satisfactory results by means of socially-acceptable forms of behaviour. Common signs of poor adjustment are hostility, unhappiness, fear of people, morbid anxiety, dependence, guilt, feelings of inferiority, apathy, withdrawal, or incompetence.

Our later years of life need not be static and unchanging. If we are prepared, personal adjustment should evolve smoothly and logically out of earlier patterns of behaviour. If a sense of continuity and identity can be maintained in spite of physiological, social and psychological changes, the process of re-engagement can proceed successfully. This is essential for adjustment and secures a more effective use of our reduced resources. Normal ageing is gradual by psychological standards, at least, and with foresight, planning and social support much can be done to ease the problems of adjustment and improve the general level of achievement and happiness.

Adequate adjustment to old age requires certain abilities of us before we can be happy.

• Our inner mental state and external circumstances are in balance. There is a degree of continuity between past and present patterns of adjustment.

• We accept old age and death.

• We feel a degree of euphoria arising out of security and relief from responsibilities.

• We have security and adequate financial circumstances to maintain the lifestyle we are used to.

Stress control and relaxation

Living in the twentieth century means that we feel more stress than any members of the human race have ever felt. We live in a success-orientated society, and competitiveness and the desire to succeed which has surrounded most of us in our working lives is something that most of us would rather do without. Much of the data that has been collected concentrates on stress as it affects men, but many women have become increasingly susceptible to stress and its related illnesses. This is particularly true of working women.

A moderate degree of stress can be good for us. Research has shown that up to a certain point it improves our performance, efficiency, productivity, and many of us thrive on it. There are some who actually need stress to function at maximum efficiency. For most of us, if stress goes beyond a certain point, we disintegrate and this can lead to both mental and physical illness. Before we can enjoy an active but serene life it is important that we come to terms with the causes of stress. We need to recognize the important part that it plays in our health and try to find out how we can either get rid of it or cope with it so that it doesn't interfere with our lives.

Flight or fight

Our immediate response to stress is the "flight or fight" reflex. This is a reflex which prepares our bodies by affecting our muscles, eyes, the rate at which we breathe, the rate at which our hearts beat, to either run from our enemies or fight them and it is primarily a hormone response. The brain sends messages to the two adrenal glands which lie on top of the kidneys. The message is recognized immediately and the body begins to pump out adrenalin. The physical effects of adrenalin are those which we all recognize.

● Our hearts begin to pound quickly so that the maximum amount of blood is being pumped round our bodies to make them ready for any kind of action.

● The rate at which we breathe increases so that our blood carries the maximum amount of oxygen to our muscles in order to make them work efficiently.

● Our blood pressures increase so that our essential organs become well supplied with blood.

● Blood vessels in our skin and internal organs constrict to make a larger volume of blood available to our bodies so that they are primed and ready to run.

● Our pupils enlarge so that we can see both what is frightening us and a clear path to get away from it.

● The blood sugar rises steeply making available a large amount of energy which we will need to use if we either have to fight or flee from an "adversary".

Our emotional responses to stress are different for different people and it's affected by our sex, cultural background, heredity, environment and the ways in which we have been taught to deal with stress. In most western societies it is acceptable for women to become upset and cry, while even little boys are encouraged to face stress with a stiff upper lip.

We come under stress because intellectually we know that stressful situations cannot be resolved by fighting or fleeing. Yet adrenalin is being pumped into our bodies which makes us ready to do both, so our bodies are switched on but our instinct to run or face the enemy is repressed. The resulting tension and frustration promotes further stress, and a vicious cycle is set up which may develop into physical and mental illness.

Results of stress

If blood pressure remains elevated for any length of time it leads to damage of the arteries and possibly a heart attack. We know that certain conditions are stress-related – migraine headaches, for instance. Skin conditions such as eczema (dermatitis) and itching of the skin, and a group of functioning conditions such as spastic colon, dyspepsia and duodenal ulcer may also result.

There are many major life-threatening diseases linked to stress such as severe, chronic high blood pressure, heart disease, peptic ulcers, arthritis, asthma and diabetes. Research has shown that when we are under stress we are more susceptible to infection, particularly viruses, and some authorities claim that the development of cancer can be directly related to stress. Certain stress-related problems specific to women include menstrual disorders, pelvic pain, sexual difficulties, premenstrual tension, unwanted hair growth and disturbance of ovarian function leading to failure to ovulate.

Dealing with stress

One of the best ways to ease stressful moments is to be active. Physical activity on its own counteracts stress. Take any kind of exercise – go for a walk, jog, play a game of tennis, tackle a household chore, even sit down and make out a list of possible solutions, probable solutions and the ideal solution to the difficulty which is causing your stress. It is better to control the stress before you react to it if you possibly can. A stress management plan will help you with your own action plan for viewing some of your attitudes, some important hurdles that you have to get over, some beliefs that you have to change along with some of your habits. This may mean a significant change to your lifestyle and the stress plan will help you to put it into practice. You are going to have to make an effort because it involves acquiring new, basic skills. Two of these skills are *deep muscle relaxation* and *mental relaxation* (see page 80). Mastering these techniques will enable you to deal with stress, change some entrenched habits like smoking and drinking and you should be able to deal with almost any of the problems that life throws at you.

When you have mastered both these relaxation techniques you might try doing the drills together. They are fairly easy to combine. You should practise the combination of deep muscle relaxation and mental relaxation (see over) initially twice a day. Once you have mastered these skills you can practise them more frequently. Don't be concerned if they take a few weeks to master completely, and for you to achieve the well-being that comes through relaxing and managing stress.

The two other things that you can do to help your body to cope with stress are *instant relaxation* and *imagery training* (see page 81). Once you are successful at muscle and mental relaxation you should be able to achieve partial, deep muscle and partial mental relaxation within thirty seconds.

Incidentally, you are well on the way to coping with giving up unhealthy habits like smoking or drinking too much. You will be able to resist the most difficult cigarettes of the day, the greatest cravings and the worst temptations.

DEEP MUSCLE RELAXATION

Deep muscle relaxation is a technique that was devised at the Stanford Heart Disease Prevention Centre. It may take us a little time and effort to learn but it will be well worth it. It will help us to cope with stress, lower our blood pressure and decrease the chance of our getting headaches, thus allowing us to sleep better and feel less anxious. This is the drill to follow:

- Find a quiet place and lie on your back in a comfortable position. If this isn't possible just sit as comfortably as you can and close your eyes.
- The next part of the drill involves your right hand if you are right-handed and your left hand if you are left-handed. Begin by tensing your right (left) hand for just a moment and relaxing it by letting it go loose. Actually *tell* your hand to feel heavy and warm. Moving up your right (left) side of your body to your forearm, upper arm, shoulder, foot, lower leg, and upper leg, go right round the right (left) side of your body. Then do exactly the same thing with the left (right) side of your body. Your hands, arms and legs should feel heavy, relaxed and warm. Give yourself a few seconds for those feelings to develop.
- Now try relaxing your hip muscles. Let the relaxation flow up from your abdomen into your chest. Don't try to tense your muscles, just tell them to feel heavy and warm. You will find that your breathing starts to slow down; wait for this to happen. Concentrate on your breathing.
- Let the relaxation flow up into your shoulders, jaw and the muscles in your face. Pay special attention to those muscles around your eyes and in your forehead. Actively get rid of any frowns. Finish by telling your forehead to feel cool.

If possible you should practise this drill twice a day, for fifteen to twenty minutes each time. If this isn't possible, three or four minutes are better than nothing. The best time to practise is just before meals and an hour or later after meals. Once you have mastered this, try mental relaxation.

MENTAL RELAXATION

This involves clearing your mind of any stressful thoughts, anxieties and worries. The drill is based on the Stanford technique.

- Just let thoughts flow through your head; let them freely associate.
- If any thought recurs, stop it by saying "no" firmly under your breath.
- Close your eyes and imagine a calm scene – such as a clear blue sky and a calm blue sea or any object that hasn't any fussy details. Blue is very relaxing.
- Concentrate hard on your breathing and become aware of its natural rhythm.
- You should be feeling calm and rested by now. You may find it helpful to repeat a soothing word such as "love", "peace", "calm" or a word with less symbolism such as "breath", "earth" or "laugh". Think of the word or even a calming sound like "ah" when you are breathing outwards.
- Keep the muscles of your face, eyes and forehead relaxed, and tell your forehead to feel cool.

INSTANT RELAXATION

• Arrange your body comfortably, sitting. You can also teach yourself to stand comfortably, even when you are waiting in a queue, or if you are facing a stressful, worrying experience.
• Take a deep breath and hold it for five seconds. Count to five slowly then breathe out. Repeat this for several seconds.

• Tell all your muscles to relax.
• Repeat this two or three times until you're completely relaxed.
• Imagine as pleasant a thought as circumstances permit, such as learning how to relax or again imagining a pleasant scene, peaceful countryside or a beautiful view or sunset.

IMAGERY TRAINING

This helps you to use your imagination by breaking down your mental blocks. You get more in touch with your body so that you can control it. Sometimes it is quite difficult to learn, but here is a simple exercise for you to follow:

• Think of your left hand and make it feel warm. Imagine your right thigh and make it feel warm. Make it feel heavy. Now try two harder tests. Imagine that one leg is heavier than the other. It may seem odd at first but it is worth practising to get control of the feelings in your body through your imagination. Once you can do these tests easily you will find deep muscle relaxation simple. You should be able to control your body to keep away headaches, migraine attacks and lower your blood pressure.

81

Depression

Depression is, to some degree, a very common, human experience – customary in certain circumstances, appropriate even if something awful happens in our lives. Nevertheless, in most cases it isn't desirable, and that in itself implies that something ought to be done about it.

Depression can also be an attitude to life. We might describe someone as "always being depressed" if he or she has a pessimistic temperament, always expects the worst out of life and usually gets it. It is not difficult to see this cynical attitude towards life growing from something which we all experience transiently into something which persists. We are all familiar with depression as a mood. The "Monday Morning Blues" might describe the sum total of all our feelings at the prospect of having the weekend behind us and the week in front of us.

All these feelings combine to make us feel apprehensive, down in the dumps, gloomy, miserable, low, lifeless, flat, fed up, cheesed off, etc. When used this way, the word "depression" combines a sense of being down in spirits, low in energy and having a sense of hopelessness and uselessness, even of loss. It suggests pessimism and apathy. The opposite would be a feeling of joy, enthusiasm, optimism and hopefulness. A depressed mood most often comes on after a disappointment. It may strike out of the blue and very often it can be accompanied by anxiety. Even becoming depressed can spark off anxiety in certain people. In others, depression arises with anxiety.

Depression is a difficult experience to put into words. It is nearly always linked to feeling depressed, but it may be accompanied by other more disturbing feelings like being devalued, not feeling appreciated or not being loved. Many of these feelings can become directed at oneself; of being useless, worthless, or not being worth loving, and we may have a desperate feeling of loss. This sense of losing something can be associated with feeling frustrated and resentful. In one way, depression can be thought of as a protective mechanism; it temporarily switches a depressed person off until he or she can cope better. If the protective mechanism doesn't work and a "fuse blows", then a depressive illness may result, and in that something has gone basically wrong. A depressive illness is much more serious than a depressive attitude or mood because it impinges upon every aspect of daily living.

It's very important to seek professional help from your doctor because most forms of depression will not respond to self-help – especially if the problem that's depressing you will not go away of it's own accord.

Masking depression

In order for us to realize that we are depressed we have to be in touch with our feelings. To be able to explain that we are feeling depressed we have to recognize that depression exists as an entity and that we are suffering from it at the time, and we have to have the capacity and vocabulary to express what we are feeling. Many of us cannot recognize depression and even if we could we would not be able to express what the depressive feeling is like. This means that many of us may be depressed without realizing it.

Just as our bodies have protective mechanisms against physical injuries, so they have against psychological stresses. When our psyches recognize that we are depressed, defence mechanisms come into play. *Displacement* is the commonest defence mechanism, diverting our attention from the thing which is most threatening to something else which is less threatening and easier to accept. Therefore, a secondary concern acts as a smoke screen for the first. For instance, someone who is very depressed may appear very anxious, and this is because the depression itself has released so much anxiety that the original depression is lost. Similarly, depression can be expressed as irritability, resentment or anger which hides it.

In the case of the classically unhappy clown, false humour is used to cover up depression. Depression can be "converted" into a physical illness – the commonest is pain. Psychological pain has been converted into physical distress and many of us mask depression simply by denial. We try to persuade ourselves that something isn't so in the hope that it will go away. We believe that if we tell ourselves that we are not depressed then the depression will go away. People who are really depressed go to a great deal of trouble to look well and happy, these are the so-called "smiling depressives".

Depression as illness

Most of us think of physical and psychological illnesses as being quite different. In fact, they have many things in common. Let's take a fairly common physical illness as a model – a fever. A fever both harms and heals the body at the same time. It commonly accompanies an infection and, as a result, an inflammation is caused in part of the body. While the high fever may make us unwell, even delirious, it is at the same time part of a defence mechanism to mobilize our defences and overcome the infecting organism. So the illness we have suffered as part of the fever has "harmed" the body while it was helping it to heal. Depression can be thought of in the same way. The symptoms of depressive illness can be the result of both strain on the person and also the person's own psychological defence mechanisms mobilized to adapt to the strain.

For many people depression can start as a normal response to given circumstances and be pushed into an abnormal one. However, abnormal depression can be potentially healing – it can lower responsiveness so that a depressed person no longer responds so forcibly to stresses. The greater the stress, the greater the depression becomes to provide a protective screen. When external stresses become overwhelming, depression can act as a cut-out mechanism so that we may stop responding altogether. If depression is accompanied by grief and weeping, it has a cathartic effect when pent-up emotions are liberated, so we can think of depression as a period of time when a person can pull up the drawbridge and use all his or her energy towards inner healing while adapting to external events.

Depression is often associated with emotional crises. These can be seen as emergencies, not necessarily to be avoided but as things which can be made use of for growth. All of us looking back can remember emotional crises which were important for us for personal growth. We can see these emotional crises as turning points without which we would not have grown and matured. Nearly all of us could describe two kinds of crises. There is the development crisis which arises at a critical stage of our own emotional development, and there are crises that can occur at any time in our lives and are concerned with events around us rather than inside us.

Developmental crises
A developmental crisis can occur whenever we are about to move from one stage of our life history into another, or from one role into another. There are crises all the way through our lives from that of going to school, having a first boy or girl friend, leaving school, going to college, getting a first job, becoming engaged, getting married or having a child. Many of these crises involve changes in the degree of dependence we feel towards others; usually we are moving to greater and greater independence, to such a point as when others then become dependent on us. They also reflect changes in the roles we play, such as being an adolescent rather than a child or becoming a fiancé, wife, husband or parent.

External influences
Crises in the outside world are potentially threatening to our safety and our well-being. They can be failures like loss of security or material wealth, failing exams, failing to get a promotion, being sacked or declared redundant and they can be of our own making or the making of others. Then there are acute losses which leave painful spaces like infidelity, abortion,

bereavement, divorce and loss of sexuality. We experience cultural transitions where there is a move from one role to another, from one way of life to another, which may involve the loss of the usual comforting guidelines. Going to college not only involves changing the role from pupil to student, but also changing one way of life to another. Moving from one country to another will involve cultural transitions.

Depression fits into all this when a person cannot cope with the change, or in someone who will eventually cope, but in whom depression appears before he or she can adapt to the change. We don't know why people should get depressed in development crises or why certain periods of life should be more associated with depression than others. Moving from one role to another, from one stage in life to another, can be seen as leaving something precious behind, rather than as moving into something new and exciting. There could be depression arising out of a sense of loss or uncertainty about the future.

Depression and ageing

It could be that at certain stages of our development we become more vulnerable to external changes and we will show this internal strain by being depressed. Our own individual vulnerability will be based on hereditary factors, our own strengths and weaknesses and our psychological make-up. It is possible to see how depression may express itself as part of the development we go through as we age and face retirement.

There is a definite loss of function and of status. A woman entering the menopause still cherishes her sexuality and her capacity to bear children. A man cherishes his power largely represented by his earning capacity. As we go through middle age we start to feel that we are lagging behind. As we retire and get older we start to know that we are lagging behind. Depression is not inevitable at any critical stage of life, but it is usually those people who have suffered an early loss in infancy, or who have not had their needs met when they were young, who are more likely in later life to become depressed when either internal or external change exposes them to stress.

Causes of depression

Depression has physical, psychological and social causes. Some of the physical causes include head injuries with concussion, and operations on certain parts of the body, particularly if they are valued parts such as the head, eyes, ears, hands and genital organs. Infections, particularly viral infections and most commonly influenza, encephalitis and hepatitis, are commonly followed by a period of depression which will last up to several months. Changes in the brain, such as epilepsy or a stroke, can lead to mood changes, alteration of behaviour and depression.

Women suffer certain biochemical changes in their bodies such as those which occur premenstrually, after childbirth and during the menopause which can lead to depression, and some drugs while dealing with one illness can lead to depression as a side-effect in certain susceptible people.

The social causes of depression are nearly always associated with separation and loss. Being poor does not necessarily lead to depression, but if poverty means a loss of status, it may do so. Bad weather doesn't necessarily lead to depression, but if bad weather means that you have to abandon a treat, then it may do so. Belonging to a minority group doesn't cause depression, but if by being so you are cut off from others, you are persecuted and lose privileges, then you may become depressed.

Most people believe that there is one social factor – isolation – which seems to be linked very closely with a tendency to depression. Hannah Gavron, a sociologist, studied women who were tied to the home. She showed that these women were socially isolated whether they were from the upper or lower social classes, and these were the ones who got depressed. Peter Sainsbury studied depression and suicide in London and showed that the incidence of self-destructive acts was higher where people were cut off from one another, whether they were wealthy or not. The isolated spinster or bachelor, widow or widower were the ones more likely to end up attempting suicide. Marriage, because it avoids social isolation, is less likely to cause suicide despite the great unhappiness it may bring.

As we get older, a wide range of social and psychological stresses may contribute to depression. Bereavement would be the most dramatic for all of us but other causes of isolation such as our children getting married or their moving to another part of the country, or our re-housing away from a familiar neighbourhood are examples which can cause disquiet.

Retirement and stress

Retirement, no matter how well managed, is also a time of stress. In one day, a person loses workmates, may suffer a tremendous fall in income, lose a major source of interest and relinquish an important family position. It may seem to society and him or herself that his or her useful life has ended. And then there are less well-defined reasons for being depressed as we get older: modern society tends to devalue the role of age in both industry and recreation. Experience is considered to be less important than vitality and originality and this can fill us with a sense of inferiority which is only accentuated by a lower income and less than perfect housing. All of this can be made worse by the pain and deprivation caused by a long-term illness, which on occasions is sufficient in itself to cause depression.

Bouts of depression in older age rarely come as a surprise for the sufferer. Most people will have been suffering from recurrences of depression since quite an early age in life. Depression may have first started in adolescence and carried on right through adult life but it is rarely in its severest form when we are older. Mild depression certainly is most common between the ages of forty and fifty, and a severe form of depression has its highest incidence between the ages of forty and sixty-five. After that, the incidence declines and it is extremely rare to have a first attack of depression in old age.

The root of the problem is nearly always difficulty in facing up to and handling change. Some people find it very difficult to shoulder the stresses and responsibilities that are peculiar to getting older. They find themselves in new territory which is unfamiliar and which has never been explained or explored before. It is even harder to bear because that territory is viewed by much of society as alien. Thus they are left standing on the outside of the workforce and the culture that goes with it, feeling very strongly that they are non-contributory members of society, feeling that they are a liability to the people who create wealth, and even perhaps feeling guilty that they are such heavy consumers of entertainment and support services. It is hardly surprising that they are besieged by feelings of self-doubt and unworthiness. Many self-possessed people are devastated to find that they are unable to care for themselves and maintain themselves through their own efforts or by self-sacrifice. Any neurotic conflicts that they may have felt earlier in life now face them in bulk. Anyone would have to be emotionally stalwart to put on a brave face and keep up good spirits when the surroundings appear hostile.

Types of depression

Depressive reactions include depressive moods, experiences and temperaments, and these can be normal or abnormal. Depressive illness, on the other hand, is always abnormal.

Depressive reaction

This is nearly always associated with anxiety; a person feels tense and restless. He or she may have palpitations, lose his or her appetite and have loose bowels. Nights may be spent sleepless because of anxiety. Sleep, when it comes, may be fitful because of unpleasant dreams and nightmares. The depressed mood is nearly always one of despair and hopelessness. There is difficulty in summoning up enthusiasm for anything, and even if the person is enthusiastic he or she cannot concentrate. People who are depressed often complain that their minds wander off and dwell on unpleasant thoughts – on rejection, despair or failure. There seems to be little point in life and little reason for going on. The anxiety and depression are often mixed with anger and resentment against a world which seems to be constantly antagonistic.

Depressive illness

Here the person is slowed up in both mind and body. All reactions are delayed which means that he or she cannot think properly because thought processes are so slow. A depressed person's body is slow, he or she moves as if in a dream. Such a person does not avoid obstacles, and even the bowels are slowed down so that he or she suffers from constipation rather than diarrhoea. Most depressed people feel worst first thing in the morning, then improve as the day goes on. Improvement, however, may only last until evening when the person feels bad again, and again on waking. Most depressed people get off to sleep all right at night, but tend to wake in the small hours of the morning unable to go back to sleep. It is usual for a depressed person to blame him or herself rather than the world outside. He or she feels guilty and full of self-reproach. Everything is their fault, even if it is due to something which has been done a very long time ago. Sometimes such a depressed person will feel so helpless, ashamed and guilt-ridden that suicide seems the only way out of the dilemma.

Symptoms of depression

Sadness and tearfulness

Sadness is probably the commonest sign of depression. Nearly all depressives look sad with their faces immobile and they express very few emotions. They rarely smile and they may complain of feeling sad. They may spend long periods gazing in front of them, looking as though they are going to burst into tears. Tearfulness may go hand in hand with sadness. Crying is often done alone and some depressives who are really agitated will cry a lot and nothing can stop them.

Sleep disturbances

Nearly everyone who is depressed suffers some kind of sleep disturbance. In one kind of illness, *exogenous depression*, people have difficulty in getting off to sleep, and in another, *endogenous depression*, they get off to sleep but wake early in the morning. Research has shown that nearly all people who are depressed spend more time getting off to sleep and more time awake in the early hours of the morning than people who are not depressed. The more depressed a person, the less sleep he or she gets each night. This, after a short time, results in the person feeling below par physically, which adds to the problem.

Loss of appetite

It is very common for depressed people to feel a loss of appetite and they may be infuriating to cook for. They tend to pick at food, complain about it, say that they are not hungry and eat very little. This can lead to a loss of weight which worries them and their families. Some depressed people can go for days without eating anything at all.

Neglect of appearance

When depression is very deep some people let themselves go and cease to care about their appearance and personal hygiene. They may become generally slovenly. Well-dressed women no longer bother to do their hair or apply make-up and just throw on any clothes that happen to be around. Men tend to remain unshaven and look dirty and ill-kempt. A person may neglect him or herself to the point where he or she smells so offensive that it is unpleasant to be with them.

Fearfulness

Depressives are fearful people and they have two major fears. They fear death and they fear being left alone. People who have been previously independent easily become housebound. A depressive with physical ailments will use complaints to curtail outings. Some depressives become afraid of driving, or have panic attacks in crowded shops, in the trains or on crossing bridges. They can't explain situations that have made them afraid, but these irrational fears can cripple not only the person affected but also his or her family. A once active husband who becomes too afraid to drive can cause a very important change in lifestyle for his wife and family. This pathetic decline turns a capable person into a fearful social cripple.

Anxiety

Very few depressives are entirely free of anxiety and many of them feel anxious most of the time. Sometimes the anxiety takes the form of panic attacks with sweating, fast breathing, palpitation and dizziness, and this may be provoked by one of the many obsessional fears or phobias that they may develop.

Depressives may develop general anxiety in anticipation of events, even those which may never happen, so that they are uncontrollably upset by the thought of something that may be hours or days off. If someone is afraid to be left alone for example, he or she begins to worry about what will happen to them days ahead of time. These worries and fears may build up to such a height that the person finds him or herself crippled mentally with ailments, real or unreal, which they can't control.

Indecision

Many depressives are unable to make the most trivial of decisions, and it can be agony to watch a depressive taking minutes over which socks to use, or which dress to put on. Sometimes they are unable to make a choice at all and may opt to do nothing rather than choose between two options. This is not because there are so many options that they cannot make up their minds, it is because a depressed person can only see negative outcomes of whichever decision is made no matter how much they try to rationalize the situation.

Coupled with this lowered ability to make decisions is poor judgement. One of the dangers of depression is that if it goes unrecognized it can lead to terrible problems. A depressed person can never be relied upon to make a sound judgement, and this has to be faced fairly early on. It is not uncommon for depressed people to have convincing and compelling ways out of their depression, for example, they don't believe that they were really suited to their wives or husbands, and so divorce is the answer; they don't get on with their neighbours, so the answer is to sell their houses and move. This is part of the painful picture which results from depression and the effect that it has on the family.

Mood changes

Some depressives are very low in mood and others can be very agitated, over-active and tense. They may pace the floor, wring their hands, jump from one activity to another; they are what we would generally describe as nervous. This is an extremely wearing kind of depression to live with, especially as they complain of physical symptoms and are very edgy most of the time. They may talk a lot and bombard people with endless questions, the vast majority of which are centred on themselves – their favourite topic of conversation. They may be so mentally agitated that their ideas flow in strings of disconnected thoughts and they may constantly suffer floods of emotions uncontrollably washing over them.

Tiredness and weakness

Most depressed people are tired and complain of weakness. The slightest effort may leave them exhausted and so they sit around a great deal. Depression slows everything down and so their thinking, feelings, actions and emotions are all damped down, in serious cases to the point of inactivity. This tiredness and weakness may become so serious that they can't even make the effort to chew their food. Depression is a psychological illness which will not get better without adequate sleep.

Poor concentration and loss of memory

Many depressives suffer from poor concentration and memory. These two symptoms are annoying and frustrating for them because they result in a very short attention span; they get distracted from any given task within a few minutes.

Depressives find that they can't think straight and that their minds often wander back to themselves and their predicament. Their memories fail, especially for recent and trivial things and they forget where they put things, what they had for lunch, and whether or not they took their tablets. Nearly all depressives lose their self-esteem and self-confidence. People who are highly confident before their illness need to get very depressed before they begin to see themselves as useless, whereas others who had little to start with soon become enveloped in self-pity and dejection. People who are endogenously depressed lose all pride in themselves and feel that there is nothing of value or worth in them. They tell everyone who will listen that they are worthless and this "negative self-esteem" may become a dominant feature of their depression. People suffering from a reactive depression tend not to lose self-esteem. They tend to feel that the world has lost its meaning and not that they themselves are worthless.

Loss of libido

One of the key features of depression is that sufferers stop getting pleasure out of life and one of the first pleasures to go is their interest in sex. Depression ranks high on the list of conditions that reduces sexual appetite. A depressed man often cannot get or sustain an erection. He then becomes anxious about this and may eventually become impotent. This only adds to his depression. Such impotence is more often experienced by an older man, who may well see himself as less of a man anyway, as he becomes convinced that life has passed him by or that he will never achieve what he had hoped.

Loss of sociability

Another main feature of depression is a feeling of flatness and loss of pleasure from hobbies and other activities that normally give a lift to life. When the pleasure is lost from these activities, the drive to pursue them disappears, too, and depressed people may be overwhelmed by their own inertia. Even favourite pastimes like football and other sports may lose their meaning and importance. Friendships suffer and eventually close family relationships cease to be important. If this condition deepens the family is rejected and the depressive person lives in a world populated only by him or herself. It is important for the family to remember that they aren't being rejected deliberately.

One has to remember that a depressive illness can control a person so totally that he or she couldn't behave differently even if he or she wanted to, and it is the very nature of the depression that the person is not motivated to behave differently or more positively.

Treatment of depression

Most depressive illness is treated successfully. Furthermore, it is treated successfully at the level of the family practitioner. Very few cases are severe enough to be referred to psychiatrists. New generations of anti-depressant drugs are highly successful. There are many different types available so that your doctor is able to prescribe one which is most suitable for you.

Drugs

Anti-depressant drugs are the mainstay of treatment and they are designed to combat the physical basis of depression. There are two main groups, the *tricyclic antidepressants* and the *monoamine oxidase inhibitors*. Tricyclic drugs may take two or three weeks to have an effect but the monoamine oxidase inhibitors, which are more powerful, have side effects. They can cause a rise in blood pressure if certain foods and drinks like meat extracts, broad beans, cheese, wine and beer are taken at the same time.

The mood elevators such as the *amphetamines* raise our moods without dealing with the underlying causes of the depression. These drugs are only palliative, and because of the risk of drug misuse and dependence they are no longer widely used. If there is anxiety with the depression then tranquillizers and sedatives may be given as well. The patient complaining of marked insomnia will almost certainly be given hypnotics for a good night's rest.

Finally there is a new drug called *lithium*. This is given in the form of its salt, lithium carbonate, and it works by limiting the degree to which our moods can alter. Also it reduces the chances of a relapse. As it has to be given for a long period, blood levels are monitored. This treatment has proven successful even in people who have suffered more than one attack of depression each year. Once lithium therapy had been started and carefully monitored, recurrences became very rare indeed.

Electro-convulsive therapy (ECT)

It has long been known that electrical activity in the brain could affect our moods. People with epilepsy often find that their moods improve after an attack and in the 1930s a Viennese psychiatrist found that severely depressed patients responded to artificially-induced fits. Nowadays, the modern form of this treatment, electro-convulsive therapy or ECT, is very sophisticated. The apprehension of the patient is reduced by using a quick-acting anaesthetic which, when given in proper circumstances by an experienced team of doctors and nurses, carries very little risk.

Although the idea of ECT may sound frightening, the patient is not distressed if it is done properly. Following after each treatment there may be a headache and a slight loss of memory, but these quickly pass. After a course of five or six treatments given twice a week, the patient will feel a dramatic release from depression. ECT is still the subject of continuing controversy among doctors and like all medical procedures it is not a universal answer to depression. It is more likely to be effective in a true depressive illness than a depressive reaction, this is particularly so in depressions of the endogenous (arising from within) type. It is quite often given in conjunction with drugs, and is useful to cover the two-to-three weeks before an anti-depressant drug takes effect.

Psychological therapy
Psychological methods are of great value in helping depression, because they bring together the mind and feelings of the person into contact with the mind and feelings of others.

Counselling is helping a patient by the joint examination of the problem. "Let the two of us sit down and talk about your situation and see if together we may be able to discover what you can do about it". A counsellor finds out the facts about a patient's case to determine what is happening at a level of reality and what is fantasy. It may involve giving advice and making helpful suggestions, though this should always be done sparingly. It means formulating a plan of action with the patient and giving emotional support while difficult decisions are being made and acted upon.

Psychotherapy is a specialized form of counselling which aims to promote new emotional learning. An easy way of describing psychotherapy is to say that it provides "a corrective emotional experience". For depression, psychotherapy is used to explore with the patient the inner conflicts which give rise to guilt and aggression. Hopefully, in the security of the relationship with the therapist, the patient will cope better with current experiences (see *Specialist help*).

Psychodrama is a fairly new technique in which patients act out feelings of being depressed in the circumstances which have led to them being depressed. As lost experiences are recreated, patients get in touch with feelings that are locked inside them and make the feelings work *for* them. One of the most important aspects of all psychotherapy methods is sharing the depression with others, and sharing theirs with ourselves. In this process healing begins to take place.

Social therapy
Yet another form of treatment uses social methods. In this context it matters less what goes on deep inside a person than what goes on in his or her interaction with others. Concern is with relationships in their usual social setting. Any way in which one person helps another or makes help available involves interaction and this can be a learning experience. Treatment for depression should be comprehensive and involve all three approaches. Only when the "whole" person is dealt with in an idealistic situation is the treatment being used well.

Loneliness

An older person who is inactive and isolated is likely at first to be bored and irritated. This state of mind may pass as he or she becomes more passive, apathetic and inert. Stagnation leads to further falls in alertness and interest, and to a loss of mental and physical use of skills through disuse. Prodding an older person into action and overcoming his or her reluctance to participate in social activities *may* be an unwarranted intrusion into his or her private life, but a change of surroundings, stimulation and guidance will often help the person to maintain an interest in life and derive a new-found enjoyment in the company of others which up to now he or she may have been lacking.

Isolation and desolation In older age an interesting and useful distinction has been made between isolation and desolation. Isolation from people of our own age may be the result of physical incapacity and disengagement, while isolation from younger people may be because of cultural change and social mobility. Through events such as bereavement, some older people are bereft of any one person with whom they can enjoy close emotional contact. Little social contact can be referred to as "isolation" though it is very difficult to quantify day-to-day contact.

To be desolated is to be left alone, neglected or forsaken by a person we deeply want to be with such as by the death of a long-standing close friend. It is a kind of emotional deprivation. It is having no-one in whom we can confide, or upon whom we can rely absolutely. This loss is far more serious because the emotional investment or attachment was strong and ingrained, and because there is unlikely to be any chance of forming a satisfactory substitute. Bereavement, however, usually brings strong support from other people. The ability to re-establish normal patterns of behaviour varies from one person to another for the same general reasons. For example, the presence of an extensive network of sympathetic friends and family members obviously reduces the severity of loss and hastens recovery because of the emotional contact available.

Physical incapacity and lack of mobility, on the other hand, will probably hinder it. Partly on account of their greater life expectancy more older women than older men are socially isolated – and desolated – and more of them are infirm. Subjective feelings of *loneliness* are more closely associated with the severance of strong emotional ties than with feeling solitary. Both psychological desolation and loneliness are remediable. Such suffering has been regarded up to now as natural and therefore acceptable, rather like the pains of illness or childbirth. Psychological distress in the later years can be and should be alleviated to a far greater extent than it is at present. Psychological distress following bereavement is associated with physical and mental ill health, and with an increased risk of death from suicide. Disengagement is thankfully met by most of us in a positive manner and so we look forward to it and plan for it. We can renew all sorts of activities that up until now we have neglected.

Suicide rates are higher for men than for women. The rate for women levels off in middle age but the rate for men continues to rise as they get older. These statistics would suggest that women cope better with loneliness, living alone and getting older than men and perhaps this is not so surprising. Women have always been the traditional housekeepers and home tenders and even if they have chosen not to take up these roles they can, across the board, look after themselves on a day to day basis better than men. They usually don't have to face retirement as a dramatic dislocation which in the case of men can lead to a disorientating drop in self-esteem. In a way women have been prepared for loneliness having, in many cases, experienced and coped with children leaving the home.

There is a fall of the suicide rate at very late ages, and for most elderly people suicide is probably never considered as a possible course of action. Its very reassuring that so few older people choose suicide as an option for trying to come to terms with life's difficulties. It would seem that the maturity, experience and wisdom of growing years prepared us to face and deal with difficulties rather than escaping from them. In other words we may be tougher than we think.

TIPS FOR COPING WITH LONELINESS

One of the best ways of coping with loneliness is to face up to it. You will get great insight into just how lonely you are if you keep a diary. Get out a piece of paper and pencil and write down the times of day and night when you feel you are at your lowest ebb, when you are the most lonely. For instance, you may realize that the worst times are evenings from about six o'clock onwards, Saturday nights, Sundays and holidays. Now that you have narrowed those times down, they may be much less frequent than you think.

Making new friends

You probably also miss physical closeness: holding hands, being touched, a gentle squeeze, a warm cuddle, and sexual expression. You may want company with the opposite sex but are uncertain about your feelings. You are uncertain about where and how you should meet other people, when you should begin dating, what you should do about your sexual yearnings, how to come to terms with guilt feelings about being interesed in people other than your lost companion. You may even feel anger towards well-meaning friends who seem to be betraying your dead partner by trying to arrange dates for you. Try to separate yourself from such feelings. It is absolutely right that you should remember your partner, and feel loyal to him or her. It is also quite normal to want another to hold you, comfort you and make love to you.

Planning time

You can start splitting up your evenings during the week by allocating them to different activities. You could go to night school on one and take up a new hobby, craft or subject for study. You could make one evening a time for having some friends into your house, and another for visiting someone else. You could make another evening an occasion for going to the cinema, the theatre or a concert with a friend. Another could be devoted to keeping fit by going along to a yoga class, having a game of squash or tennis, or going to a gym for a workout. Another could be for a home hobby like painting, gardening, carpentry, or just doing odd jobs around the house. Saturday night could be something special. You could join a local club whose members are interested in the same things as you. It may be the local golf club, singles club, bridge or dancing club, with special activities on Saturday nights. Sundays should be carefully planned. Unless you invite distractions, or go out to meet others, it is a long day because it is not easy to shop or do errands. The best and most satisfying ways of occupying your Sundays is to invite friends into your home for lunch or brunch. Make it a very relaxed occasion and arrange the food so that people can come and go as they like.

Finding new interests

You are never going to meet people staying alone at home. You will have to get out to meet people, otherwise you will have to rely on friends bringing new acquaintances to your own home. One of the best ways of getting yourself out of the house is to decide to take up one of your pet passions. Have you always been interested in politics? If so, go along to the next local political meeting. Have you always wanted to paint, or sculpt? In that case enroll at evening classes at the local school. Is clay pigeon shooting something you have always hankered after? Join the local rifle club and buy yourself a gun. If you have oodles of self-confidence, go along to the local singles club. If you are really interested in making yourself physically acceptable, accessible and striking up acquaintances with people, you could go on a cruise, take up a travel-study programme where you can travel and learn while taking a holiday in a foreign country.

Bereavement

The grief associated with bereavement is not always a feeling that's easy to describe. There may be a good deal of ambivalence at the time, for example, sorrow and disappointment may be mixed with anger, guilt and anxiety. Bereavement is a stress which can precipitate psychiatric disorders, psychosomatic illness or suicide. Many widows, for example, experience feelings of guilt about their role in the events leading up to the death of their husbands, and widowhood reduces life expectancy. The psychological and social aspects of widowhood have been the subjects of systematic studies. The reorganization called for following the death of a spouse introduces an added source of stress with regard to emotional deprivation and living arrangements, and the increased risk of death of the bereaved person. There are good reasons for supposing that preparation and psychological support help to alleviate the distress which leads to personal conflict. In older people the awareness of dying has developed slowly. There has been enough time to adapt to the prevailing circumstances and time to learn appropriate strategies of adjustment. Without such adaptation, bereavement and the awareness of dying may evoke feelings of dread associated with a sense of isolation or rejection.

A certain amount of sociological research has been carried out in connection with bereavement in general, and widowhood in particular. The situation faced by women widowed in later life is eased somewhat by their realistic anticipation of this eventuality, and by the companionship of other women of comparable age who have also been widowed. This provides opportunities for receiving support and consolation and sharing of advice, help and so on. Widowers are usually in a less favourable situation.

The importance of grief

Bereavement is the loss of someone very precious; grief is the resulting emotional experience of being bereaved. Most people think of grief as a natural response to bereavement. Indeed, they would be suspicious of someone who denied or hid his or her grief. Nearly all of us see grief as therapeutic, and we are often told "Get it off your chest and have a good cry".

Grief is a more complicated process than that. It is dynamic and we live through it. We go through several steps each of which is hard work. It is not a passive process of letting out pent-up feelings. It is an active process of adjustment. It is a positive "letting go" of something or someone that has been very precious to you for a long time.

Grief is important in that it is a half-way stage between the experience of losing something and coming to terms with the loss. When we are grief-stricken we have strong feelings which we have to deal with so that the wound can heal. I personally have found grief easier to understand and live with since I read of Ross Mitchell's stages of grief. Perhaps if these stages were talked about more freely then the subject of death would not be taboo. These feelings come in clearly-defined stages, each of which has to be endured and these are listed below.

Anticipation

It is uncommon for bereavement to strike out of the blue. Most of us live in the expectation of death, though at some distance, but there is still a shock when death confronts us and our imaginary fears become real. Even when death comes at the end of a long illness there is still the reality and shock of loss. When death and bereavement is sudden the shock is greater still.

Loss

This encompasses a feeling of emptiness. We are very aware that something has gone, that someone has been taken away. There is an empty space where that person used to be. No matter what our feelings were towards that person, there is still a feeling of loss. It is obviously greater if the person was well loved but it can still exist even if the person was hated.

Numbness

This is a protective mechanism. It is a primitive shutting down of all our emotions. All our vital functions become extremely depressed. It is a kind of mechanical cut-out which stops us from feeling any more hurt.

Anger

Here we get indignant, rebellious and resentful that something we cherished so much has been taken away. We may want to grab it back. We may feel self-pity and wonder why it has happened to us. We may wonder what we have done to deserve this grief. We may feel that we have been unfairly singled out. We want to take revenge so we look around for someone to blame because we feel we may be in some way at fault.

Searching

This is where we set out to find what we have lost. We keep looking and hoping to find the person, even though we know we will never find him or her again. This is a way of denying to ourselves that our loved one has gone for good.

Denial

Here we deny to ourselves that we are not going to find our loved one. We keep on making excuses for the fact that we can't. We may believe that he or she is just round the corner. We will find him or her tomorrow. We will just have to wait and see. He or she will come back. It is a desperate game that we are playing with ourselves and with other people.

Acceptance

This occurs when our anger eventually burns itself out. The searching ceases when we realize that we are not going to find our loved one and our denial subsides. We face up to reality.

Letting go

At last, with acceptance, we know that our loved one has gone. We start to bury them in our minds. We no longer enshrine our lost one. We start to feel hope that new life has to be created. We move forward into a new stage of living.

Regrowth

This stage takes a long while to complete. We don't always look forward, we sometimes look backwards and even return to previous stages. Ultimately, if we have gone through all the different stages, regrowth takes place and we gradually return to normal.

In life these stages are not separated – they overlap. The length of time we stay within each stage varies for each person, and in every circumstance. Numbness may last a few hours, a few days, a few weeks. Anger, searching and denial may go on for months. Acceptance, letting go and regrowth may take another six months, so it may be a year from the death that grieving is complete. There may be anniversary reactions when temporary renewals of grief appear for a time, these may lessen in intensity as time goes on.

Indications of grief

There is no right way to grieve. Grieving varies from person to person and from culture to culture. The point about grief is not *how* it is done but that it *should be done somehow*. Things may go wrong. Grief may be denied totally, or it can begin and then be inhibited. It may be turned inwards into the body instead of outwards to relationships with other people. We quite often see a person who appears not to be affected by grief, but know that such good spirits are superficial, false and brittle. If grief is delayed or inhibited, superficial relief is only gained for a short time. When grieving does start it is often more severe because it has been delayed. If grief is denied altogether, the person may slip from grief, which is normal and healing, into a depressive illness which is distressing and abnormal. When grief is turned inwards into the body, the person may complain of physical illness. Research has shown that during the first six months after bereavement, widowers often complain of heart trouble which may literally go on to death from a broken heart. Widows tend to consult their doctors with gastric upsets and rheumatic conditions.

It is very easy to confuse grief with depression. The bereaved person feels sad and lost. Appetite goes and sleep is interrupted. There may be reproach for not having cared more for the lost one. Kind friends may tell the person not to cry, not to be upset and to try to forget it all. That is exactly what a person must not do if they are to go through the natural stages of grieving. They must be allowed and encouraged to grieve.

Practicalities of bereavement While no bereaved person should have to take major decisions concerning the future immediately, there are a few things which require immediate action concerning statutory responsibilities and personal arrangements for funeral burial or cremation, and sometimes this need for immediate action can be helpful rather than burdensome.

Statutory responsibilities

Your family doctor has to be informed of the death which he or she will certify and issue a death certificate. This then has to be taken to the Registrar's office and the death will be registered. The medical certificate of death is filled in and given to you by the doctor who looked after the person during his or her life and during the final illness. Your doctor will report the death to a coroner if there are any unusual circumstances surrounding it. When a death has been reported to the coroner, death cannot be registered until the coroner authorizes the registrar to do so. This may mean that a post-mortem examination has to be performed, but it is not inevitable. A coroner's decision to hold a post-mortem examination is final and no appeal can be made, and the body does not become the responsibility of the family until the post-mortem has been carried out. The post-mortem examination is usually carried out to establish the cause of death. An inquest is held to establish who the dead person was and when and where they died. A coroner usually requests an inquest when there are grounds for suspecting that the death was not due to natural causes, however, this does not necessarily mean that he suspects the death to be caused through anything sinister.

COPING WITH BEREAVEMENT

- It is important to realize that the feelings you are experiencing are normal. It is normal to feel rage and anger. You wouldn't be human if you didn't feel guilty, so don't spend a lot of emotional energy on self-recrimination.
- Try and find an understanding person to talk to. You can work out quite a lot of your anger, guilt, shame and grief on someone who will just listen, correct you when you over-react and sympathize with what you are going through. At this moment when you are in the depths of despair, an objective viewpoint which doesn't see life as entirely white or entirely black is one of the best helps you can have.
- As I have already said it is important to grieve. Grieve in your own time. Don't take any notice of people who encourage you to snap out of it or get back to normal. You will know when your grieving work is done, because you will feel it has worked its way out of your system and you will feel like starting afresh so if you really want to have a good cry, if you want to even have a conversation with your dead partner, go ahead and do so.
- Once the grieving is over, it is important that you start to think about regaining your identity, or even possibly building a new one. Resist the temptation to live in the past and to continue living through your dead partner. You should try to become your own person and to assert your own identity. Start shaping your life as it suits you by doing things that you are really interested in rather than continuing a past way of life.
- Don't make any big decisions quickly, rather let yourself grow into them gradually. Some decisions may be quite hard to take at first. If left for several months or a year, a problem which seemed insoluble will have a very ready solution. Trust your own judgement and go on your own gut feeling which has always served you well throughout your life. Don't

choose this moment to start doubting yourself without reason.
- Whatever you do try to stay mobile. Don't find yourself chained to a house unable to get out. Not only see people but do essential shopping to give yourself vital changes of routine. Keep the family car. Or if you don't have one it may be worth using up some of your precious financial resources to buy one. If you don't drive consider taking driving lessons. If you haven't driven for a little while get a friend to accompany you on the roads to give you a bit of confidence. If at all possible take the car out several times a week so that you regain your confidence on the roads. Don't deprive yourself of the self-satisfaction that you can take yourself off anywhere anytime if you want to. This knowledge in itself is comforting and morale building.
- Don't neglect your finances. This is not a time for them to get out of control and find yourself in debt. So keep an eye on them, budget your expenses and keep a good check on all your sources of income. If you have never had to budget before in your life ask a friend to explain the rudiments of budgeting to you and to have a crack at organizing yours along with you. If you have the money and your affairs are complicated, get the help of an accountant immediately. Start keeping records of all your income and of everything you spend and try to balance the budget at the end of each week or each month.
- Though it seems unlikely while you are grieving, life does go on and you will live again and you will be happy again. Meanwhile you should take good care of yourself. Reward yourself with a holiday. Take the holiday you dreamed you might always take. Perhaps a world cruise. Treat yourself. Perhaps spend some time in your favourite surroundings or take a course to study a hobby. Try and get out and see members of the family and perhaps stay for a few days.

Funeral arrangements

Once you have a death certificate from the doctor, you can make arrangements for burial or cremation, and this requires that you fill in four additional forms. It may be as well to ask a funeral director to take over the arrangements for you from this point. You have to inform the director of your various wishes for different aspects of the funeral. Funerals are always somewhat more expensive than expected, and it may be a wise precaution to contact several firms to ask them for written quotations and to make sure that you have the arrangements as you want them.

Financial and legal consideration

It is possible that you are entitled to government grants which will help towards meeting the expenses of the funeral and they may also help you with long-term finances. Yourself, children and other dependents may benefit. To find out exactly what you can claim you should get in touch with your local government departments. If necessary, you will have to go through your partner's papers and insurance provisions to claim on policies which covered funeral expenses, life insurance and mortgage payments. If you have any difficulty, contact your partner's solicitor immediately to discuss any bequest.

Medical help

Don't hesitate to turn to your family doctor for help. Doctors are very aware of, and sympathetic to, the apathy, lethargy and depression which can obstruct your chances of recovering from bereavement. Whilst they should never be given in the long term, short courses of sedatives, hypnotics and tranquillizers can help you over a very upsetting week or so.

The help of others

When the acuteness of your initial grief has subsided do try to prevent yourself from becoming a recluse by seeking the company of friends and relatives. One good friend my be sufficient. It can take a lot of courage and energy to pull yourself out of your despondency but your life has to go on and it will return to normal all the more quickly for having the comforting words and presence of others.

So draw up a schedule of visits, short trips, holidays, friends to stay which will fill up the next few months. Telephone relatives and friends and arrange visits, either you to them or vice versa. You'll find that just looking forward to this future programme of being with others helps to soothe your grieving and brings you gradually back a normal lifestyle.

A lifetime of loving

As we get older we don't feel very different inside about anything, but particularly about loving; we love just as strongly and as passionately and as tenderly as we did when we were youngsters. While a loving older couple may look odd to people on the outside, it doesn't seem so very different to the couple from when they were young. However, we often find new ways of expressing love.

As loving and being loved do not stop when we reach a certain age, many of us have the time to search for its expression in different ways. We may develop companionship without passion or develop the way we express ourselves sexually. Such sexual development may be personal and private or it can be in tandem with a partner. It can be a very thrilling time.

Of the many good reasons for maintaining fitness and health throughout life, one of the best is that fitness allows, and may even encourage, continuation of sexual activity. Lack of fitness certainly inhibits it, and may even preclude it. Chronic ailments affecting the lungs and the heart, muscular strength and joint mobility act as deterrents to sexual activity. So, it is worth planning well ahead of time to have a fit, healthy and agile body as we get older, in order to be able to enjoy all the benefits of fitness including sexual activity.

Partnerships

A couple who has always shared strong physical affection is more likely to share caresses as they get older than a couple who has lost the habit of touching each other in middle age. The frequency of sexual contact is much less important. As we get older the meaning of sexual contact and its frequency have little to do with each other. Between a devoted couple, sexual union is an affirmation of something that goes well beyond momentary pleasure. Years of giving and receiving love strengthen the occasion. For many couples, only one contact a month may be fulfilling enough, reflecting three, four or five decades of intimacy. It also helps each partner to have a sense of being desirable, and to create the self-image of someone who is sexually alive. Anyone who has had an enduring relationship will miss the satisfaction and meaning of this kind of experience. Maintaining sensual awareness as we progress into older age makes us more vital and attractive in all sorts of relationships, not just sexual ones, and staying sexually alive helps us to avoid the drabness and greyness which a great many people wrongly associate with old age.

It is not surprising that this should happen. Research has shown that couples who experience middle age together feel a profound increase in personal satisfaction. This is not because partners improve miraculously, but we all develop greater tolerance which may become spontaneous once we stop blaming our partners for our own shortcomings.

At last we know our partners really well and we now have the opportunity for true companionship – something that we might not have had the time to enjoy up until now. We know now how to strike a balance between shared interests with our partners and privacy. It's a good feeling to realize that we have the chance of growing old with someone with whom we can share memories, friends, odd pleasurable moments like walking in the rain or simply recapturing earlier joys which for many years we did not have time for, by spending some time together.

Everyday occurrences such as a visit to the shops can be a celebration if we are able to respect each other's privacy, but still keep the door open for companionship. It gives confidence to feel certain that we will look after each other and helps to prepare for the future with a feeling of serenity and contentment. This contentment brings security and independence. As we grow older our engagement with the world is more and more narrowed down to engagement with a partner. This is part of becoming a more private person. If a person is content with him or herself, this act of drawing back brings a new stability, especially when a loving partner thinks the same way. There again partners can take up new roles. One's mate is not only a valuable companion, he or she can take up the role of a substitute parent, if you both wish.

Sex and sexual relationships

All of us are the richer for loving and expressing love. Sexuality is one part of that love – the capacity to respond to another person physically. There are many misleading and damaging myths about what happens to our sexuality as we grow older and I should like to explode a few of them.

Sexual myths Many people are persuaded that men approaching fifty become paunchy, consider themselves less attractive and fear impotence. Women, once the fertile period of their lives is over, feel that the sexual aspects of their lives will dwindle quite rapidly into apathy. They fear they will be bereft of sexual excitement and pleasure. Naturally enough, men and women wonder and worry about life without the special closeness that comes through a physical relationship.

These misconceptions are supported by the popular belief that as we get older, sex becomes more and more wrong, even indecent, or, at the very least, not quite the thing for older people to do. The physical side of life during our older years is generally disapproved of and is quite frequently labelled "dirty". This may be a hangover from an age when sexual activity for carnal pleasure rather than child-bearing was thought unpardonable. Today, however, we recognize that with her child-bearing life behind her, a woman can look forward to many years of a different kind of sexual activity, more beautiful, more relaxed and more leisurely than ever before. She may even discover that sex takes place more often for enjoyment than for the sole purpose of procreation.

One of the problems with the dissemination of information about sex is that the good news is kept secret. In a recent survey undertaken by *The Observer*, it was found that many people in their seventies and older not only need to have, but actually do have, active sex lives. Unfortunately this news is not widespread, remaining unknown to most of us.

However, as we grow older, we can counter negative attitudes with the thought that we are beyond the reach of public moralizing and bigoted attitudes towards sex. That is all, thankfully, behind us.

WHAT THE MEDICAL TEXTBOOKS SAY

Men aged 50-89
- An erection takes longer to develop and may not be as full or as firm as it was when he was younger.
- Ejaculation lasts for a shorter time and is not as forceful.
- An erection subsides more rapidly after ejaculation than in younger years.
- The volume of semen is nearly always less than it is for younger men.
- It takes longer before a man can have another erection and another orgasm.

Women aged 51-78
- A longer time is needed to respond to sexual stimulation.
- Lubrication is less effective and generally takes longer than in younger women.
- The vagina is less capable of stretching than in younger women.
- After the age of sixty the clitoris shrinks but may still remain responsive to stimulation.
- Orgasms are generally shorter and less intense than they were in younger years.

Despite what the textbooks say you can take each one of these statements and find valid research to show that it does not apply to the majority of people. This is what should be publicized. Instead of being terrorized with the prospect of advancing years, we would look forward to them with joy and curiosity. If we did, growing older would be a great deal easier and we would do it a lot more gracefully.

What is kept secret is that more and more of us lose our inhibitions as we get older (there are surely no good reasons why we should retain them). Many of us feel a need and a freedom to enjoy sexual pleasures which we kept hidden when we were younger. There may be the feeling that time is running out so we should do as we wish as long as we don't hurt anyone. Other activities which used to use up a great deal of energy like parenting and tight domestic arrangements have been left behind so there is more energy left over to be invested in pleasurable activities, including sex. Furthermore, one often finds in later life that intimate situations are easier to control. There is more privacy, there are very few interruptions and many couples feel that they have the time to go more slowly and savour the most beautiful moments in sex.

There are two statements in the Starr-Weiner report, which, the authors claim, are fairly commonplace and which demonstrate how inaccurate is the old-fashioned picture of an older person being resigned to a life without much sexual pleasure (see page 110).

Another important finding in this report was a clear demonstration that the frequency of sexual intercourse does not decline markedly from early adulthood. In his report, Kinsey stated that the average frequency of intercourse at thirty was 2.2 times per week and at sixty 0.5 times per week. In the Starr-Weiner reports which covered people age sixty to ninety-one there were average frequencies of 1.4 times a week and this figure matches the one that Kinsey reported in his forty-year-olds. Desire was even higher.

The facts challenge the widely-held belief that older people are beyond having sex. Unquestionably, most older people still find sex a thrilling and energy-giving exercise. Contrary to the myths, neither the desire nor the capability vanishes. It may wane a little in frequency and vigour but not in sweetness and satisfaction. Just as in relationships at a younger age, attraction and love are followed by sexual desire and sexual fulfilment. These basic qualities in a relationship don't seem to falter, rather they strengthen as we get older. This is something we can all look forward to in our maturing years and feel confident enough to carry out for many years to come.

THE TRUTH ABOUT OUR SEXUALITY

There is nothing but good news about sexuality in our later years. In fact, recent research has confirmed that sexual drive, sexual enjoyment and sexual pleasure is greater than it was when we were younger. This is why it is accurate to describe the years after fifty as our prime time.

• Sex is commonly considered a crucial part of life during our older years and provides a sense of well-being and a positive feeling about ourselves.

• Sex makes older people feel beautiful, desirable, exhilarated and mystical, and for some who attach importance to the youth cult, it makes them feel young. Also, sex is relaxing and relieves tension. It may be one of life's exquisite moments, driving every other problem and care out of our minds temporarily or even permanently.

• Only a minority of people (less than 30 percent) feel there is a decline in sexual response and feelings. This is especially true of men who have problems with erection and, therefore, withdraw from sexual activities.

• Nearly three-quarters of older people feel that sex is the same as it was when they were younger; more than a third of older people say that sex is better than when they were younger.

• For those of us who find sex more gratifying when we are older, the key is having the right partner, loss of inhibitions and a greater understanding of sex.

• For couples who get married for the first time or remarry in later life, love, caring and sharing and companionship are emphasized; so is sex. The majority of people consider that sex is very important in later life.

• About 80 percent of older people are sexually active; half of the people who are sexually active have sexual intercourse about once a week or more; 30 percent have sexual relations three times a week; 20 percent report sexual relations twice a week.

• Sex brings love, faith and trust, approval and warmth; these are the same needs and desires for every age.

• A staggering 99 percent desire sexual relationships at a varying frequency if they could have sex whenever they wanted to.

Mature sexuality

As long ago as Kinsey's research in the 1940s, well-worn facts chronicling the decline of sexuality were being eroded. Masters and Johnson gave us excellent scientific data which proved that the traditional medical picture was wrong; Shere Hite made this even clearer in terms of what older people experience, feel and question. The recent Starr-Weiner report shattered the myth once and for all with an excellent detailed survey of sexuality in a large group of people aged between sixty and ninety-one. On the basis of these reports, a clear picture of sexuality in our older years emerges. It is almost the exact opposite of long-held beliefs (see page 107). It is not a picture of decline and deprivation but one of continuing desire and fulfilment.

HOW WE VIEW SEX

- The majority of us are satisfied with our sex lives the way they are.
- We consider orgasm, which may be stronger than earlier in life, to be an essential part of our sexual experience. Most women have had orgasms in their younger years, and are still having them.
- Masturbation is a perfectly acceptable outlet for our sexual needs.
- Many of us are very happy to live together without marriage. The majority of us, including widows, widowers, divorcees and singles, remain sexually active in the last third of our lives.

- Many of us vary our sexual practices to achieve satisfaction.
- Many of us consider oral sex to be the most exciting sexual experience.
- We rarely show embarrassment or anxiety about sex if left to ourselves, and not bombarded by negative messages from the media and social opinions.
- The majority of us like to be naked and enjoy nudity with our partners.
- When we think of an ideal lover, we choose someone near to our own age.
- Most of us see our sex lives remaining just the same way as we grow older.

Furthermore sexual problems are not an inevitable result of ageing – the same factors that lead to sexual problems in younger people are important for older people too: factors such as fatigue, emotional problems, drug abuse, alcoholism, disease, over-eating, and these should be taken into account.

Most of us see our sex lives remaining just the same as we grow older. This is not surprising. Our older years represent a large part of our lives – one of the biggest. Many people today live well into their eighties, which means that the years from sixty to eighty-five are a quarter of the total life span. Most of us, therefore, look forward to having one-third of our lives left after we pass our fiftieth birthday. We spend relatively few years at the beginning of our lives without sexual activity. Why should we expect a curtailment of sexual activity towards the end? Despite what society and religious teaching have programmed us to believe, we never lose the need to be touched, stroked, cuddled and caressed. It has been known for years that physical contact is a basic human need, starting in the newborn infant, and, if anything becoming more powerful in sixty-, seventy- and eight-year olds. A basic human need which we need to fulfil.

"I was a widower for five years. Six months ago I remarried and everyone said to me, 'It's good that you married again because you need companionship.' Everyone tells me about companionship. It gets me mad. So I want companionship, but I also got married for sex. I always had an active sex life and still do, and I am eighty-two."

A good sexual experience was described by one sixty-one year old woman from California as "To be really horny with a partner who is just as horny, to take plenty of time and when you can't stand it another minute, make it!"

The older woman

Older women are wrongly characterized as sexless by society, but science has recently shown that up until the age of sixty, sexual responses in women don't change at all, and even after sixty what changes take place are extremely slow and gradual. Add to this the fact that many men withdraw entirely from sexual activities because they fear that they may be impotent or that they might have a heart attack or a stroke during sexual intercourse and this leaves us with too many women over the age of sixty desiring sex, but with partners who won't fulfil their needs. Many older women find themselves without a regular sex outlet. Research has shown that for an older woman the only barrier to a more active sex life is the availability of a partner.

Another fact which has failed to filter through to the common consciousness is something which was first described by Kinsey. He established the sexual superiority of women by stating that a man reaches his peak early in adolescence and then shows a steady decline throughout life. This decline is consistent whatever age he is; in older years it is no faster than it was in earlier ones. On the other hand, a woman reaches her peak in her late twenties or thirties, and *remains at that plateau through her sixties*. It is only after seventy that she may show a slight decline in sexual response.

Orgasm   Nearly 40 percent of women say that orgasm is the most important part of the sexual act. This should not be surprising. Much has been written suggesting that the female is superior to the male both in her capacity for, and her ability to sustain, orgasm. Dr Jane Sherey described the human female as "...sexually insatiable in the presence of the highest degree of sexual satiation".

Masters and Johnson have reported on a woman's capacity for "...a rapid return to orgasm immediately following an orgasmic experience", and of "maintaining an orgasmic experience for a relatively long period of time". Though there are physiological changes, like vaginal lubrication taking only fifteen to thirty seconds in a younger woman, but perhaps one, two or even five minutes in an older woman, we are yet to have objective evidence that there is any real loss in sensation or feeling. The clitoris in both older and younger women remains the main organ of sexual stimulation, and the excitement generated by clitoral stimulation is exactly the same in older women as it is in younger ones. A woman of eighty *has the same physical potential for orgasm as she did at twenty*. Another finding which emphasizes that orgasm is a real part

111

of the sex lives of older women, is that the proportion who have not experienced orgasm is smaller than at any other age – less than two out of a hundred women, and amazingly not one of the women in the eighty-or-over age group reported that they were non-orgasmic; 86 percent of respondents in the Starr-Weiner survey said that the frequency of their orgasms was the same or better than when they were younger.

Sexual responses

Masters and Johnson also had something to say about older women and their sexual responses. Most aspects of arousal remain identical. The arousal and erection of the nipple occurs in exactly the same way in older women as in younger ones, though engorgement of the areola (the pigmented area around the nipple) is not so intense as in younger women. What is more important, however, is the fact that the clitoris remains as responsive at least until the middle seventies, and while there is a thinning and loss of elasticity in the vaginal walls with advancing age, plus a shortening of vaginal length and width, these changes have been shown to have little effect on orgasm.

Many people have accepted as fact that intercourse in an older woman results in pain and discomfort because of a lessening in vaginal lubrication. This appears to be wrong, as more than 80 percent of women report no such pain.

The conclusion is that far from it being age, it is interest, opportunity and availability which control the body's response. "Use it or lose it," is an adage which is particularly applicable to the older age group and we must try to overcome the fact that our culture exaggerates the importance of menopausal changes which makes women's fears into self-fulfilling prophecies. There is absolutely no question that powerful feelings of sexuality extend two decades or longer beyond the menopause.

Attitudes to sex

These have changed quite a lot as a result of the feminist movement. Prior to that, the majority of women accepted that sex was mainly a male domain and they were fixed in the role of passive and submissive partner. To fulfil this role, many women repressed their sexual desires and they believed they were behaving in a ladylike fashion when they did this.

Today many women, particularly when older, have come to the conclusion that they have just as much passion and sexuality as men and, more importantly, that they have the right to make choices. Among older women there is a less willing acceptance of the old-fashioned male view of sex as being measured in performance only – how much, how often. Many women are now seeking equality, quality and variety. They are quite prepared to wake up their partners when they feel in the mood.

The older man

Sexual potency This is by no means a problem for every marriage but impotency can be very demoralizing if it does occur. This can be worsened when incorrect advice is given by a doctor. The news that a sixty-year-old man will no longer be able to sustain an erection can be horrifying for both partners. After all, it is tantamount to saying that their sex lives are over. The blow to a man may be so great that advice coming from a sympathetic wife to seek a second opinion may be spurned.

What is more shocking, if anything, is that doctors themselves fall into the trap of believing that it is perfectly normal for a man in his sixties to be unable to maintain an erection. Most men in this situation would be understandably depressed and needlessly feel a failure.

A doctor who takes the time and trouble to study information would be very thorough in examining such a man and he would find out as much as he could about his past medical history. It may be that the man has had his prostate removed and is looking for an excuse to end his sex life. It may be that he has had a heart attack and is afraid of having another if he attempts intercourse. This fear prevents him from having an erection. When this has happened several times, a man quite wrongly feels he is impotent.

Though the work of Masters and Johnson was widely publicised their precise findings were not. One of their most important statements was that any kind of therapy programme for impotence or premature ejaculation is as applicable to older men as it is to younger men, because most of these problems are psychological in origin and not physical. There is a lot of help available for older men and women and it should encourage us to know that the success rate in this age group is extremely high.

Masters and Johnson even made a practical suggestion to older men on how to make frequent sexual intercourse possible. They point out that it is unnecessary for a man to ejaculate every time, that men need rest periods of several days before they can have another erection and orgasm. If older men hold back instead of feeling forced by macho instincts to have frequent sex then the frequency of sexual relations is more under their control. It becomes easier for them to adapt their sexual relationship to suit their own personal needs as well as those of their partners. To feel comfortable with this changing pattern of sexual activity it's important for men to be open and honest with their partners so that there is the understanding to maintain a loving relationship. This is the foundation upon which loving relationships are built.

Helping a man

You can help a great deal to make sure your man doesn't believe that his sex life is coming to an end. The most important thing that you can do is to understand the changes in the way your husband is functioning and to see them as perfectly normal. You should recognize his altering patterns of erection and orgasm as normal too. Both of you should discuss what's happening so that your expectations are realistic, and so that you can adjust your sexual behaviour to whatever changes occur.

You should not become afraid because your partner takes longer to attain his erection. Should you sense that he is apprehensive you should reassure him that all is normal and if he takes longer it doesn't mean that he is unable. Your partner may become less aroused by seeing you naked or thinking about sex; skilful manual and oral caresses can overcome this. Whatever you do, don't feel rejected and panic-stricken. Don't think that because he can't attain an erection rapidly he is no longer attracted to you. Don't worry if he does not ejaculate but seems sexually satisfied. When your partner cannot attain a second erection within a short time, don't think that this is the first sign of impotence. In such a situation a woman can be a creator and an initiator. She can lead the way and introduce a changing pattern so that both partners create a new kind of sexual loving. A woman can find new ways of doing things which will fit her partner's new mood and will help to build his self-esteem rather than erode it.

Helping a woman

Few women have any difficulty in reaching an orgasm through masturbation. You can make your lovemaking techniques more successful by modelling them on the woman during masturbation. Even on a small sample, Masters and Johnson concluded that there is no time limit to female sexuality drawn by advancing years. Shere Hite argued convincingly that an orgasm achieved through intercourse is not necessarily a better orgasm than one achieved by other means. She also said that women can have an orgasm whenever they want. If intercourse doesn't work, you can help your partner reach a climax through manual or oral stimulation and this release is just as easy to accomplish for a woman as a man. Women appreciate tender stroking and kissing of the breasts and clitoris; your partner will appreciate long, leisured embraces.

POSITIONS FOR OLDER LOVERS

Experience more than compensates for any lack of energy that we might feel as we get older and there is no reason why we should not enjoy sex even more than we did when we were younger. We now understand our partner's bodily responses more fully than ever before and feel confident and considerate enough to concentrate on pleasing our partner in the years ahead.

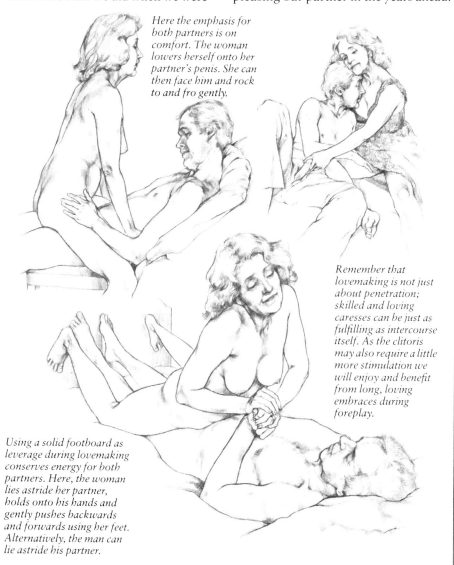

Here the emphasis for both partners is on comfort. The woman lowers herself onto her partner's penis. She can then face him and rock to and fro gently.

Remember that lovemaking is not just about penetration; skilled and loving caresses can be just as fulfilling as intercourse itself. As the clitoris may also require a little more stimulation we will enjoy and benefit from long, loving embraces during foreplay.

Using a solid footboard as leverage during lovemaking conserves energy for both partners. Here, the woman lies astride her partner, holds onto his hands and gently pushes backwards and forwards using her feet. Alternatively, the man can lie astride his partner.

115

Sexual activity in chronic disease

Heart disease
There is absolutely no need to eliminate sexual activity altogether unless heart disease is very severe. In fact, in many cases of heart disease sexual activity can be beneficial, since sexual activity can be the equivalent of performing moderate exercises with an increased heart rate, slightly increased blood pressure and improved oxygen consumption. In 1975 a study was made which showed that less than one percent of all coronary deaths occurred during, or after, intercourse. Most doctors believe that the therapeutic benefits outweigh the risks. Total abstinence can bring a great deal of psychological stress which will worsen any heart condition.

All in all, the news on heart disease is extremely good. Doctors now realize that a normal sex life can actually benefit many men who suffer heart attacks, but it is important that they don't get overtired. It is possible that the pattern of sexual relationships has to change to mornings or after a good night's sleep, when both partners are feeling rested. One of the great things about being retired is that you don't have to jump out of bed at 8 a.m. The job no longer beckons and the house can wait, so you can use the mornings for sexual enjoyment.

A change in position can also help people with heart conditions. Lying next to each other on your sides, face-to-face, is more restful than the missionary position. You can find positions that avoid muscle cramps and tension, with the woman on top so that she can do most of the moving, which will avoid the man getting overtired.

High blood pressure
Many people with high blood pressure believe that sexual activity is dangerous for them. This is not necessarily so, although quite a number of patients who take drugs for high blood pressure say that they suffer loss of potency. Most authorities attribute this impotency to the drugs. It is not known that high blood pressure itself reduces sexual desire, and when doctors are prescribing treatment for high blood pressure in older people, they should try to make sure that they are using one of the drugs that will not affect sexual potency.

Diabetes
Impotence is a fairly common occurrence amongst diabetics. Men find that they have difficulty in attaining erections and ejaculation and women may have difficulty with vaginal lubrication. Research has revealed lower testosterone levels in diabetic men and it has been suggested that male impotence may result from malfunction of the nerves which supply the penis. Premature ejaculation may be a symptom.

116

Arthritis You may find that arthritis affects your sex life by causing discomfort during sexual intercourse. Painful, stiff joints may make the ordinary face-to-face position difficult but the adoption of a new position – such as with the woman on top (if the male is arthritic) can often bring success. Taking pain-killing drugs before having sex can also help. Even if the problems involved in making love are so severe that you decide to forego full intercourse, you should never abstain from indulging in other sexual activities if you and/or your partner desire them. Physical closeness through touching and caresses can provide a great deal of comfort and reassurance. If you are used to sleeping with someone it's better to get in an extra single bed for the occasional troublesome period, than to switch to twin beds permanently. This way you need sacrifice your physical closeness only on those occasions when you feel pain.

SEXUAL POSITIONS FOR ARTHRITICS

Experimenting with some different positions for sexual intercourse is the best way to find comfort. This may lead to different feelings of intensity.

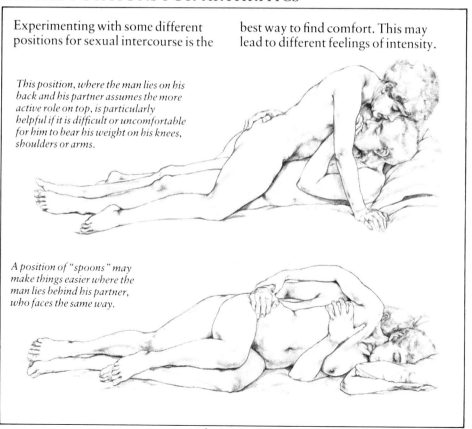

This position, where the man lies on his back and his partner assumes the more active role on top, is particularly helpful if it is difficult or uncomfortable for him to bear his weight on his knees, shoulders or arms.

A position of "spoons" may make things easier where the man lies behind his partner, who faces the same way.

117

Divorce

Divorce is often harder for people when they're older than it would have been if they had gone through it when they were young. In the aftermath of divorce many people feel that they are "over the hill" and unattractive. They may fear that no one will ever want them again. Many dislike going alone to dances and parties after so many years of living with a secure partner. Some people are bitter because they are left alone after thirty or more years.

The divorced woman

Women, especially after being deserted for someone younger, may feel ferociously protective about their alimony, particularly if they haven't been trained for a job and feel they are too old to begin a career. Salt is rubbed in the wound if a woman can remember it was she who put her student husband through his professional training so that he could make a good salary for the two of them. Some women feel that after bringing up the family for a man, and helping him achieve success in his career, they deserve every penny they can get.

This pessimistic approach may end up making women believe that divorce is the end of their lives. But having lived through the despair, pain, self-hatred and even self-pity, many of us find that life is better after divorce. Some get their first full-time job to keep busy and sane. Some feel self-confident enough to have dates with other men. It is possible for women to discover sex for the first time after having lived a claustrophobic life in a claustrophobic marriage. Prior to divorce and meeting men, some women wrongly believe that they have a low sex drive. They believe sex can never be really enjoyable. Sometimes they feel reborn when they have a fulfilling relationship with a sympathetic partner.

It's easy to feel cheated for having spent a long time with a rather stodgy partner, but the best view is that there is a good number of years ahead. It is the prime time of life, there is no worry about becoming pregnant, the menopause has passed. The children are married and therefore you don't have to worry about taking care of them. It is possible to have a small, efficient apartment which takes a short time to maintain. You may find that the only worry you have is how best to go about having a good time – just like your old bachelor days.

The divorced man

Now that they have discovered that they can look after themselves economically, women are leaving men more frequently than before. More and more men over fifty are being left behind by wives who always wanted to get out of the marriage. It is no longer safe to assume that an older man who is divorced is the guilty party and has left his ageing wife for a younger woman. On the contrary *she* may have left him for a younger man. Men in this situation feel depressed and deserted and many seek a lasting relationship for the years ahead. Men seem to be very well suited to the marriage state. Health statistics show that they are happiest, in the best health and least depressed when they are married. So they tend to re-marry.

Remarriage and new partnerships

Widowers are much more likely to get married than either bachelors or divorced men, especially if they were happily married. Once they have got over the initial shock of losing their wives, widowers begin to miss domesticity after the years of companionship and loving. Women may be deterred from marrying men over forty because they think that they are marrying a potentially disabled person, especially if their future husband has diabetes, a heart condition or high blood pressure. However, even a healthy man if he is over fifty is risky too. Women over the age of fifty are something of a health risk but these facts need not spell pessimism.

You have to decide whether the companionship of a few years of remarriage is worth the risk of living with chronic illness later. Only you can decide this for yourself. Separation is much harder when you are older and there is a lot to be said for having someone to chat to, laugh with and share life with.

Against this, you may be reluctant to share your assets, be it your salary or your alimony. Only you know how secure or insecure you feel if you have to manage on this income. Only you know how much or how little you really want to get married. Examine the kind of person you are. Be entirely honest with yourself and examine your feelings about this particular man or woman. Then make your decision. There is one golden rule which should be applied during your older years, if not at all other times – there is no point in marrying *anyone* unless you would trust them with everything of yours, and unless you are attracted to them. You are going to spend an awful lot of time with your new partner.

If you are over fifty your new partner may be ready to retire. He or she may already be semi-retired or fully retired. This means that you will be thrown together much more frequently than a younger couple. A woman won't have the hours off while her man is at work. Nor will he have respite from his partner's company. It will be a good deal easier if you are excited about each other and have a good time in each other's company. Being together all day and every day from breakfast until bedtime is a very long time.

In the end obstacles can be overcome just as triumphantly by older people as young. It is difficult to overestimate the importance of a long-standing loving relationship in old age. Sex on its own is not to be slighted, but love brings much more than physical pleasure. Each partner is sure of their identity as a person and feel that they can offer something valuable and worthwhile. A body which is no longer young can still be a means of giving and receiving pleasure. Older lovers like and understand their bodies. People of fifty and over who enjoy an active sex life have more confidence in themselves than those who decide to go into their old age celibate.

Through a loving relationship, two people who have shared intimate years of sorrow and joy can buffer each other from the contingencies of the outside world. Through a loving partner we can find the reassurance that we are still individuals and that our emotional needs have not been forgotten. In each other's arms we can be ourselves, rather than the image of an old person which society forces us to be. This sense of togetherness against the world, the joy of small, shared intimacies and quiet conversation, that insulates us from the rest of the world, is life-affirming and precious. Society's oppressive attitude towards sexual intimacy in old age is a reflection of its own insecurities and misconceptions. Most older people have come to realize this and have decided to please themselves rather than adhere to the mores of others. A few may feel the pressure to conform to society's mould, but should resist it. The fifty plus age is the last chance to achieve happiness because with it comes the necessary experience and maturity.

The family

Most of us became adults at a time when family, friends and neighbours automatically came to each other's rescue with whatever resources they had no matter how little. Although bureaucracy has grown and many social services exist for older people today, the greatest strength and help for them is still the family even though family relations are not always easy. Interactions between the older and younger generations can cause stress and disturbance for both families and friends. Situations are often complex. Not enough research has been done on what happens between families and their dependents but we know that the assumption of responsibilities by younger members for their older relatives is a severe emotional, physical and economic drain and it causes a great deal of anxiety.

Most of us would confess to having questioned ourselves about failing in our responsibilities to older relatives. The children of very old parents may themselves be sixty or approaching seventy and are therefore limited in the support that they can give. By old-fashioned standards, present day families in the Western world tend to be small and have only a few relatives. The mobility of today's society means that the family is not localized in one village as it used to be, but can be scattered widely, perhaps over the whole world. Even a few minutes of travelling time can make support difficult. This can be specially so when there are commitments to other members of the family and to work which is the case for most of us and those are very difficult to avoid.

There are two studies, however, which contradict the common belief that relatives fail to meet their responsibilities to older people. They were done in Glasgow and Edinburgh and show that less than one per cent of families were unreasonable in not providing support. In contrast, there were many families who took on substantial burdens in looking after their relatives, compared to their other commitments. A small percentage of people, of course, refuse help from their relatives, and a very few families who, having taken on the responsibility to look after an older person, give inadequate support. Most families who have undertaken care of an older family member find that the breakdown in relationships is nearly always due to some factor which they can't control for instance, alcoholism, prostitution, or a disturbed marriage. We can take the optimistic view of the future that families will continue to support elderly relatives. And where family support is given, it is usually a far greater contribution than can be provided by our health service.

Family problems There are several well-recognized situations in which the interaction between family members can cause great upheaval. The mother/daughter syndrome is one. A daughter lives all her life with her mother, is adoring and dependent. She seeks her mother's advice on most issues that concern her and does most of what her mother tells her to do. She bears this benign tyranny because it is stable. However, as the mother grows older, the relationship becomes strained due to anxiety and depression which may develop or because of physical illness. For the first time the daughter sees her mother as dependent on and subordinate to herself, and she may not be ready to assume

121

command. When tensions arise, it is usually due to the daughter assuming more and more responsibility in the absence of any real power. Thereafter, the resentment on both sides may be rather child-like.

Another pattern is the "fallen dictator". It is usually a father or husband who falls into this role. He would be described as powerful, domineering, good at his job, usually well thought of by colleagues at work; but overbearing, tyrannical and rigid at home, usually maintaining his superior position by the use of fear. As such a man gets older, ill-health and loss of income and status at work remove the basis of his power. To make things worse, increasing demands for help at home undermine his position further. He then tries to retain command in a radically different situation. His behaviour often creates crises and even rejection by the rest of the family.

"Power reversal" affects the ideal husband, constantly helping in the house, handing over the wage packet unopened, not drinking, not smoking, not going out with the boys. He is the perfect handyman, working to improve the house, and taking great pleasure in doing what his wife and children want. He may even be viewed by the family with amused contempt. At an older age he becomes an invaluable family member, but then he may develop a heart attack, a cancer or other life-threatening disease. Then, for the first time, every minor illness and symptom demands the attention of the whole family. When he survives his illness, he will have learnt a lesson. He will be aware that he has the power to be the centre of attention, to frighten and to stir up feelings. Once having learnt this lesson he may not be willing to return to his previous humble position in the family. War has been declared and the older person may attempt to retain power by being childish.

One of the problems is that doctors tend to label any emotional crisis between an older person and their family as a "social problem", so older people with anxiety, hypochondriasis, phobias, or depression may be misguidedly offered practical help in the form of home help, meals on wheels, voluntary visiting, outings and holidays, when it is really psychotherapy that they need. However, the outlook for older people with family problems is normally good. A person with a pleasant personality in the past and stable family life, very often has the basis for a rapid return to normal behaviour.

The family's changing nature There is no doubt that the structure of the family is constantly changing. For many older people, the time when they really need stability and continuity may be the very time when they are confronted by a family upheaval with divorce, remarriage and

A changing family pattern often means that the members have more people of all ages to rely upon.

new relations from various children and children-in-law. Moreover, they may have to face changing relationships with former sons and daughters-in-law of whom they are very fond. It is possible that there will be the added strain of having to decide with whom and near to whom they are going to live. The family is gradually being reconstituted and is reaching a new equilibrium. This is difficult enough for young family members to cope with, but extremely difficult for the older ones.

The new extended family will probably include children and young adults who have grown up with the idea that their parents are fixed points in the universe. Suddenly they may acquire new grandparents. In the same way, grandparents may

123

find themselves with new children. Neither may be able to understand the situation very well. As with many other aspects of changing family patterns, people often overcome these difficulties through love and generosity, and some of the newly-formed family ties can be strong and good, even better than the old. However, a family upheaval can seriously affect the support system which older people receive from their relatives when they need it most.

When things go wrong in our relationships, it is not uncommon to hide them from our parents for as long as possible, so as "not to worry or bother them". Usually there is another part of us that feels guilty. The younger generation, and even some adults, often underestimate the capacity older people have for forgiving and forgetting. It is possible that our childhood fears and anxieties linger on and stop us from communicating, even as middle-aged people with our parents.

It is not only older people who experience their children's marriages breaking up, parents are still quite often middle-aged. In either case the effects of shifting membership on families needs close attention and any older members must be included in this. There are those people who think we should give up the term "nuclear family", and talk instead of the "modified extended family". Some think that this label represents the family situation of many people in our society today more realistically. Even though there is greater geographical mobility than ever before, there is no evidence to suggest that kinship networks are breaking down in an emotional sense. The way we help older people when their children's marriages break down, may directly affect their confidence at a later stage when they are less self-reliant.

Stresses and strains within the changing family will be for the most part private and handled between family members themselves. Very often there is no thought or place for social workers, but in matters of divorce and child custody, they do become involved. Older family members may be called upon to take an active part. Grandparents may have an important role to play in divorce. Their case is now being raised to the point of there being special legislation for grandparents to apply to courts for custody of grandchildren when one or both parents have died. A social worker thinking positively about what help could be offered to children might well recommend grandparental custody with benefits to children, parents and grandparents. With grandparents becoming younger all the time and with an increasingly closer identification between children and grandparents, this option of grandparental custody could become more and more common.

Being a grandparent

One of the joys that most people have in store for them as they grow older is that of becoming a grandparent. Once past the childbearing age, many women begin to look forward to their second chance for mothering, and find that few experiences exceed those of being with, teaching, and learning from their grandchildren. To my mind, grandparents are an extremely important part of the family, be it nuclear or extended. I personally see a family as a fundamentally stable structure encompassing strong and lasting relationships among an extended group in which a child can grow up feeling secure and loved, to which he or she must contribute and in which his or her voice is heard. I also consider it important that a child becomes able to relate to people of all ages, and, therefore, should meet relatives and friends who are older.

Grandparents are vital in helping a child to do this. They also play a unique part in enabling children to develop their personalities, and are a valuable asset to a family. By virtue of their age, they are generally more philosophical, long-suffering and sympathetic than parents. Long practice means that they have learnt the knack of handling children with ease.

Being a good grandparent The best grandparents can interpret warning signs, anticipate problems, and head them off. They pacify by distraction not by insistence, and so obtain obedience more readily. Unlike those parents who rule by force, grandparents will more often than not persuade with patience. It is said that grandparents spoil their grandchildren. This must be a misuse of the word "spoil". If spoiling a child means giving explanations instead of dismissals, suggesting alternatives instead of negatives, and helping instead of ignoring, then grandparents do spoil children. The presence of grandparents in the house can often be a boon to the family and, given that they don't cause friction with the parents, are often welcomed.

Grandparents can renew earlier joys with their grandchildren. A grandmother can teach her young granddaughter the art of sewing, bird-watching or gardening. A grandfather can once again enjoy tranquillity while he is teaching his grandson to fish, and discover a new sense of purpose and usefulness if he can take the young baby for a walk and chat to his friends on the way. Grandparents should live along *with* their grandchildren but it is important that they don't live through their grandchildren rather than through their own direct experience. If they do, they may suffer an emotional setback if misfortune strikes the younger generation.

The role of grandparents

This has changed enormously since the turn of the century. Then, children, parents and grandparents frequently lived in the same house and it was assumed that the latter, as elders, were the authorities on what was right and wrong. This is no longer so. Grandparents no longer have that role. In fact, as a grandparent you may find yourself casting about as to what you can do to help. The best thing you can do is to show your children and your grandchildren how to cope with change. You have lived through the most drastic changes the world has ever known. You have lived longer than any of your family so you have had to cope with a rapidly changing society more often than anyone who is close to you. Your granddaughter may be very depressed because she can't get a job. Only you with an historical perspective on unemployment, and knowing how much it demoralizes people, can help your granddaughter to develop a healthy critical distance between the refusal she gets at job interviews and her feelings about herself. You can share with her what you remember about the depression and unemployment in your time.

You can allow your grandchildren to see you as a real person for the first time, drawing a parallel between their development and yours. In a conversation on politics, for instance, you can stop being a wrinkled, white-haired old person and describe how you were a young soldier in the army during the First World War. You can recount some of your experiences, possible moments of glory. There isn't a grandchild in the world who won't be riveted by that kind of story, and learn much from it.

You can show your family that you are not a doddering and useless grandparent. You can be independent and act so. You can be mobile and agile so that you can join younger members for a walk, or take a leisurely stroll around the golf course while they play a few rounds. You can also listen. Parents don't have a lot of time for that. But you can listen without giving advice, you can tell yor family what experience you have had in your life and what it has led you to believe.

You will also find that you have a lot more in common with teenage grandchildren than you ever had thought. At opposite ends of life you are both searching for changing identities, and both asking the same questions "Who am I?" "What do I really want to do?" "How shall I do it?" Very often adolescents have more in common with grandparents than they do with their own parents. Parents often are too busy or too ambitious forging ahead in life to be self-examining and introspective. The relationship with younger grandchildren, even babies, is also very special. Grandparents can give a unique kind of loving and

127

caring which can only come from them. Young children usually adore them, and also enjoy knowing that they have a very special place in their grandparents' lives.

You mustn't be surprised if it turns out that you and your partner are different as grandparents. After all, you might have been different as parents. One of you might have been the disciplinarian and the other more permissive. Or it might be that one was strict with a daughter, but lets a granddaughter get away with murder.

In a family this ability to change roles is a very good thing. It means you and your partner have different strengths and make different contributions to your family than you have made in the past. This results in rich relationships which are special.

Social relationships

Everyone, whether young or old, needs an active, stimulating environment and dynamic interaction with people of all ages. When youngsters are faced with lack of visual stimulation and hearing or lack of human contact, they begin to show certain signs of *old* age after only ten days of this monotonous environment. They become apathetic, mentally confused, and they may have loss of memory. One effective way of preventing, reducing or postponing social and mental deterioration in older age is to make sure that life is full and active and is set in stimulating surroundings.

Many of today's major problems connected with getting older are preventable in that they are either social or economic. Some of our present customs, such as compulsory retirement, may cause difficulties of both those kinds. A person who has been enthusiastically and gainfully employed may at the age of sixty or sixty-five suddenly drop into the oblivion of compulsory retirement with economic and social deprivation on the grounds that they lack the ability to carry out a productive role. This stems from a value judgement which is common in present-day society, that personal worth can only be judged in terms of economic productivity even though it is well known that people of retirement age are able to work and learn new skills. Furthermore, they are perfectly able to adjust to such changes given the chance.

There are many opportunities for older people who are fit and mobile to enjoy an active social life beyond their own homes. Day centres and luncheon clubs, which usually provide some care for older people, can be a marvellous opportunity for

Day centres and luncheon clubs often organize trips to places of interest.

meeting others, having chats, comparing notes, making friends, etc. They can be particularly helpful when relatives need to be at work for several hours each day and also when they need a break from everyday routine.

The day centre, if the older person wishes, can provide a meeting place for local friends where everyone can socialize and be looked after. Day centres may cater for hobbies. There may be opportunities to participate in hand work, or games such as cards, billiards, bingo or drafts. There are some day centres which are organized in the form of workshops so that older people can earn enough money to give them a sense of purpose. Another type of day centre provides a full daytime care where there are meals available at reasonable prices. Transport is often provided by volunteers to and from these centres.

Luncheon Clubs are an extension of the meals-on-wheels service, and usually meet in a local community hall or home where you can buy an inexpensive hot lunch. There are clubs for people with special interests and hobbies. If you hear of a club for workmates when you retire, think seriously about joining. You may get a great deal of enjoyment from joining Old Girls' Clubs or Old Boys' Clubs run by your old work place.

I think it's important for you to make the first move otherwise other people will be unaware of your existence let alone your needs. Once known it's surprising how readily people will rally round you.

129

Caring for a changing body

Most experts who study ageing (gerontology) agree that getting older is a continuing process which happens to us and everything else that lives – plants and animals alike. Ageing can be viewed as something which goes on throughout life, beginning with conception and ending with death. It is not something affecting people reaching the age of sixty, but everyone from babies, children, teenagers, and young adults to older people. The reason for studying ageing is not that it is a phenomenon which happens in any one particular phase of life, studying ageing gives information about youth and middle age as well.

In addition to describing changes in individual organs and systems, this seems a good place to discuss the *menopause* – an event of great significance for both men and women. This is also the chapter to mention how we might best maintain our appearance.

General effects of ageing

Our body organs show general signs of wear and tear as we continue through life. We become more aware of the physical changes in ourselves and in our partners.

Body changes   This is not to say that all functions diminish at the same rate for every individual, quite the opposite, they are different for almost every person, and of course, the figures may be lower at seventy-five than those stated if there is some pre-existing organic disease.

One of the most significant changes which occurs as we get older is an alteration in the temperature response of the body. As we age, our bodies are less able to respond to loss of heat; we produce heat less efficiently by shivering and our reflex to shiver is slower. This can result in a serious fall in body temperature if we are exposed to cold. In addition, we begin to cope less well with an excess of heat. When we were younger, as a reflex to a raised body temperature, we lost heat by opening up the blood vessels in the skin and sweating. As we get older, the response to this reflex is slower and we cannot sweat as efficiently.

There are other functions associated with ageing which means that less oxygen, nutrients and antibodies are carried to the weakening parts of the body. As we grow older we are less able to move minerals like sodium, calcium and potassium around our bodies as efficiently as we did when we were younger. These solid metabolites may become deposited within and between cells in pigments – a crude analogy would be that our systems become blocked in the way that a furnace is choked with clinker, so that it becomes difficult to maintain. This accumulation of metabolites may be a mechanical hindrance to the normal activities of the cell and the normal functioning of our bodies, causing adverse reactions.

As we get older there is a gradual decline in the function and reserves of our bodies; this increases the likelihood of our becoming ill. Most of our stabilizing mechanisms become less sensitive and less efficient as we age. The decline differs from one organ to another and from one individual to another.

Our bodies are less well able to adapt to stress, injury and disease and we take longer to recover from physical stress such as exercise, psychological stress such as anxiety and health stress such as disease. When there is increased demand during an acute, stressful incident such as surgery or an infection, this may go beyond the normal reserve capacities of our vital organs; the same stress could be easily surmounted by a younger adult. One theory on ageing propounds that it is this precise "slowing down" of our bodies' ability to recover and adapt to a variety of stresses which finally kills.

Many of us don't show the signs of strain when we are resting. It is only when we are subjected to stress, or exercise, that our various functions show a decline. At one time these decreases in function were thought to be an inevitable part of getting older. Mental confusion and signs of senility were considered to be unavoidable. Now we quite rightly question this idea of automatic decline with age. Certainly, some decline can be attributed to our getting older, but much is dependent on the deconditioning of our bodies due to our increasingly sedentary lifestyles.

Skin

Our outward appearance undoubtedly alters as we get older and for most people the condition of the skin and hair is the final arbiter of age. Some of these alterations in our appearance are due to factors which are not easily controlled: the loss of the

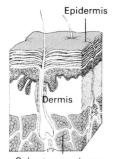

Epidermis

Dermis

Subcutaneous layer

Hair emerges from the epidermis. The dermis nourishes the skin. The fatty subcutaneous layer holds the skin to the muscles.

layer of fat underneath the skin, the decrease in the number of cells which produce pigmentation, the gradual withering away of sebum and sweat glands, and the hardening of, or simply fewer, blood vessels which we have to nourish the skin. Such things as heredity (if either one of our parents has a good skin, we had a 50/50 chance of inheriting one ourselves), and hormone balance are largely beyond our control, too. However, nutrition and prolonged exposure to sun, wind or chemicals are things which we can do something about.

The skin is the largest organ in the body and it serves us extremely well. With its suppleness (its collagen bundles give it almost unique elasticity), it allows us to move freely and to express our feelings. It prevents poisons from getting into our bodies, it is the major organ which keeps our bodies at a steady temperature and it carries messages to our brains by a series of interconnecting nerves.

Wrinkling

Wrinkling is traditionally thought to be the most obvious sign of ageing skin. However, wrinkling actually begins as early as our twenties and continues at a fairly steady pace for the rest of our lives. We use our facial expressions as a way of communicating with others and recording anger, rage, disappointment, happiness, surprise, consternation, etc. These expressions are captured on our faces by lines which begin to form in the places that move most. Very few of us get to our forties without any of these tell-tale signs.

LESSENING THE EFFECTS OF WRINKLING

For both sexes
● Splash water on your face and keep it there with a moisturizing film to prevent your skin dehydrating.
● Never go out in the sun without wearing a sunscreen - the higher the number, the greater the protection. Remember, a day on the ski slopes can do as much damage as a day on the beach.
● If you have tiny surface veins on your face, avoid eating hot, spicy food and drinking alcohol; these will aggravate face flushing.
● Stop smoking. Cigarette smoking may hasten crow's feet and causes deep lines.
● Keep your body well rested by adequate sleep to improve your complexion.

● Facial exercises can help to relax the facial muscles which cause "tension" wrinkles and lines. They can also help keep facial and neck muscles mobile and relieve tension headaches. They cannot, however, *stop* wrinkles forming. Try a smile all the time instead of a frown as it exercises more muscles.

For women
● If you don't wear make-up be sure to wear a fairly liberal covering of a heavy moisturizer which prevents water loss.
● If you can put on some make-up, it will help to reduce water loss from the skin. Avoid astringent toners; switch from cleansing soaps to creams.

Wrinking is caused primarily by a thinning out of the subcutaneous fat which gave our skin its original plumpness. At the same time, the disintegration of collagen bundles, caused mainly by the sun, produces a loss of elasticity. Long-term exposure to the sun unquestionably hastens ageing of the skin (and more seriously is a major cause of diseases of the skin). Given a thinning, loosening skin, the force of gravity does the rest. Professions which demand an outdoor life, such as gardening, farming and construction work, would normally be thought of as healthy, but sunworshippers are simply behaving illogically. What they are really saying is "Here I am, age me" and yearly suntan can result in an irreversible leathery skin.

FACIAL EXERCISES

These will relax your facial muscles and help to prevent "tension" wrinkles and lines. First put some moisturizing cream on your face and neck.

For your chin, upper lip and cheeks
Move the corners of your mouth upward towards your temples. Keep you mouth closed, your teeth unclenched and your lips relaxed and use very tiny, controlled movements. Carefully release your muscles in reverse.

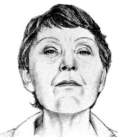

For your chin
Jut out your chin and lower your teeth upward and forward using your chin muscles only. Relax slowly and repeat.

For the muscles in your cheeks, chin and around your mouth
Place your fists under your chin, with your face in a relaxed, normal position. Gently press down with your head and up with your fists, maintaining an even pressure.

Shortly, with practice, you will be able to wrinkle your nose upwards while smiling.

For the contours around your eyes
Focus your eyes upwards and very slowly raise the lower lids both upward and inward (as if you were trying to close them from the bottom only). Slowly lower your lids.

MINIMIZING WRINKLES WITH MAKE-UP

● Use a light-textured foundation diluted with a moisturizer and water which won't accumulate in lines and wrinkles.

● Don't use powder on wrinkled areas – it exaggerates them. If you must, use it on oily areas only; brush it on lightly.

● Use a lipstick pencil to define mouth shape and keep the lipstick from oozing into fine lines on the upper lip.

● Lightly brush on light ivory or white foundation at the bottom of a deep furrow and blend it in very carefully to the rest of your foundation.

Major treatments for wrinkles As the description implies, these are major procedures and should only be practised by expert medical personnel. Never go to a clinic which advertises such treatments. In inexpert hands any of them can result in permanent scarring. Best of all, seek medical advice and consult a dermatologist who may give you the treatments. For full advice see *Specialist help*.

Dermabrasion
This is a surgical treatment which involves removing the superficial surface of the skin with a rotating, cutting instrument. Only surface wrinkles will be removed, not scars or deep pits. It is especially good for removing fine wrinkles around the mouth, eyes and brows.

A special instrument, similar to a dentist's drill, is moved over the surface of the skin. The end of the instrument has a rapidly rotating end shaped into a convex surface with a cutting edge. This planes off the skin layers. The operation takes about 30 minutes and leaves the skin baby-pink and raw. A few days of post-operative attention and bandaging may be necessary.

Skin peeling
This is a chemical treatment which involves using a highly corrosive agent on the skin to remove wrinkled layers. A more hazardous procedure than dermabrasion, you should always go to a highly-skilled expert who should take care to avoid deep burns. The scabs which form will drop off to leave red skin and this must be kept out of the sun until it fades.

Face lifts
Pulling up loose facial skin and tightening or removing fatty tissues in the face and neck can eliminate wrinkles, jowly and wattling effects and sagging skin. Both plastic surgeons and dermatologists can perform such operations which require general anaesthetics and take about three hours. Any incisions are concealed under the hairline or around the ears.

COSMETIC SURGERY

Before considering either of these
operations do read my advice on
pages 197-198.

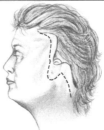

Blepharoplasy
*This involves removing any excess sagging skin
from round the eyes. An incision is made under
the brow bone and the fat is removed. It's
unlikely that there will be any scarring and the
operation will last for up to ten years.*

Face lift
*This affects three facial areas: loose chin and
neck; drooping eyebrows and frown line; and
slack cheeks and mouth-to-nose lines. Skin is
pulled back behind the ears, with any scars
fading after three months.*

Recuperation may involve a week in hospital and there is
much discolouration of the skin. Overtightening of the skin is not
desired as the expression becomes artificial. They are nor permanent and they may last eight to ten years; the skin will
continue to age and sag as before. It is not uncommon for
people to have repeated face lifts.

Silicone injections
Some practitioners inject small amounts of liquid silicone into
wrinkles, deep lines or furrows to smoothe them.

Eye lifts
Excessive skin of the upper eyelids and baggy skin of the lower
eyelids can be removed to restore your youthful look. The
operation known as a blepharoplasty can be performed by
ophthalmologists as well as by plastic surgeons. Excess tissue is
removed along the fold of the eyelid or underneath the lashes.
Following the operation there will be discolouration and the
sutures are not removed for about four days. The results of the
operation will last for up to ten years.

*Dry and
sensitive skin* Normally, subcutaneous fat acts as an important insulator
against loss of body heat, but when it is lost certain functions
can no longer be performed efficiently. The greater the loss of
subcutaneous fat, the greater the amount of body heat which
escapes, leaving us more susceptible to cold. As we get older we
often complain of feeling cold because our skin becomes drier as
the blood circulating to it becomes more sluggish.

Our temperature regulation is affected in the other direction too and the older we get the more likely we are to suffer from heat exhaustion. This is because we have less capacity to perspire and cool off. The loss of oil-secreting glands may cause the skin to dry and crack, perspiration is less, the moisture content is reduced and chapping often results.

• Always keep your hands warm in the winter, particularly the fingertips which, being the furthest extremities of the body, are the last to get nutrients and oxygen, so the skin becomes vulnerable to cold or rapid changes of temperature.

• In winter a humidifier is useful for keeping the room moisture at a good level for your skin.

• Wear smooth materials next to your skin.

• Contact with water is drying to the skin – no water gets in, water is drawn out. Don't lie for a long soaking in the bath. Shower, if possible. Keep your hands out of water as often as you can possibly manage.

• Only use sufficient soap when washing, as soap is defatting and can cause itching, soreness and scaling, especially around the genitals. Don't use soda crystals or bath salts of any kind.

• It is particularly important as we get older to keep our skin supple and moist so keep jars or tubes of handcream in convenient places around the house so that you can rub cream into your hands whenever you remember. Every time you get your hands wet, put on a liberal amount of handcream.

• Wear rubber gloves for dirty jobs, but make sure that you wear an inner lining of a cheap cotton glove soaked in hand cream or hand lotion.

Brown patches Most of us have a few "brown spots" on our skins. These blotches are areas of irregular pigmentation affected by ageing and exposure to sunlight. Typically, such spots appear on exposed parts of the body – the face, neck, backs of the hands and upper arms.

They are not dangerous but may be considered unsightly. We can cover them with cosmetic sticks or creams. Personally, I follow the golden rule that a brown spot should never be interfered with unless a doctor says so and after, only after, you've consulted a dermatologist to check that such treatments are suitable for your particular spots, they can be removed by various medical skin treatments (see page 206).

Itching and inflamed skin After forty, itching can result merely from our skin being dry due to frequent, overzealous bathing in hot water and strong soaps and sunbathing. Sometimes, however, redness of the skin with itching and raw patches – *intertrigo* – is due to the skin

137

creases caused by the build-up of body fat. Where skin surfaces touch each other – as between the legs, around the armpits and, in women, under the breasts, friction and lack of ventilation can cause intertrigo and the skin gets raw and smelly and may host fungus infections.

Self-help involves keeping such areas dry and cool and not becoming overweight. Once the skin is red and sore, you should see a dermatologist who can prescribe drying and anti-yeast medications. Better you should lose some weight. If you have a skin irritation apply a cooling lotion such as calamine, never use an itch-relieving spray which may contain local anaesthetics.

NECK EXERCISES

Perform these once a day to relax muscles, improve deportment, prevent stooping and maintain good posture.

Neck rolls (3 times)
These relieve tension in the back of your neck while thoroughly exercising your neck muscles. Sit in a straight-backed chair or cross-legged on the floor and keep your neck and back straight and shoulder down, your face ahead. Tip your head forward and without turning your neck at all, roll your head loosely on your neck round to the other side and then back.

Chin lift (12 times)
This exercises your chin and jaw line. Sit up straight and look straight ahead without lifting your head too high, say "eee" and then "ooo".

De-sagger (6 times)
To exercise and relax your neck muscles, lie on your back on a table or firm bed with your head hanging loosely over the edge.
Now, slowly pull your head up until your chin is as close to your chest as you can get it. Hold for a few seconds and then slowly let your head fall back, but don't let it flop.

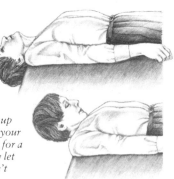

Now, put your hand lightly under your chin and feel the muscles pull and relax to the sounds.

"Crepey" necks

All of us will eventually notice that the skin of our necks is getting "crepey". This is due to two things: the neck has to be a very mobile organ, moving in all directions much of the time; its skin gets more stretching than skin elsewhere so it becomes loose. The neck is often neglected from a beauty routine, gets no special cleansing, no special moisturizing. At the same time, it's nearly always exposed, so it bears the mask of ageing from the elements. The most efficient moisturizer that we can use contains sebum, which holds water in the skin.

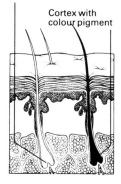

Transparent cortex cells

Cortex with colour pigment

The root of the hair is buried deep inside a hair follicle.

Hair

Hair is constantly being renewed from below the skin's surface; normally, 20-60 hairs a day fall out but these are replaced. Hairs remain on the head for a period of two to six years. The rate at which hair grows, half an inch a month, slows down as we age. Also, the rate of hair loss begins to exceed that of new growth so some thinning is inevitable. However, it is felt that at least 40 percent of our hair must be lost before thinning becomes apparent.

Greying hair is a normal part of ageing and most people have some noticeable greying by the middle forties. While some people may have no grey hair until their late fifties, hardly anyone at seventy has none. Grey hair is just as healthy as pigmented hair and needs no special treatment. "Old" hair does not lose its colour – we don't turn grey – but rather new hair grows in without pigment. '

Hair care

Use the mildest shampoo you can find and only ever shampoo your hair once. Make sure your head is thoroughly wet, mix a small amount of shampoo (two teaspoonfuls) in a glassful of warm water and pour this on, massaging the shampoo into your hair very gently. Make sure all the hair has been covered by the shampoo solution; it is not necessary to work up a lather. Leave it on for about a minute and then rinse thoroughly until the hair is squeaky clean. If you like, you can add a conditioner afterwards. Here are a few basic tips:

● Do not scrub the scalp with your fingertips as you will loosen hairs from the soft wet hair follicles;

● Do not tug or pull at your hair as you comb it when it is wet; this will remove or tear it. Use a wide-toothed brush.

● Do not brush or comb your hair too frequently, this may irritate the scalp and the oil glands;

● Do not treat any dandruff yourself, see your doctor about it.

139

Hair colouring

Temporary or permanent colouring can be used to hide grey hair, though nothing can restore hair to its original shade once it greys. All the types of hair colouring below are marketed for both sexes or can be obtained from any good hairdressers.

Comb-through colour "restorers", or liquid metallic salts, are sprayed onto the hair. However, they do little more than discolour hair and cover it with a dull coating which often causes the hair to become brittle and easily damaged.

Temporary colours, which can be dry or liquid, are actually rinses which can give highlights to grey hair, hide dull yellow streaks, brighten faded hair and blend streaked hair. They do not lighten or last beyond a shampoo.

Semi-permanent colours can blend grey hairs into your natural colour or enhance hair that is drab. They fade over a period so re-application is necessary every few weeks.

Permanent colours penetrate the hair shaft and chemically alter the pigment so that it cannot be shampood away. This process should not be repeated more than once a month as it can damage hair or produce undesirable colour shades. Permanent hair colours containing PABA have a warning on them in the USA about a possible association with developing cancer.

Hair loss

Baldness affects men most, though women may be affected to a lesser degree. If there is a familial predisposition to baldness it cannot be prevented and there are no "cures". Some diseases, especially those which involve defects of the thyroid gland and anaemia, also cause hair loss but in these cases the hair is restored when the disease is treated.

Many people who suffer from baldness are under psychological stress. A loss of hair can cause a reciprocal loss of morale making the depression worse. A belief widely held is that baldness is connected with virility both positively and negatively but such a belief is entirely untrue.

A trio of factors including heredity, hormones and age are responsible for causing baldness; this process varies from man to man but is irreversible and progressive.

Many men suffer from male pattern baldness and some women also go thin on top – it's part of the body's genetic programme. The hair gradually recedes from the forehead, temples and crown of the head, leaving a reasonably thick fringe around the sides and back.

Male baldness

Baldness usually begins in the early twenties and is pretty well established by middle age. Typically, the earliest signs of baldness are noticed in the areas on the sides of the forehead – complete lack of hair is preceded by the presence of fine downy hairs which can be seen by holding a flashlight parallel to the head's surface.

Female baldness

Although total baldness is extremely rare in women, considerable thinning does occur at the temples and over the top of the head. Again, this pattern is usually inherited although the use of hair clips, combs and bands which tug at the hair may be responsible as may be damaging hair treatments such as permanents or dyeing. Psychological upsets, particularly around the menopause, can cause loss of hair which may take nine months to a year to recover.

You should take care to avoid using rollers and heavy bristle brushes which may break hairs and pull at the roots and also keep permanents, frosting and teasing to a minimum.

Many women, too, find that as they age they also lose hair from other parts of their bodies, especially from the pubic area, under the arms and from the legs.

Dealing with hair loss

Hairpieces

This is the safest and least painful way (in terms of health and money) to camouflage your hair loss. A wide variety of well-cut and well-matched items are made to suit both men and women. Some hairpieces can be permanently attached to the head, either by being tied to existing hairs or by being sewn onto the scalp. These latter may result in infection and are therefore not recommended. Some wigs or hairpieces may contain adhesives to which the wearer is sensitive, other than this they cause no damage to the remaining hair.

Hair weaving

This is a non-surgical procedure which adds replacement hair to existing hair in order to cover a bald patch. The new hair is braided strand by strand on to the edges of the hair *in situ*. Hair weavings require maintenance and careful cleansing.

Hairpieces have been successfully designed to blend in with natural hair for both men and women.

Hair implant

This is a quasi-surgical procedure where strips of hair are attached to the scalp in the form of surgical threads implanted in the balding area. The implants are normally synthetic so a hairdryer mustn't be used.

141

Hair transplant

This is a surgical procedure which generally results in a permanent replacement of hair – though even when established it is not as luxurious as the hair you've lost – and has become increasingly available. Plugs of hair are cut from remaining healthy hair on the sides and back of the head and implanted in bald spots. This hair normally falls out after the transplant but it is replaced by new hair. Quite a few hair follicles must be transplanted at the same session, and the process needs to be repeated for the bald areas to be covered.

Excessive hair   Just as with hair loss, the tendency to develop excessive hair is hereditary and is usually due to hormonal influence. It is particularly common in people with Latin or Mediterranean backgrounds. This is mainly a problem for women, as men usually worry about a lack rather than an abundance of hair. Hair may begin to appear in one or more places – chin, upper lip, around the nipples, or from the navel downwards. Men often find hair growing in their ears, nostrils and on their backs. Eyebrow hair gets thicker and more noticeable.

Superfluous hair is often upsetting but there is little that can be done about stopping the growth. Remedies include lightening it with make-up or bleach, or removal. The hair's rate of growth is not affected whether it's shaved or plucked, contrary to any old wives' tales you might have heard.

Neither plucking, wax removal nor shaving will make the hair more wiry, darker or thicker; nor will they prevent its regrowth. If you find any hair growth distressing, electrolysis is a permanent method of removal which can be used successfully on most parts of the body.

Women with very severe, unwanted hair can be investigated to see if hormone imbalance is the cause. An endocrinologist can perform a hormonal profile and, if it's advisable, hormone therapy can be tried as a remedy.

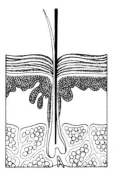

An electrical current travels down a needle which is placed adjacent to the hair shaft. The current destroys the follicle and prevents growth.

Eyes

The eye is one organ which does not necessarily change as we get older; this means that not all of us will suffer from deteriorating vision as we mature. Indeed 80 percent of people over sixty-five who have a visual impairment can be fitted with glasses so that they can go about their normal activities. However, it becomes more important for us to have regular checks on our eyesight as we get older so that we receive expert advice.

PRESBYOPIA

A lot of people in middle age develop a tendency to be far-sighted because the lens is less able to change its shape to bring into focus what we are looking at. This phenomenon is known as *presbyopia* or "old sight".

Normal eyesight
When the eye focuses on an object, the image is projected on to the retina upside down and back to front. The brain alters this to the way we see.

Presbyopia
This results when the lens becomes less accommodating and is less able to change its shape in order to bring objects into focus.

Eyesight with glasses
In order to remedy presbyopia your optician will prescribe convex (outwardly curved) lenses to increase the power of your own lenses.

Our senses (seeing, hearing, tasting and feeling pain) become less acute and this affects the way we function, our activity and our responses to stimuli.

Another difficulty ageing brings is that the lens begins to yellow. This makes it difficult for us to distinguish between different colour intensities. The most difficult are the cool colours such as blue, green and violet which are filtered out by the yellowing lens. It is generally easier to see warm colours such as yellow, red and orange.

Bear in mind, too, that as we get older it takes a longer time for our eyes to adjust when we go from a well-lit area into a dark one. Don't forget that we also see less well in the dark, so don't be afraid to ask someone to go in front of you if you have to navigate steps or a bumpy path. I do.

Wearing glasses

Presbyopic eyes may require "reading glasses", which are normally focused for about 14 inches. These will reinforce the power of the natural lens of your eyes but they will have to be replaced every few years.

Half glasses may be useful for near correction but not distance. They can be worn all the time, you simply look over them to see any distance.

Bifocals contain two lenses, the long-distance lens is on top and the reading lens on the bottom. They have a thin, visible dividing line. The reading lens can be of a variable size according to taste and you should discuss this with your ophthalmologist before ordering glasses. It can take some time to get adjusted to bifocals.

143

Contact lenses can also be worn to improve vision, though people over forty may find that they cannot read or see things closely with them and they may need to wear reading glasses over them. It is also possible to get bifocal contact lenses; these can be fitted after you have adapted to single ones.

Sun or tinted glasses may be useful in forestalling the development of cataracts or retinal disease, as exposure to bright light is now thought to be harmful. They should not, however, be worn while driving at night to correct the dazzle of headlamps. They will only make matters worse. Nevertheless, it is useful to wear sunglasses during the day if you expect to drive back from the beach in the evening. If headlamps do dazzle you, this may be an early sign of an impending cataract (see page 244) and the best solution is to keep your glasses scrupulously clean and windscreens clear.

Loss of visual acuity

The loss of visual acuity can prove a serious problem when communicating with other people. As we go through life we become quite dependent on our eyes for receiving and processing messages about what is going on around us through books, newspapers, magazines and television. During our daily lives we have to perform tasks which largely depend on good vision. Simple things like sewing on a button, watching out for the bubbles as the gravy comes to the boil, and making sure that we have the same coloured socks on each foot all become difficult, undermining our sense of security and self-confidence.

Anyone who suffers *sudden* loss of vision needs patience and sympathy if he or she is to avoid feeling afraid and isolated. Remember that anyone who is losing his or her eyesight may be hesitant in trying to do anything, especially anything new, because he or she is feeling self-conscious. Such a person feels slow and gauche in striving to do well and may draw back from getting involved in things.

Living with visual impairment

● Fit more powerful bulbs in all the lights throughout the house, especially in reading lamps and those in dark hallways; *however,* if you have glaucoma don't make your lights too bright as this can cause glare and deepen shadows. Tell those close to you what your needs are so that they can come to your assistance if necessary.

● Never leave the house completely dark at night. This can make any journey from the bedroom unnecessarily hazardous. If you can afford it, get dimmers fitted to your electric light switches in the bedroom, bathroom and upstairs hall, so that you can leave a dim light burning all night.

● Put fluorescent tape around your electric plugs and light

switches, door handles and keyholes. It will also make it easier for your to pick them out when the light is poor.

● If you suffer from glaucoma, have your eyes tested to see how much your field of vision is restricted, and then ask advice about whether or not you should drive a car. Don't forget that our reflexes slow down as we get older and in today's fast-moving traffic we can't afford not to see passing cars.

● If your peripheral vision is restricted, ask someone who is talking to you to face you directly, or if you can, make sure your face is directly in front of him or her. If someone is demonstrating something to you, make sure that all the movements are in your line of vision.

● Explain the kind of visual loss that you are experiencing to your family and friends and any social or health care workers who are helping you. They will then try to make adjustments easier for you.

Ears

At the age of about fifty most of us will have noticed some hearing loss, usually to the higher-pitched sounds. The majority of us do retain fairly normal hearing beyond the age of sixty but in our seventies and eighties we are three times more likely to have lost some of our hearing.

In the Western world men suffer much more from hearing loss than women, possibly because of a higher noise level at work. This is supported by studies of primitive villagers who do not have the kind of age-linked hearing impairment which we get in cities nor any difference in the hearing of men and women.

Hearing loss is usually due to changes in the inner ear involving the transmission of sound to the brain. The cochlea is the hearing organ in the the inner ear and it transforms sound vibrations into nerve impulses through delicate hair cells. These hairs have the capability of transforming sound waves into electrical impulses which are carried via the auditory nerve to the brain, where they are transferred back into sound. The most common cause of loss of hearing is thought to be due to loss of hair cells. This loss obviously cannot be helped by a hearing aid.

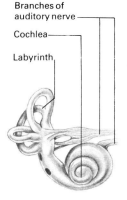

Branches of
auditory nerve

Cochlea

Labyrinth

The brain receives signals from the cochlea via the auditory nerve.

Impaired hearing

Patience and kindness are automatically shown to a blind person, but someone with hearing difficulty often meets with impatience and embarrassment. People hard of hearing can see the irritation they cause, which is something spared the blind. Even long-standing relationships may be disrupted.

145

It is vitally important for our mental well-being, as well as of those whom we love, that we keep in touch with the world about us. As loss of hearing jeopardizes this ability, any reduced hearing should be reported to your doctor as soon as it becomes noticeable. Loss of hearing in a young person is nearly always forgiven, but impaired hearing in an older person is frequently interpreted as stubbornness, senility and eccentricity.

When hearing begins to wane, our ability to hear higher frequency speech sounds may be affected. Consonants such as K, CH, F, SH, S and Z have higher frequencies, while vowel sounds A, E, I, O and U have lower frequencies. If there is disparity in hearing these vowels and consonants, a person can hear conversation but cannot make out the words precisely. Thus a phrase like "clean dentures" may be perceived by the person with early hearing loss as a chain of vowel sounds which he or she cannot comprehend. This presents a lot of difficulties for both the listener and the speaker. Most people try to make themselves heard by shouting which only results in a chain of booming, unintelligible sounds. It does nothing to clarify higher frequency sounds.

A common cause of hearing impairment is failure to conduct sound waves across the middle ear through a chain of tiny bones: the hammer, the anvil and the stirrup, so named because of their shapes. *Otosclerosis,* caused by the fixation of the stirrups, can lead to a loss of hearing.

A trivial thing such as wax can harden and dry and block sound waves getting to the eardrum. Some people's ears make more wax than others and any excess is not an indication of lack of cleanliness. Hearing can be vastly improved simply by having the ear canal syringed and wax collected and removed by a doctor or nurse. Never attempt to remove wax by poking any object into your ear.

Hearing aids and their problems

If hearing impairment is not due to damage to the auditory nerve then a hearing aid can help, though it is not a perfect substitute for hearing normally, nor can it give the listener a full range of sound frequencies.

It is normal for people newly fitted with hearing aids to complain that the sound seems unnatural and also that they pose problems in adjusting. If you are helping someone through this adjustment period, bear in mind that hearing aids amplify all sounds and a wearer may have difficulty in distinguishing speech patterns from any other noise in the room, such as television, radio, jumble of conversation by several different people, sounds of washing up, cooking, etc. If you are given a hearing aid, seek advice as to how it works properly.

HEARING AIDS

Hearing aids are supplied free by the National Health Service at the ear, nose and throat departments of hospitals. It is also possible to buy them privately, a commercial hearing aid centre may offer a range of styles.

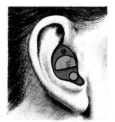

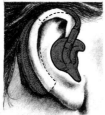

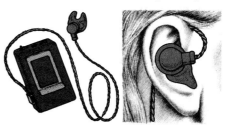

Internal aid
This fits snugly into the outer-ear canal and it is hardly noticeable.

Behind-the-ear aid
The earphone fits into your outer-ear canal and seals it up so that no sound is lost.

Body-worn aid
In some more powerful hearing aids, the amplifier and battery are kept in a plastic case which you can clip to your belt or place in your pocket. It's unobtrusive and connected to the earphone by a thin, plastic-covered wire.

If you don't, you might be tempted to discard it and cut yourself off from the social intercourse and companionship of others.

Another fairly common problem with hearing aids occurs when the ear-mould is fitted incorrectly. It should be an exact replica of your ear.

Making the best of your hearing

- Go and have your ears checked fairly regularly, say once every six months and have any wax removed by your doctor.
- If your hearing is going and you cannot successfully master a hearing aid, try to learn to lip read. This can be of great help in conversation. Ask the person whose lips you are reading to face you, making sure that the light falls on his or her face. It is important that you can see him or her clearly and not to exaggerate lip movements as you will find this confusing.
- Don't become defensive and withdrawn when somebody is shouting to help you hear better. Ask him or her to speak more loudly but to lower his or her voice so that you can pick up the lower sound frequencies and to speak clearly and slowly.
- If you have difficulty in hearing one particular word, ask the speaker to use another word to say the same thing.
- It does no harm at all to point out that non-verbal communication is extremely good for getting messages across. Encourage people to use facial expressions as these can tell you about their moods, feelings, excitement or disapproval when you can't get this from the tone in which the words are said.

147

Mouth, tongue and teeth

As we get older we begin to lose sensitivity to pain and irritation in the mouth. Many irritations, therefore, we disregard and any which we notice are shrugged off in the false belief that they will heal quickly. This, combined with infrequent visits to the dentist, can lead to poor oral hygiene. A touch of arthritis too can prevent good care of the mouth and teeth and lead to the loss of a positive self-image and problems in the mouth.

As we get older our mouths tend to dry out because we secrete smaller quantities of saliva; the lining gets thinner and can't hold water, and we may be deficient in certain vitamins (such as vitamin A) which are responsible for the integrity of lining inside the mouth.

Loss of taste sensations As we go through middle age we may experience blunting of our tastes due to a gradual withering of the taste buds on the tongue. A stroke, or hardening of the arteries in the brain, can also affect the way we taste.

It is possible that people of seventy have 70 percent fewer taste buds than they had at thirty. As we approach old age, in our late seventies and eighties, we feel almost an 80 percent reduction in our ability to taste. It is not until after sixty, however, that we notice any real deterioration. Salty taste does not appear to be affected by age but sweet, bitter and sour do decline. As one might expect, what goes is the ability to detect subtle differences within sweet, bitter and sour tastes. There is a loss of touch sensitivity in the mouth and any lessening of our senses of smell will also affect how we taste things. As taste becomes duller, we may find ourselves increasing the flavouring of food by adding spices and seasoning. We often eat dishes which, when we were younger, we would have considered over-seasoned and avoided at all costs.

One of the dangers of losing the ability to savour food is that our appetites may lessen and we become in danger of not eating sufficient quantities of the right foods. All of these things, plus loneliness, isolation and a loss of spirit, deter us from spending enough time shopping for nutritious foods and preparing healthy meals.

The "older" mouth While a forty-year-old mouth may not be perfect, it should be healthy and efficient. By middle age almost all our mouths will contain fillings, inlays or crowns and we may also have a bridge or partial denture. Even a full set of dentures is no longer an indication of old age (see *Specialist help*).

Teeth have several functions. They masticate food and help to mix saliva with it so that digestion is started in the mouth. Certain sounds involve contact between the teeth and the tongue and so they are important for good speech. Even today, when there is emphasis on dental conservation, nearly 50 percent of people living in the Western world have lost most of their teeth by the age of sixty-five and about 75 percent of all people are edentulous (toothless) by the time they reach seventy-five. The main causes of this attrition are a poor diet rich in sugar, and neglect by the individual and by his or her dentist and/or hygienist to make sure that the teeth are regularly cleaned and scaled, the gum margins looked after and teeth repaired as soon as their conditions deteriorate.

As we go through middle age we begin to show a different pattern of dental problems from those we had when we were thirty-five and forty. Dental cavities which reached their peak when we were thirty-five are present now to a lesser extent. But after forty the most common cause for losing teeth is pyorrhoea (infective disease of the gums). During middle age the gums begin to recede and more of the teeth show so that they look longer, hence the phrase "longer in the tooth".

The commonest dental changes are missing teeth, worn teeth, teeth becoming slack in the gums and badly-fitting dentures. All these affect the functioning of our mouths and teeth and can lead to cosmetic changes in the appearance of our faces and to subsequent loss of self-image.

Restoring teeth New developments in dentistry have concentrated on the restoration of adult teeth. Plastic, composite materials are available for filling and building up front teeth in an "invisible" way. New plastic-covered wire braces and those which are attached behind the teeth have led to a big increase in the number of adults wearing braces to correct their dentition. Oral surgeons can also realign jaws, making possible the correction of gaps and protruding jaws. Moreover, permanent implants have been used successfully to hold dentures in place.

Dentures Failure to fill any gaps caused by loss of teeth can lead to complications; if dentures are not worn, any remaining teeth adjust to fill the spaces and there may be resulting changes in the underlying bony structure of the jaws. The same problems can occur if dentures are badly fitted.

Dentures are socially well accepted, and amongst some communities are even status symbols. The best-fitting denture is one for the upper teeth. The lower one never fits quite as well because gums recede and so the denture has to be altered.

149

LOOKING AFTER DENTURES

Nowadays, most bridges (see page 205) and also dentures are designed to be kept permanently in the mouth except when they need cleaning.

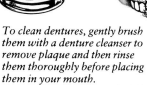

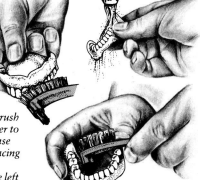

To clean dentures, gently brush them with a denture cleanser to remove plaque and then rinse them thoroughly before placing them in your mouth.
Removable dentures can be left to soak in water overnight.

This means that you should go along to your dentist for an assessment of your dentures about every five years.

Dental adhesives are almost universally unpleasant and their effects last a fairly short time. They should never be used as a substitute for periodic rechecks by a dentist.

Looking after your mouth and teeth

• More regular visits to your dentist for the purpose of conserving your teeth and maintaining the health of your mouth. This lowers any chance of your having trouble, like developing an ulcer due to irritation by sharp tooth edges.

• Any sore on your tongue or gums or the inside of your cheeks which lasts two weeks should be seen by your doctor.

• Drying out of the mouth can lead to problems, so if you find that this is happening to you, irrigate your mouth by sucking a sugarless sweet or having a cup of tea or coffee.

• Pyorrhoea is largely caused by calculus, the chalky-white, hard deposits around the margins of your teeth where they enter your gums. You can keep this at bay by removing plaque with regular tooth brushing at least morning and night and after eating sweet food, and visiting your dentist at three-monthly or six-monthly intervals for mechanical removal of the plaque, depending on its seriousness.

• Always have the sharp edge of a tooth attended to by a dentist as soon as you feel it. Don't put off your visit.

Legs and feet

Special attention must be paid to our legs and feet in order to have an active lifestyle. Gradual hardening of the arteries and increasingly poor circulation due to ageing are expecially hard on feet. Feet take a great deal of wear and tear and a regular programme of foot care is vital.

Looking after your feet
- Avoid blisters and sore areas on your feet or toes by wearing comfortable, supple, low-heeled shoes. Well-fitting shoes should grip your heel and instep but not press on your toes.
- Sit with your feet up whenever you can so that any fluid can drain out of them and their nourishment can be increased. This is particularly important if you get any kind of abrasion, cut or sore on your foot.
- Minor injuries tend to take longer to heal than anywhere else because of their dependent position. Treat even a small sore promptly with a simple antiseptic cream (no hot water soaking, please). If it doesn't clear up in a few days consult your doctor. Consult him or her *immediately* if you are a diabetic or suffer from any circulatory disease of the veins or arteries.
- Don't keep your stockings up with garters, especially tight ones, as they may make a poor circulation poorer.

EXERCISES TO AID CIRCULATION

Our extremities are the first to suffer as our blood circulation slows down, so it is important that we take care of our legs and feet.

Foot bending (10-15 times)
Point your feet and toes upwards as far as you can manage and then point them down. Repeat this action vigorously.

Leg raising (20 times)
Keeping your legs straight, point your feet and toes upwards and raise one leg 45° Hold to the count of 3 and then slowly lower it to the floor. Repeat the exercise with your other leg.

Foot circling (15 times)
Working from your ankles, turn your feet in a circle in one direction. Repeat in the opposite direction.

151

Chilblains   The older we get, the more we tend to be subject to chilblains (areas of itching, swelling and redness). You can help to avoid these by wearing thick woollen stockings or socks and, in the coldest weather, fleece-lined shoes and slippers. However, make certain that any lined shoe or boot will accommodate your foot comfortably as tightness retards circulation and may encourage chilblains. Warm trousers can also be protective. You can also help discourage chilblains by starting the day with a warm bath and massaging your feet gently with a rotary movement using foot oil before drying with a rough towel.

If you do develop chilblains, never put your feet or legs near direct heat – such as a hot water bottle. Try bathing the chilblains alternately in hot and cold water.

Nail care

Hardening of the arteries and poor circulation may make skin cool to the touch and it also leads to thickening fingernails and toenails. It is important to trim them regularly, say once a week to keep them in the best condition.

When you are cutting your toenails, never cut them down deeply at the sides; keep the nails straight all the way across – this helps prevent ingrowing nails. If they are very thick you can file them frequently and attempt to thin them down as well as shorten them.

If you have difficulty in looking after your toenails and feet, regular visits to the chiropodist is a vital investment if you want to remain agile.

Muscles and joints

Changes in our muscles and bones are important because they can greatly affect our lifestyle by making certain everyday functions harder to perform. Even though some degenerative changes may cause pain, stiffness and difficulty with movement, there is no need for them to be disabling as long as we get the correct diagnosis, treatment and maintenance therapy. Bones and muscles give stability to the body, help it keep its shape, provide support, protect the vital organs and enable us to move and walk, jump and run freely. As we get older we find that we take these functions very much for granted; as our musculo-skeletal systems can no longer take the stresses and strains of younger life we become prey to bad posture, stooping, loss of power in our muscles, stiffness, painful and even mis-shapen joints, loss of mobility and we may become prone to falls and fractures.

Bone and muscle disorders are among the commonest conditions affecting people over the age of sixty-five. It is dangerous to bracket all bone and muscle symptoms together as part of getting old, otherwise the pain of osteoporotic bones (ones which have lost protein and calcium) or the stiffness and crouched stance characteristic of Parkinson's Disease, may be dismissed as normal ageing and proper treatment delayed. At no age are long-term recurrent joint and muscle pains natural. Anyone experiencing such symptoms should seek medical advice (see *Special medical problems*).

The amount of muscle in our bodies decreases as we get older. This is partly due to hardening of the arteries and a sluggish circulation which is a result of the slowing down and/or loss of nerve cells which send messages from the brain to the muscles, and partly due to a reduction in the amount of physical activity we manage to undertake each day.

So, as we get older we may take longer to complete a job. Muscle deterioration can affect other body organs which you might not suspect. For instance, if the muscles involved in breathing become weak, this will predispose to chest illnesses. Weakening of the bladder muscle means that it never completely empties so we feel the need to pass urine more often.

It is important that we make our limitations known to friends and colleagues so that they will recognize what we are capable of – and give us sufficient time.

Posture   Often, our posture deteriorates as a result of normal ageing, with gradually softening bones and loss of muscle flexibility. Our chins begin to jut forward, our backs become humped and our knees and hips bend. If this continues our breathing and lung capacities can lessen, our gaits can become shuffling and there's often a greater likelihood of fractures. The good news is that exercise can prevent, or remedy, such changes and it can help to ensure that the deterioration normally associated with old age is forestalled (see *Keeping physically fit*).

Backache can be prevented if the back muscles are kept strong by simple exercises and good posture to support the spine. Improved bearing substantially contributes to a youthful appearance (see page 37).

Posture is a matter of balance; if the body segments are properly aligned then less strain is put on the muscles. It must be maintained when sitting and walking as well.

153

EXERCISE FOR CO-ORDINATION AND BALANCE

Good balance helps posture; if our body segments are properly aligned then less strain is put on muscles.

Stand against a wall with your head, buttocks and heels touching it and stretch up with your hands over your head until you are raised on your toes.

Move away from the wall, keeping your feet 6in (15cm) apart and your arms by your sides. Tighten leg and stomach muscles, extend your chest and clench your fists bringing them chest high. Take a deep breath, let it out slowly without relaxing and rotate your arms for a count of 3 (5 times).

Make sure your chair is comfortable and upright and sit back on the seat with your head and shoulders balanced over your hips. Use your hips as well as your arms when you reach for something. When walking, centre your body over the balls of your feet and lead by your thigh.

Looking after joints and muscles

● Always take an injury to a muscle or joint seriously. Consult your doctor or a specialist in order to get an accurate diagnosis and specialized treatment. Make sure that once the injury is healed you learn about a maintenance programme of exercising for endurance, strength and mobility from a physiotherapist.

● Most treatments for joints involve a programme of combined rest and exercise. This applies just as well to healthy joints. Rest plus exercise means resting the joint at night in the position of optimum relaxation (this also prevents the joints from becoming stiff and immobile in an abnormal position) and a series of exercises repeated during the day. Anyone who feels discomfort and stiffness beginning should start on this kind of programme.

● If you feel a joint becoming stiff and uncomfortable, the worst thing that you can do is rest it for any length of time without consulting your doctor. You will hasten the speed at which it stiffens and becomes immobile.

• If you find that joint or muscle pain is disabling, do consult your doctor so that any discomfort can be relieved and so that you can get appliances to help you do everyday tasks. There is special cutlery, for instance, for those who are beginning to feel stiffening joints in their fingers. There is even a gadget which can help you turn on and turn off the tap (see page 308).
• A programme of exercise is important at all stages in our lives because it helps to increase the blood flow and promotes the health of our bodies. It lowers the blood cholesterol and it makes the burning up of calories more efficient. It also suppresses appetite. As we get older it is important to maintain a programme of at least gentle exercise. People who are bedridden must be actively exercised to prevent loss of muscle strength (see *Living with long-term ailments*).
• If you fail to or cannot exercise, mobility aids such as crutches, walkers and canes become more difficult to use.
• There are conversions which you can make to your home which make life easier if you suffer from muscle or joint complaints. These are discussed in *Adapting your environment.*

Gastro-intestinal tract

In the gastro-intestinal tract some of the changes are specific to the various parts of the mouth, stomach or intestine, while others are due to general ageing of the body. Digestive juices decrease in quantity and the gut doesn't move as energetically to digest and push our food along. The muscles lining the various parts of the digestive organs become weaker and when nerve function fades, messages about enzyme and hormone release don't get through to the brain efficiently. There is also less response to pain and internal sensations.

Vague symptoms from the gastro-intestinal tract such as heartburn, indigestion and discomfort at the lower end of the breastbone increase with age. Many of these symptoms are caused by normal changes but as we get older they can be linked to serious conditions which may be life-threatening. Don't be put off by a doctor who attributes rather vague stomach or intestinal symptoms to getting old. Ask for a second opinion.

Changes in the stomach   From middle age onwards there are changes in the structure and function of the stomach which affect digestion, but research has not yet revealed exactly what these changes are and how fast they occur. The stomach, however, gradually stops producing a normal quantity of acid which is essential for carrying on

155

digestion and it may become short of acid. Mucin, which is secreted by glands in the stomach and stops the stomach from digesting itself, has a tendency to be produced in smaller and smaller quantities.

Gall bladder and liver Most gall bladder problems don't increase in frequency until after we are sixty-five. When we get older, two things happen to gall bladder function which both predispose to inflammation (cholecystitis). Firstly, the gall bladder no longer empties efficiently, and secondly, the bile becomes thicker, richer in cholesterol and less in volume. Certainly, gall stones increase with age. By the time we are seventy between 15 and 30 percent of us will have gall stones.

The liver is the largest gland in the body and it is important to our health. It has been described as a "chemical breaker's yard" because it undertakes so many functions. It builds up carbohydrates into a form which can be stored; it also acts as a reservoir for proteins, vitamins, minerals and fats; it is a chemical sieve which filters out and renders bacteria harmless. The liver is in control of how much bile we secrete and it makes certain blood cells and antibodies. These are important in the eradication of infectious and other diseases.

As we get older our livers increase in size in proportion to the rest of the body, so that the liver's percentage of body weight remains constant until the age of seventy. Only then does it start to decline slowly up to the age of a hundred.

Changes in the intestines There is a family of conditions which affects the large intestine and it is often thought to be the natural outcome of growing older. Quite a lot can be done with plain common sense to prevent them from developing into anything serious.

Along with many other linings in the body, the lining of the intestines becomes thin and its glands get fewer in number. The resilience and elasticity of the intestines diminish as collagen becomes thinner and disintegrates and also muscles become a good deal weaker.

The large intestine serves as a storage organ. It is the major site in the whole gastro-intestinal tract where water is absorbed from the stools and where waste collects. Both of these functions can become less efficient because the movements of the bowels weaken and slow down as we approach seventy. Constipation is an almost natural consequence unless we take care to have the right diet (see page 243). Adding bran to semi-liquid dishes, for instance, will help to overcome the discomfort. Mention the fact that you have constipation to your doctor and he will advise you which drugs to avoid, and if necessary, which laxatives are gentle enough for you to use.

Looking after internal organs

- Your stomach and liver may be less able to cope with a large, rich meal, so eat little meals, say six a day, often.
- Never medicate yourself for gastric symptoms, even mild ones, for longer than 10 days without seeing your doctor.
- When considering a diet, don't stick to a rigid plan. Accommodate your own tastes, attitudes, abilities and needs.
- If possible, in early middle age, take precautions not to become dependent on alcohol, with the inevitable development of cirrhosis and death. It is never too late to stop drinking if you have a liver problem. The changes that have already occurred are not reversible but you can prevent further damage.
- If you are suffering from haemorrhoids consult your doctor about treatment, and in the meanwhile ask him or her for something that will soften the stool and increase its bulk. You can do this yourself by adding a spoonful of bran to your breakfast each morning. Do not use proprietary haemorrhoid products from the supermarket shelves.

Heart, blood vessels and chest

For certain heart conditions it is virtually impossible to distinguish whether they are due to age-related conditions or to heart disease. In other words, it is difficult to tell where normal changes end and disease changes begin. Finding a distinction is not merely an academic exercise – certain symptoms in an ageing heart may only indicate slight weakening and not a serious threat to life.

The heart nearly always remains the same size as we advance through life, but malnourishment, confinement to bed, and the rigours of a long illness, may produce some shrinkage. There is, however, a gradual lessening of elasticity in the main arterial trunk of the body, the aorta. At seventy it is only about half as elastic as it was at twenty. Also, there is a slight reduction in heart muscle cell size and a progressive weakening of the heart muscles. This leads to a reduction in the amount of blood which the heart is able to pump around the body but these ageing processes of the heart don't start in middle age, they start after the age of twenty. From then on there is nearly a one percent loss of heart muscle strength for every year lived.

Reduction in the strength of the heart muscle and cardiac output does not mean that there is an inadequate blood flow around the body. Output usually remains adequate because body requirements have fallen and there is a lower metabolic rate. The important part of cardiac function which becomes defective with increasing age is the ability to respond to stress. The response is always inadequate, but it will be sufficient if the rest of the body is not stressed. However, it may be difficult to provide for the whole body's increased fuel needs as the heart cells no longer respond as rapidly or as strongly to the chemicals which are produced when the body is under stress.

Symptoms of wear and tear

Our heart valves tend to thicken with age and there may be signs of calcium deposits. Blood pressure also rises with age. The systolic pressure usually stabilizes in the late seventies and the diastolic pressure stablizes from the early sixties onwards. Some authorities feel that a normal blood pressure for an older man is in the range of up to 160 millimetres of mercury systolic pressure and 100 millimetres diastolic pressure; for women these figures would be 170 and 90.

In the face of this list of age-related changes, you may be tempted to feel that the outlook is black. It is not. Usually, the changes in the heart are continuous and do not significantly interfere with heart function as long as the coronary artery system (the circulation which supplies the heart muscle itself with oxygen) is not damaged. However, diseases of the coronary arteries (ischaemic heart disease) can restrict cardiac function so that symptoms such as getting out of breath on exertion, racing of the heart, palpitation and breathlessness at night when you lie down, may show themselves. Fortunately, the power of the heart lessens in parallel with the demands that are made upon it.

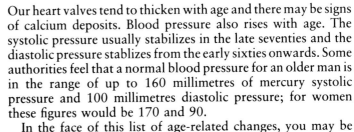

Coarse artery wall

Atheroma

Blood flow

Deposits of fatty material collect at the point where the artery branches. This interferes with the flow of blood.

The following are the most important factors in heart disease: heredity, high blood pressure, diabetes, lack of exercise, cigarette smoking and being overweight. Diet is also thought to be an important factor (see page 268). Much coronary artery disease is caused by *atherosclerosis*. This consists of deposits of fatty material in the wall of arteries, thereby narrowing their cores; this can start very early in life – there are fatty streaks in the aorta of a child when only three years old. One pathologist found evidence of atherosclerosis in infants as young as three to four months. In the Korean war the average age of soldiers who were examined was just over twenty-two and more than three-quarters of them showed extensive atheroma.

Arteriosclerosis

This is synonymous with hardening of the arteries and describes loss of elasticity in the arterial wall. Arteriosclerosis occurs in every population regardless of the factors listed above. It is progressive and related to age. As soon as there is hardening of the arteries there is a decrease in blood flow to areas supplied by them. Arteriosclerosis and atherosclerosis may exist together. Atherosclerosis, however, is not the cause of loss of elasticity in the arteries.

Hypertension or high blood pressure This also increases with age in Western society. Diagnosis of whether blood pressure is high depends on a person's sex, age and state of health. It has been defined as a rise of pressure in the arteries which causes symptoms and this can be relieved with medication. In both men and women high blood pressure is closely correlated with the risk of coronary heart disease.

The most important causes of high blood pressure as we get older are arteriosclerosis and atherosclerosis (see page 219). Both conditions narrow the diameter of arteries and their ability to stretch and the amount of blood which they can carry. They mean that our hearts have to work harder to push the blood through the narrowed vessels to nourish our bodies.

Of course, high blood pressure need not be an inevitable consequence of getting old. More primitive races than ours do not show the same trend as we in the Western world. There is no tendency for blood pressure to increase with age.

Diseases of the lungs In our lungs the most important change is a reduction in breathing power and this means that the older we are, the more easily fatigued we get. These changes rarely cause symptoms when we are resting. This kind of "normal change" does not affect our lifestyles as we get older because our bodies need less oxygen; there is absolutely no reason why we should be disabled by these changes. With increasing age the airways and tissues in the lungs, including the alveoli or air-sacs, become less distensible and more inflexible. The size of the chest cavity may be reduced by a gradual softening of the bones in the spine, osteoporosis (see page 232), and the spine may become curved forwards so that the chest cavity may lessen in size, making forward and downward movements of the ribs more difficult. Added to this the respiratory muscles lose some of their power as do the abdominal muscles. This means that there is extra demand on the diaphragm.

As we go into old age, diseases in the lung become more prevalent than when we were younger. The threat of a serious infection in the lung does increase with age, as does chronic bronchitis, emphysema and lung cancer. Our tendency to have lung infections is partly due to our loss of resistance to bacteria, viruses and fungi because our immune systems become weaker as we grow older. Lung cancer is not related to age. It is much more influenced by smoking and by being exposed to polluted air in our everyday environment.

159

Breast self-examination

The point of regularly examining your breasts yourself is to find any lumps at an early stage. One of the few ways which modern surgeons have found of improving the cure rate for cancer of the breast is to treat the tumour while it is still small. When you are examining your breasts you are trying to detect lumps about ½ inch (1 cm) in diameter if possible.

Remember, most lumps are not malignant. You should also remember that most breasts become naturally lumpy during the week before a period. They usually become heavy, enlarged and tender when squeezed, and the nipples may tingle. If you are still having periods, your breasts will go through these normal monthly changes. When you feel their consistency just before a period with your fingertips you will find that there are small lumps similar to orange pips in their substance. These are only swollen milk glands which enlarge in the second half of each cycle. They shrink again when menstruation is over. If you have stopped menstruating this cycle will not affect you.

BREAST EXAMINATION

Do examine your breasts regularly. Observe them carefully and look for any dimpling of the skin over the surface of a lump; any change in the size, shape and colour of your nipples; and any discharge from your nipple.

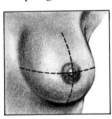

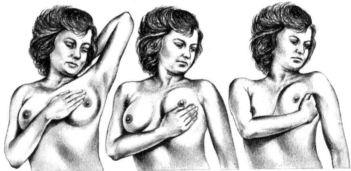

Lie on a flat surface with your head on a pillow and your shoulder slightly raised. Hold your fingers straight and examine the four quadrants of each breast as they are illustrated above.

Starting from the outside, feel your breast with your fingertips in a circular, clockwise direction. Use your right hand to examine your left breast. Keep your left arm loosely by your side when you examine the outer parts.

Examine the inner surface of each breast with the same movement. Extend the arm you are not using behind your head to stretch the breast tissue as this will make any lump easier to find.

Feel for lumps along the top of your collarbone and in your armpit. Now repeat the examination using your left hand to feel your right breast.

Brain

The number of brain cells which we have starts to drop from twenty-five onwards. In parallel there is a slowing down of nerve impulses travelling to and from the brain so messages come and go more slowly. This can lead to less stimulation of all five senses: taste, smell, touch, hearing and vision and may result in confusion and social isolation in the oldest years of life. Even with arteriosclerotic and atherosclerotic changes in arteries which supply the brain, nourishment can still be quite adequate as we get older. Any impairment in the circulation of the blood to the brain is called *cerebrovascular disease*; when part of the brain is deprived of blood a stroke results. The commonest underlying cause is atherosclerosis which can lead to cerebral thrombosis in exactly the same way as a coronary thrombosis, and causes a stroke (see page 221).

If atherosclerosis of the carotid artery (the main branch to the brain via the neck) has made it so narrow that it may be denying blood to the head and neck, ask your doctor if you can be referred to a surgeon who might consider an *endarterectomy*, in which the inside of the artery is cleared of fatty plaque with something resembling the brushes which chimney sweeps use.

Urinary tract and genitals

The bladder capacity of someone in their seventies is less than half (about half a pint) than that of a person aged around twenty-five (about one and a fifth pints). It also holds about a fifth of a pint of residual urine most of the time. The desire to urinate in older people is slow to come and this can cause leaking away of urine and mild incontinence; the bladder has to be very near maximum capacity before they feel the desire to pass urine. In younger people the bladder only has to be half full before the reflex to empty the bladder is activated.

In very old women the pelvic diaphragm is weak so support around the edges of the bladder wall is deficient. The outlet may become funnel-shaped so that the bladder cannot close off completely when urine has been passed. Whenever there is an increase in pressure in the abdomen, such as during coughing, straining at stools, doing strenuous exercises and laughing, urine will leak away causing stress incontinence. Stress incontinence can occur at any age, certainly in women, where it is often due to damage caused during labour. I will discuss the problem more fully in *Living with long-term ailments*.

A prolapse, or pelvic relaxation

A prolapse, or "pelvic relaxation" as it is called in the USA, occurs when the pelvic musculature becomes weakened and allows part of the pelvic organs to protrude or drop out of position. It is especially noticeable when intra-abdominal pressure is increased on coughing or straining at stool, or it occurs simply due to the downpull of gravity. The affected organs include the uterus, bladder, rectum, and urethra; the uterus is the most likely one to collapse. The various types of prolapse include:

Urethrocele is a bulge of the lower front wall of the vagina, which contains the urethra. If it irritates the urethra lining it leads to a frequency of urination.

Cystocele occurs when the bladder bulges into the upper front wall of the vagina.

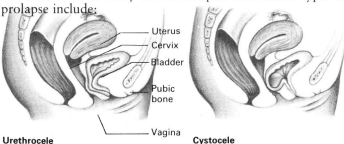

Uterus
Cervix
Bladder
Pubic bone
Vagina

Urethrocele
Cystocele

Diverticula of the bladder

These occur in about 30 percent of older men and are usually caused by an obstruction beyond the bladder, such as an enlarged prostate gland (see page 217). In women, bladder diverticula are rare.

The kidneys remain quite normal in the absence of disease, although kidney function does decline with age and the rate at which the blood is filtered slows down. The other functions of the kidney such as the reabsorption of valuable minerals and the excretion of urine decrease in line with this. There is a decrease in kidney function from our twenties onwards. This rate accelerates as we approach old age. For instance, at thirty we had double the number of functioning units in our kidneys as we will have at seventy.

Infections of the urinary tract

As we age we leave a larger amount of urine in the bladder after emptying and this can act as a perfect medium in which bacteria multiply; a urinary tract infection can follow on. Infections occur most commonly when people are taken into hospital for some reason and are bedridden. The symptoms of a urinary tract infection are a burning sensation when urine is passed, having to get up out of bed at night to pass urine, an increased frequency of passing urine during the day, not being able to get to a lavatory in time (precipitancy), and possibly having a raised temperature and a feeling of nausea and a headache. Incontinence does not lead to infection; the high volume of residual urine does. This means that prostate problems have to be treated promptly and adequately (again see page 217).

The appearance of bacteria in the urine of elderly people is fairly common and it is not necessarily the cause of symptoms. Symptomatic cystitis is very often brought on by an enlarged prostate, diverticula of the bladder, bladder stones, arteriosclerosis of the blood vessels supplying the bladder and a bladder which is just more irritable than average. Cystitis at all ages is commoner in women than in men, because of their having shorter urethras and the greater possibility of trauma to the urethra during intercourse, doing gymnastics, or while riding a bike. Other characteristics of the female may contribute – features such as the close proximity of the urethral opening to the anus, dilation of the ureters and the urethra during pregnancy, the enlarging womb during pregnancy pressing on the urethra, the bladder and the ureters. In men, a predisposing factor is the gradual lessening of fluid from the prostate gland with its anti-bacterial qualities. There are also social and cultural factors which increase the chances of getting a urinary tract infection such as the kind of sexual activities and the type of personal hygiene you practise, socio-economic status and abuse of pain killers. Some metabolic diseases such as diabetes and bladder and kidney stones will also predispose to infection.

Prostate gland   There are age-related changes here. Some start to occur after the age of forty which are internal to the gland and can only be felt by an examining doctor. A gland becomes rather irregular in shape and can be nodular when felt through the rectal wall during a rectal examination. The nodular kind of growth in the prostate is fairly common from the age of fifty onwards and most corrective surgical operations are carried out between fifty and seventy. Surgical removal of the enlarged prostate does not affect a man's potency.

Later on, after sixty, these changes get worse and occur throughout the whole gland. Many elderly men suffer from one kind of prostate problem or another. When the gland enlarges and obstructs the exit from the bladder a man may experience hesitancy, and then later on have to get up at night to pass urine. He may also find that the stream of urine is very thin and weak and finally he may go to the stage of not being able to pass very much urine from the bladder.

Just as cancer of the breast is the most common cancer in older women, cancer of the prostate is the most frequent tumour in older men. You should be ready to spot symptoms and go along to your doctor as soon as they are causing difficulty. Prostatic enlargement is said to be less common among Indian than Western men because of the oriental tradition of rarely abstaining from sex.

163

Looking after your urinary system

The following are straightforward steps which you should take in order to keep your urinary system in a healthy condition.

• As we get older we all need to empty the bladder more frequently. Avoid embarrassment by doing so *before* you feel the urge – say every two to three hours, more often if you're drinking a lot of fluids.

• Wear a special sanitary pad if you are incontinent (see page 292) and don't drink too much coffee; it makes your kidneys produce more than usual quantities of urine and will increase your desire to empty your bladder.

• Treatment of urinary infection should always begin by getting an accurate diagnosis so that your doctor can choose the right drugs to ensure success in treating the infection. It is essential to give an adequate amount of antibiotic or urinary antiseptics, and fourteen days' treatment is preferable. Anyone with a urinary tract infection must take his or her medication exactly according to instructions, and not stop when the symptoms *seem* to disappear.

• The antibiotic of choise is *ampicillin*, though many infections are successfully treated by mouth with many antiseptic medicines. If your doctor prescribes *tetracycline*, by all means query it, as this drug can lead to rising levels of blood urea in some individuals.

• It is essential to drink a lot of fluid if you have a urinary tract infection. This helps to flush through the urinary tract and get rid of bacteria. It also relieves your symptoms because it makes the urine less concentrated.

• Because cancer is the most frequent tumour in older men, you should go along and have your prostate checked by your doctor (this is simply done by your having a rectal examination) whenever you get symptoms.

Hormone system

Abnormalities in the hormone or endocrine system are not at all frequent in old age; most endocrine disorders have their peak in early and middle adulthood. None increases as we get older. This system exhibits fewer disorders related specifically to ageing than any of the other systems we have discussed. The commonest are diabetes (see page 237) and abnormalities of thyroid gland function. Despite the fact that diabetes was described in Egyptian papyri as long ago as 1500 BC, it is also a disease of civilization. It becomes more prevalent with Western work patterns, life in communities, lifestyles with little exercise and a Western diet. Diabetics will also benefit from modern technology and are living much longer lives. There is, therefore, an increasing number of older diabetics.

There seems to be a steady increase in the number of people with diabetes if we track them from childhood to old age. The peak occurs late in the decade between sixty-five and seventy-five and then drops again. Many cases of diabetes in old people are due to being overweight. There is a school of thought which believes that diabetes is the only disease related to excess weight, a fact worth bearing in mind when you think about improving the quality of your daily diet.

Thyroid gland

This decreases in weight compared to total body weight as we get older. There are very few other functional changes. Thyroid disorders are not that common and they are most frequent in young and middle-aged people. When changes in thyroid function occur in older people, they take up quite a different pattern from that which they exhibit in young people. Many physicians believe that problems caused by an underactive thyroid may affect as many as 40 percent of the general population and they cannot be detected by conventional tests. Some go as far as saying that hypothyroidism can be related to many chronic diseases with unlikely symptoms ranging from joint pain to mental depression.

Looking after your glands

• Being overweight has the strongest association with diabetes – while it is always important not to put on weight – as you get older it becomes doubly important for this reason. So you should reconsider your diet and take up more exercise.

• An over-active thyroid can usually be managed by treatment with drugs alone. Most doctors favour carbimazole as the anti-thyroid drug of choice. Treatment with radioactive iodine, which is selectively taken up by the thyroid, may be necessary. With one or other of these régimes, 50 percent of patients with *thyrotoxicosis* are cured within two years.

• With an underactive thyroid you need hormone replacements, usually for the rest of your life. The thyroid hormone, *L-Thyroxine*, is the safest and simplest drug to take. The usual starting dose of L-Thyroxine is very small but this is very gradually increased by very small amounts per day until a suitable maintenance dose is reached.

• If you are taking any kind of thyroid therapy, you should have regular check-ups: every three months for the first year or so, then less often.

• Diabetics should be regularly and fully checked every few months without fail.

The female menopause

The word "menopause" is usually used to describe the time in a woman's life, between the ages of forty and fifty, when her fertility declines and her menstruation stops. The word literally means "cessation of menstruation". This obviously cannot be applied to men, but if we consider the word "climacteric", which defines the years before, during and after the menopause, lasting anything up to 15 or 20 years, then there is a parallel to be drawn between women and men. The menopause has quite rightly been given a good deal of attention because it is a dramatic event. There are many changes: hormonal, physical, mental and emotional, which occur during the change, and there is the obvious and inescapable punctuation mark of no more menstrual periods. To feel confident it is necessary that we know what is taking place in our bodies, so that we can understand that the mechanism is normal.

For men and women, the climacteric is closely involved with gaining new insights, maturing, changing standards, choosing new lifestyles, and emergence of new opinions and priorities. It may be a confused state, or it may be plain sailing. We must draw on our reserves of serenity and maturity.

Onset of the menopause

In the UK the average age for menopause is fifty but it can occur anytime between thirty-five and sixty-four. At any one time there are about ten million women over the age of forty-five in the British Isles. This means that about a fifth or sixth of the population is in the menopausal age group and may be suffering unpleasant symptoms because of the following body changes.

The first half of each menstrual cycle is controlled by a follicle-stimulating hormone (FSH) which ripens an egg in an ovarian egg follicle. This ovum produces oestrogen. Before ovulation a surge of luteinizing hormone liberates the ripe ovum from the follicle. From this point on the follicle produces both progesterone (in large quantities) and oestrogen (in small quantities) for the rest of the month. Three or four days before menstruation begins both these hormones decline. It is this drop in hormone levels which results in shedding of the endometrium as a period.

As women approach the menopause, the ovary becomes resistant to FSH which no longer responds with a growing egg. Over the age of thirty or forty the ovary may become almost depleted of eggs and eventually it stops working altogether.

After this the levels of oestrogen and progesterone swing around in an irregular way in response to the varying levels of follicle-stimulating hormones and luteinizing hormones which are attempting to coax the ovary into functioning for a little longer. It is this swinging of hormone levels which results in many of the symptoms we experience during the climacteric.

Periods stop during the menopause and there are several well-recognized and acceptable patterns which cessation usually follows. *It is never normal to have frequent, heavy periods during the climacteric. The passage of clots of blood is never normal. Bleeding between periods or after intercourse is abnormal.* You should consult your doctor immediately if any of them occur. These are the ways periods usually stop:

● Very rarely do they stop suddenly. You may have regular periods right up to the day when you miss one and from then on you will have no more.

● It is much more common to continue to have periods for a few months and then miss a few, have a few more normal bleeds and then go longer and longer between periods until they eventually stop.

● You may find that your periods simply become scantier and scantier and shorter and shorter until they stop.

● By definition, if you are under the age of fifty and do not have a period for 12 months, if you are over the age of fifty and don't have a period for 6 months, then it is likely that your periods have stopped for good.

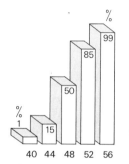

Percentage of women who have experienced the onset of menopause at various ages.

Symptoms of the menopause

Not all women suffer symptoms at the time of the menopause. There are three classical ones – hot flushes (sometimes referred to as hot flashes in the USA), night sweats, and loss of lubrication in the vagina. Nearly all of these symptoms are thought to be caused by low levels of oestrogen in the blood. It is these low levels of female hormones which are also responsible for the gradual loss of calcium and protein from the bones, osteoporosis (see page 232) and approximately 20 percent of women develop osteoporosis after the menopause if they don't take oestrogen supplements in some form (see page 69).

"Classical symptoms"

A hot flush it just what is sounds like. The skin becomes hot and pink. You will feel very hot and you will start to sweat. This can be particularly bad during the night.

Night sweats can prevent you from sleeping for much of the night, making you resort to throwing off the bedclothes and getting out of bed to cool off. They can even cause sleepless nights for your partner as well. Eventually one or both of you may become exhausted through lack of sleep.

Soreness, dryness and thinning of the vagina can be very troublesome during and after the menopause and many women feel shy of discussing these complaints with their doctor. The vagina is usually kept healthy, plump and lubricated by oestrogen, but when levels fall, the vagina may change dramatically. The cells of the lining become thin and dried out and they cannot protect themselves against invasion. The vagina, therefore, becomes prone to infection with the vaginal discharge. The urethra may be affected as well as the vagina, and menopausal women may suffer from cystitis or pain and burning when passing urine.

One of the most demoralizing side effects is that sex can become difficult when there is insufficient vaginal secretion and intercourse may be painful (dyspareunia). This can lead to reluctance to have sex or avoidance of it, and a consequent deterioration in your relationship with your partner. In this way dyspareunia may lead to a loss of libido.

Always try to discuss these problems with your partner and get him to understand that they should be seen as a natural part of the menopause. As a practical step you can start using a lubricating jelly. The best non-hormonal lubricant is KY jelly. It is used by surgeons and doctors to lubricate their vaginal instruments. Your own doctor may help you by giving you a hormone cream which is only available on prescription; this may help to relieve vaginal soreness and itching.

Bone changes

One of the most important changes which occurs during the climacteric is change in the bone. Oestrogen contributes to a healthy calcium balance and sturdy protein architecture of the bones. As the oestrogen levels fall, however, the bones become thin, weak and prone to fractures, and aches and pains may arise in the bones and joints. These bone changes can be entirely arrested by the use of hormone replacement therapy (HRT) given as a combination of oestrogen and progesterone.

Oestrogen on its own is very rarely prescribed in the UK in contrast to the USA. It has been shown by British doctors that the addition of progesterone will guard against most of the harmful side effects, such as the association of oestrogen with cancerous change in the uterus, and therefore a combined régime is always employed in this country. Hormone replacement therapy cannot repair weakened bones, but it will prevent the condition from getting any worse.

HRT should always be given along with calcium and vitamin D supplements. Calcium on its own, without HRT, is not effective. After the age of sixty-five, however, it is calcium and vitamin D which become important and they alone are probably sufficient in keeping our bones healthy.

Emotional and psychological difficulties

Women can have emotional problems which may be the predominant symptoms of the menopause. Depression, moodiness, tearfulness and irritability are common. Some intellectual functions such as memory, decision making, speed and accuracy also deteriorate and a woman may find that she is more prone to accidents than she used to be. She is generally less stable and she may suffer a serious loss of self-confidence.

It is possible that this physiologically-induced emotional upset may be worsened because of personal crises. A woman may feel that her children have grown up and left home and she is no longer needed. If she hasn't continued with her career she may feel a useless member of society. Parents may be becoming more and more dependent and this is a heavy burden, but it is not a problem which can be solved in any way by hormone replacement therapy.

Hormone replacement therapy

Of course, depression and anxiety and the menopause may respond to anti-depressants and tranquillizers as they would at any time, but you may need HRT as well. Specialists in the field regard HRT as the mainstay of medication and consider the menopause to be a hormone deficiency state in which the deficiency should be corrected by hormones.

The benefits of HRT are well documented. Night sweats, hot flushes and a dry vagina, with its accompanying problems, are nearly always relieved. Very often sleep improves, there is a lessening of anxiety and depression which helps with improving a woman's mental and physical state.

Of course there are some risks associated with HRT and it is particularly unsuitable for you if you have had blood clotting problems, high blood pressure or if you have a strong family history of heart disease. Before you have HRT you should discuss this whole matter with your doctor.

Doctors vary in the length of time for which they are prepared to treat women with HRT. Some doctors are so prejudiced that they won't use it at all. If this is the case you can try going along to a menopause clinic, so that a doctor can assess whether or not your symptoms may be relieved by the use of HRT. Sometimes it is necessary to be treated for two or three years, though most doctors agree that courses should not be given continuously. Breaks are advocated. While you are taking HRT you should have regular medical checks, your breasts should be examined both by yourself and by your doctor. You should also have an internal examination and a cervical and vaginal smear.

HRT is not a way of putting off ageing and preventing wrinkles and flabby breasts and it must not be used casually.

169

The male menopause

Even now, little is known about the male menopause, or better the male climacteric. We still don't know when it occurs, or if it truly develops, and if it does whether or not it is similar to a female's. Do all men experience a climacteric? If there is such a thing, what are the symptoms? Drawing a parallel from the menopausal symptoms in women, should men be the beneficiaries of hormone replacement therapy? Once this question is advanced others follow. What would happen to the male climacteric if hormone replacement therapy were widely used? What would the success rate be? What are the harmful effects? What are the long-term effects? There are very few answers to any of these questions because so little research has been done in this area, though this is sure to change in the near future as more people take an interest in the symptoms.

The male menopause hasn't the same drama as a woman's. It is more gradual, gentle and in a way more insidious than a woman's; nor does it occur during exactly the same years. It is much better thought of as a male climacteric, which envelopes all the changes going on in the body and mind as the male genital system begins to wane.

Male sexuality Masters and Johnson made a very detailed study of the psychological and physiological factors which might contribute to a decline in a man's sexual prowess as he grows older. From their studies it became obvious that there are factors which affect a man's sexual responsiveness.

• The primary factor is monotony, described as being the result of repetitious sexual relationships.
• A close second is his preoccupation with career and economic pursuits.
• Mental or physical fatigue no doubt contributes to a decline in sexual response.
• The older man's penchant for over-indulgence in food and drink plays its part.
• Any physical or mental infirmities in either of the partners may lead to a further decline.
• A fear that his performance does not come up to scratch may be greater than at any other time in his life, especially during a time of stressful career decisions.

Monotony is quoted most often and most constantly as the factor which leads to a loss of interest in sex and sexual performance. The end result of this may be one of dutiful indulgence and the need for sexual release. This sometimes arises from a failure of the sexual part of a relationship to grow throughout the marriage. Overfamiliarity with a partner is often blamed; the female partner may no longer be stimulating to her man. If a woman ceases to see the necessity for making herself sexually interesting and attractive she may well trigger off this sexual boredom. It is not difficult to see why this may happen. The female herself may be engrossed in her domestic situation, looking after the children, in a career and in social activities. Furthermore, women generally do age more during their forties and fifties in terms of physical appearance than men. Without care to physical appearance, a woman may become physically older looking than her partner. I have outlined some useful techniques which will easily counteract this on pages 179-183.

Almost all men between the ages of forty and sixty are going through the most competitive stages of their careers. The tensions brought on by competition at work are not eased by the financial necessity to look after a growing family with multiplying needs and activities. On the one hand, men are striving for personal eminence, and on the other they are preoccupied with the security of the "family". A man in this situation often finds that he spends more time following his professional career than with his family. This leaves a smaller amount of time for loving relationships with his partner and stress may lead to a gradual lessening in sexual activity and this may eventually stop completely.

Both mental and physical fatigue are important elements in the decline of male sexuality and beyond middle age they have an ever-increasing influence on sexual activity. An active sex life in the middle years means being in good condition, for if a job requires a great deal of physical effort, a man may simply not be fit enough to have stamina left over at the end of the day to enjoy an active sex life. Sometimes, if a man is not fit, a weekend of recreation is more exhausting than the demands of his job, particularly in the age group of fifty and over. Again, this leaves very little energy for sexual activity. If a man is exposed to unaccustomed or excessive physical activity he may feel a loss of sexual responsiveness for a day or so which will add to his feeling of despondency.

As men grow older they eat and drink more. Excessive consumption of food or drink has a tendency to repress their sex drives. Also, if men feel satisfied from good food this lowers their capacity to need to achieve in other areas. Over-indulgence in alcohol has a particularly negative effect on potency. Impotence developing in an otherwise potent man, often makes him drink excessive alcohol and otherwise behave in a way that has not been in his nature.

Most men become unable to accept that a lessening of sexual drive is normal and they try to compensate for this.

Most men approaching middle age become concerned about performance. One of the ways of handling any concern is to withdraw from having to perform. This leads to total avoidance of sex within the marriage. If a man is also drinking excessively it only makes matters worse. A problem may arise within the marriage. A man may find that he is impotent with his wife but with another, who cannot measure present sexual performance against past, he is perfectly normal.

At any age, physical or mental infirmity can lower or even eliminate sexual drive. After the age of forty, however, physical or emotional difficulties have a very much greater effect, and above the age of sixty a tremendously negative influence. Being physically disabled in the short or long term lowers sexual responsiveness in either sex, but if the illness is acute, such as pneumonia, loss of libido is usually transient and accepted by both partners. With more long-standing disabilities, such as arthritis or emphysema, interest in sex and sexual performance may decline slowly and until it becomes non existent. Some conditions, such as long-standing diabetes, can lead to impotence in men for medical reasons. These problems do need to be discussed with a partner.

There is no doubt that"fear of failure"plays a very important part in the ageing man's withdrawal from sexual activities.

Once a man has noticed that his potency is declining, or he experiences one occasion when he is unable to achieve sexual satisfaction through impotency, he may withdraw voluntarily from any kind of sexual activity. This is mainly because most men are unable to face the "ego-shattering experience of repeated episodes of sexual inadequacy". Most men are unable to accept the fact that a lessening of sexual drive and a lowering of sexual performance are parts of the normal ageing process and they make all sorts of excuses and will blame many different kinds of external factors rather than face the truth that their bodies are maturing.

Masters and Johnson hypothesized in 1970 that a man who finds his potency declining may be showing signs of lowered levels of androgens which may amount to a deficiency. They went on the say that until studies had shown that there was a general requirement by the body for androgen (testosterone) replacement therapy during the male climacteric, cases had to be treated on an empirical and individual basis.

There are endocrinologists in many parts of the world who make a special study of the male climacteric employing hormone replacement therapy for their male patients. The whole area however, still awaits clear definition and guidelines. Until then HRT for men will remain a highly-specialized field not generally practised. In this respect women are better off than men. It may be because women are honest and courageous enough to declare that their bodies are deficient, whereas men, particularly in the sensitive area of sexual activities, have yet to come to terms with their bodily changes.

Danger signs

The chart on pages 174-6 indicates certain signs and symptoms in medicine which indicate changes that become commoner as we get older. As I explain in *Special medical problems* these changes are not serious in the majority of cases and your doctor will be able to put them right. Symptoms such as a change from your normal bowel habit, change in your digestive pattern, a sudden bout where you cough up blood-specked sputum or a sudden severe headache attack are signals that the body is not working as it should and needs investigating. They are not meant to be a cause for alarm.

By noting what symptoms you have and asking yourself the questions provided you will perhaps be able to put your mind at rest. Do see your doctor if you show any of these symptoms.

DANGER SIGNS

What to note if you have:

Blood in sputum	Blood in vomit	Blood in stools
Colour and quantity	Colour and quantity	Colour and quantity of blood; colour of stools; presence of mucus; any pain on passing

What to ask yourself

Have I had a sore throat, cough, chest pain, or recent chest infection?	Have I taken drugs? Have I eaten anything unusual, drunk a lot of alcohol or had indigestion recently? Do I have a duodenal ulcer?	Do I have piles? Do I have a duodenal ulcer? Have I had stomach or abdominal pain? Have I recently had indigestion or an intestinal infection?

What to do

If there is a lot of blood, call an ambulance; otherwise make an appointment to see your doctor. Keep sputum to show doctor	If there is a lot of blood call an ambulance; otherwise make an appointment to see your doctor. Keep specimen of vomit to show doctor	If there is a lot of blood call an ambulance; otherwise make an appointment to see your doctor. Keep specimen of stools to show doctor

What your doctor will do

Question you about your chest. Examine your sputum and X-ray your chest	Question you about food, your stomach and digestion. Examine your abdomen, look at your vomit and your stools. Possibly order a barium meal	Question you about your stomach and intestines. Examine your abdomen and rectum (internally). Examine your stools. Possibly order a barium enema

What tests will be done

X-ray, throat swab, lab tests on sputum	Lab tests on stools, possibly on vomit; barium meal	Lab tests on stools; barium enema

What it is likely to be

If you are coughing, it's probably a small, burst blood vessel. It could be the aftermath of bronchitis or similar chest infection	The commonest causes are aspirin and other drugs, alcohol and duodenal ulcers	The commonest causes are piles or severe diarrhoea; it may occur with diverticulitis. Black, tarry stools occur when a duodenal ulcer bursts

Blood in urine	Sudden onset of indigestion	Sudden onset of diarrhoea, constipation, pipelike stools
Colour and quantity of blood; any pain on passing	Relationship to food; if alkalis bring relief	Colour and shape of stools. Any mucus or blood – quantity and colour
Have I had kidney or back pain; have I had a recent urinary infection?	Do I have any pain elsewhere? Have I taken any drugs, alcohol or strange foods recently? Is there any change in my bowel habit?	Have I started taking any drugs or different foods? Have I got a temperature; am I in pain?
If there is a lot of blood, call an ambulance, otherwise make an appointment to see your doctor. Keep a specimen of urine to show doctor	If it persists for more than 3 days, see your doctor	Take your temperature; if it is raised, make an appointment to see your doctor. Keep specimen of stools to show your doctor
Question you about your bladder, urine and kidneys. Examine your urine and arrange an intravenous pylogram (IVP)	Question you about food and digestion. Ask for a stool specimen for analysis. Try a course of treatment; order a barium meal	Question you about food and digestion. Examine your abdomen and stools. Do a rectal examination. Try a course of treatment; possibly order a barium enema
Lab tests on urine; IVP	Barium meal; lab tests on stools	Barium enema; lab tests on stools
The commonest causes are cystitis or severe kidney infection	The commonest causes are starting to take medication for the first time or strange foods	The commonest causes are strange food, infection or diverticulitis

175

DANGER SIGNS

What to note if you have:

Onset of persistent headaches	Sudden pain in chest	Sudden onset of breathlessness
Position and frequency. Any related signs, e.g. pins and needles in the skin, flashing lights, nausea	What makes the pain worse: breathing, coughing; or better: rest	What makes the pain worse: breathing, coughing; or better: rest

What to ask yourself

Have I had shingles of the face, or toothache, recently? Does anyone in the family suffer from migraine? Have I been working hard or am I worried?	Have my lower legs swollen recently? Do have high blood pressure or bronchitis?	Have my lower legs swollen recently? Do have high blood pressure or bronchitis?

What to do

Take analgesics; see your doctor	Take your temperature. If high, call your doctor or an ambulance, especially if you are breathless	Take your temperature. If high, call your doctor or an ambulance, especially if you are breathless

What your doctor will do

Question you generally. Give you a full physical examination. Take your blood pressure. Examine your eyes and your urine	Question you, examine your chest, heart, sputum, blood pressure, chest X-ray; give you a course of treatment. If you are breathless, send you to hospital	Question you, examine your chest, heart, sputum, blood pressure, chest X-ray; give you a course of treatment. If you are breathless, send you to hospital

What tests will be done

None necessarily	Chest X-ray, sputum tests; investigations of legs and lungs to see if there are any clots	Chest X-ray, sputum tests; investigations of legs and lungs to see if there are any clots

What it is likely to be

The commonest causes are migraine, tension headache, postherpetic neuralgia (related to shingles) and dental problems. If pain doesn't respond to analgesics it is probably psychosomatic	The commonest cause is bronchitis or tracheitis, as part of a virus or chest infection	The commonest cause is bronchitis or tracheitis, as part of a virus or chest infection

Maintaining appearance

Both men and women, but especially women, are often upset by the effects of ageing on the face and body. Sometimes, people are so affected that they no longer make any effort to help themselves. There can be few things as depressing as looking in the mirror and hating what you see, but on the other hand, if you look in the mirror and *like* what you see, your whole outlook and demeanour will improve. Such a positive sense of self-esteem becomes increasingly important as we get older, and looking after our appearance is one of the best ways of achieving this. In addition to the beneficial effects of a good diet and regular exercise, proper care of the skin and hair and attention to your figure and clothing can help you both look and feel younger. It can also help you maintain an active sex life which again can keep you feeling younger.

Hair loss in men
Whether or not it is comforting to know that human hair is probably superfluous and will disappear in future generations, it is safe to say that some men would keep their longer if they worried less about losing it. A positive way of looking at baldness is to realize that it can be quite flattering and may give you a forceful air – like the strong-willed personalities reflected by Telly Savalas and Yul Brynner. But there's also nothing wrong in attempting to cover up hair loss as long as your solution looks natural (see page 140). However it's often better to be bald than to look extremely artificial.

When hair loss is gradual, some camouflage can work very well. By letting the hair grow slightly longer than usual, a thinning area on the crown may be disguised; if you comb your hair forward, you may be able to cover a slight recession at the temples. A permanent can also be useful in giving body to the hair so that it looks much thicker, but if balding is severe, a permanent may only contribute to further hair loss. Probably the most successful solution is having your hair properly styled; even with relatively little hair, a good stylist can make a vast improvement to the way you look.

When there is less hair, it's usually wrong to grow the remaining hair longer as it can look stringy and unkempt. It is also a mistake to grow large sideburns as this only calls attention to what little is left on the head. Furthermore, hair which is forced into an unnatural shape not only looks wrong, but can put added strain on the hair remaining, gradually resulting in more hair loss.

On the positive side, it is a good idea to keep hair short. Short hair has more life and resilience. Trying to create a new focus in

177

a haircut, like changing a centre parting to a side one, can also be successful; even avoiding a well-defined hairline can be an improvement. Or, you may try going with the baldness and foregoing style with hair cut very short and, if necessary, bleached so that it doesn't look like stubble.

Grooming for men

For all your life you have probably been conditioned not to look critically at yourselves and you may have allowed your partner to choose your clothes, with you perhaps not even being present! Now is the time to take a good look at yourself full-length in the mirror to see which areas are unkempt and could be improved with a little grooming.

There is no secret formula for looking good, it is a question of thinking carefully and logically about how best to go about making the most of your good points and successfully concealing your not-so-good points. There is certainly no need to spend lots of money on expensive cosmetic products, it is much more important to look natural. Remember there are no prescribed roles for you to play. There is no set of rules for you to follow. You need not pay attention to cosmeticians' sales talk if you don't want to. As with most other things you should be starting to please yourself, so interpret the following suggestions as loosely as you'd like to. When it comes to choosing clothes, comfort need never mean shapelessness.

TIPS FOR LOOKING GOOD

- Be meticulous about hygiene; take special care of your hands and feet.
- Make sure your hair is regularly looked after – cut and styled to suit you. Grey hair can be quite attractive and you may not want to fuss with colouring.
- Keep a young figure, if you possibly can.

There is nothing that gives the impression of age more than obesity and shapelessness.
- Avoid garments or shoes in stiff inflexible materials.
- Pay attention to your posture and gait. Few things are so ageing as stooped shoulders.

Clothes for women
As we become older, comfort becomes a more and more important prerequisite of clothes. I personally am no longer prepared to go for hours in tight-fitting garments, or even to wear a belt on the tight side. This doesn't mean that a figure is not well-defined. But you may like to consider going for comfortable fabrics – that is, soft, thin ones and not hard, thick ones. You might consider skirts which are gored or gathered and tops which are blouson. Never buy a size too small and avoid waistbands which are too tight. Where possible, choose natural fabrics like cotton so as not to feel sweaty.

If you are interested in clothes, try to be fashionable – it has some important pay-offs. It keeps you looking young, and more important, feeling young. It also tells the world that you are not living in the past. It has a stimulating effect on you, yourself forcing you to look at yourself in a new light.

Scan the fashion magazines and spot new fashion trends, be it in the width of the shoulder, where a belt is placed – high, low or on the waistline – the shape of the silhouette, straight, flared, A-line, or the length and shape of the sleeve. As an older woman you should never ever go for exaggerated trends, but in any outfit try to include at least one fashionable feature which will give your proportion and image a current feeling.

179

Avoid matronly fashions whenever you can. Any outfit which is safe, pale, with an indistinct outline, helping you to fade into your surroundings and conventional in terms of colour and fabric, is unadventurous. Try to add a bit of drama to what you are wearing, possibly by colour combination or with an accessory. Never be afraid to accent your femininity. Try to remember that a mature woman finds it hard to look good in a classic style, in a drab colour, in a thick masculine fabric. Yes, you can wear a classic, tailored style, but in a bright colour. But whenever you can, avoid thick, inflexible fabrics; they make your body look stiff and unsupple, quite the opposite of young. If you have a good bustline, show it. If your waistline is attractive, display it. If your ankles and legs are good, make sure your hemlines are not too low. To stay abreast of fashion, buy cheaply, often, rather than expensive, rarely.

There are some useful tricks to flatter mature women. You should wear pretty colours next to your face and avoid too much jewellery. Go for ease and simplicity, perhaps wearing fewer pieces, parts and complications. If you body is younger than your face, draw attention to your figure and try to keep your walk youthful; avoid a drooping posture.

The most important parts of your figure which give the impression of youth are your *bustline* – it should be midway between your shoulder and your elbow; keep it there with a well-fitting bra, and your *waistline* – if you are short-waisted and get dumpier as you get older you will look older. Stay younger looking by choosing clothes which don't have any waistline at all or have a dropped waist, and always choose one colour from top to toe. If your abdomen protrudes a bit, don't wear clingy fabrics or any that will hang heavily over your stomach. Wear A-lines or sewn-down pleats rather than straight skirts. Slash pockets are useful because they divert the eye from the stomach.

Make sure that your bra isn't so tight that there are rolls of flesh overhanging at the back, and never wear too clinging a fabric if you have a large bottom – every bulge will show. If your buttocks are too big, disguise them with long jackets and tunics and overblouses. Wear skirts and trousers which are slack over your bottom and don't pull tightly around your buttocks. Avoid garments with a flat yoke flaring out at the hips because they will give you more than ample proportion.

If you have a double chin, stay away from big earrings and avoid high chokers at the throat. Wear a long pendant low on the chest to provide distraction. Simple and flat collars which rest on your shoulders are preferable to large, stiff collars which will crowd your neck.

MAKING THE MOST OF MAKE-UP

In my opinion a mature face cannot get away without wearing make-up. The older we are, the more we require some; not more in quantity, but more in finesse; I don't think there is a feature on our faces which we should leave unmade-up if we wish to look our best.

You might try out different cosmetics to find out what will accentuate your good features best, and what will camouflage your bad ones. If you haven't changed your make-up in the last twelve months then you should, and you should start experimenting now. This is especially true of eye make-up: nothing marks a woman's age like it. You can quite easily guess the age of another woman by the kind of make-up she wears on her eyes.

If necessary, take yourself off to a make-up expert (not a make-up salon attached to one of the cosmetic manufacturers) who will show you how to alter your bone structure with contouring; for instance, to make a fat nose less podgy, to minimize a square jawbone, to lengthen a face and to bring out your eyes.

None of these things requires layers and layers of make-up. Quite the opposite. As with good medicine, the minimum effective quantity for the maximum possible effect is all that you're after, and it need not be expensive. If you go to a make-up expert, they will show you how to use a particular type of cosmetic and you can either choose to buy that specific product or try to duplicate it less expensively elsewhere.

Foundation
Always apply a film of moisturizer underneath your make-up base to allow easy, smooth spreading which is less damaging to the skin.

Use a moisturized liquid or cream make-up base in a beige tone (never pink or tan) which is one shade *lighter* than your own skin tone. This will help to reflect the light and minimize lines. Try and use a sponge if you can; all make-up experts do and it really does make a difference both to the staying power and the set of your make-up. It also stops you pulling the skin around too much.

To camouflage baggy areas under your eyes, use a light-textured shadow coverer (not the stick variety, they are much too heavy and only accentuate wrinkles) and apply this underneath your eyes, over the upper lid and the whole of your brow area. Extend it out to the upper surface of your cheekbone to cover broken veins, but then wing it out up beyond the corner of your

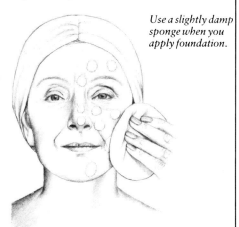

Use a slightly damp sponge when you apply foundation.

eyes towards your hairline. This takes the eye of the observer upward and outward over your face and counteracts any droopiness. Also apply it on top of the laughter lines which extend from your nostrils down to the lower corners of your mouth to lighten up these shadows.

MAKING THE MOST OF MAKE-UP

To make a plump nose look thinner, apply a thin line down the whole of the length of the top of your nose and put a small spot on the front of your chin to make it look more delicate.

Don't apply too much powder when high-lighting your cheekbones or it will leave patches.

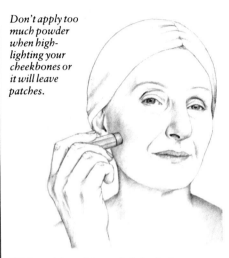

With a stick make-up slightly darker than your make-up base, draw in a triangle under each cheekbone with the point winging up towards your ear, and blend it smoothly into the rest of your make-up. This will accentuate the shape of your face.

Use a minimum of colourless powder to set your make-up. Powder, if applied too heavily, clogs in all the wrinkles and makes them seem more obvious than ever. Never repowder during the day, simply blot dry with a tissue or cotton wool.

Experiment with cream or liquid shaders and blushers. Never use a pink blusher, and never use too much blusher at the first application, you can always add more. Make sure it is well blended in. Go for a rather tawny apricot shade and place it just on the high point of your cheekbone and then smooth it away upwards and outwards towards your temples, a trick which also leads the eye of the observer upwards away from your nose.

Eyes

Stop using eyebrow pencil today. There is nothing more ageing than a heavily-arched eyebrow drawn in a hard line with a dark pencil. Your eyebrows in general should be well plucked underneath to form a fairly high arch, again to give that upward and outward look to your face, with a fairly short downward curve. Unless your eyebrows are very sparse, all you need do is darken them with mascara. Your eyebrows should be the shade of your hair.

Try not to use an eyeshadow with an obvious colour. Stick to muddy, murky, indefinite tones. There is hardly any need for anyone to vary from grey or brown as these are the most natural colours and have the most dramatic effect if used properly. Try leaving off your eye shadow from the eyelid. Eye shadow here makes the eye look smaller in the first place, but secondly, it is very old-fashioned. Eye shadow is much better applied just at the outer corner of the eye and in the eye socket and then smoothed out. A little can also be applied and smudged under the lower lashes.

If you've never worn false eyelashes, you are missing one of the greatest beauty aids that a middle-aged woman can use. They don't have to be dramatic.

When putting on your false eyelashes it is safer to use a close-up mirror.

They should be invisible when you have them in place. Start off with thin, longish eyelashes and trim them down to a natural look once they are in place. Mascara them along with your own eyelashes. Never wear black false eyelashes unless you are naturally very dark. Brown eyelashes are more flattering. Make sure that you find the best eyelash glue you can. Use an eyeliner or kohl for definition.

Lips

Place your foundation over your lips, powder them and blot thoroughly, brushing away any surplus powder. This will also help prevent lipstick bleeding.

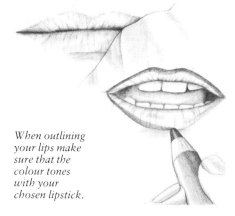

When outlining your lips make sure that the colour tones with your chosen lipstick.

If you have never used a lip pencil to outline your lips before applying make-up, start doing so now. It has two great effects. Outlining your lips and filling them in with a slightly paler shade of lipstick clearly defines them and gives your mouth a more attractive look. Also, lip pencils are generally rather dry and they stop the lipstick leaking down the small creases of the lips on to the skin of the face (known as "bleeding"). Use make-up suggestions as a basis for experimenting.

Hair

Hair, as long as it is fairly thick, looks younger if it is unpermed, loose and fluffy, and is not lacquered. If you can't run your finger through your hair and still look good, then it needs cutting, shaping, and restyling.

Keep hair in an up-line to give it a lift and keep it away from the face. A twist or chignon is often effective as is a short feathery fringe. Pulling back the hair with barettes and other simple, straight styles is often quite successful on older women.

Get rid of all facial hair, preferably by electrolysis, but pluck it, if necessary. Shave your legs and under your arms at least once a week, and every time you wear an evening dress or something which leaves your armpits bare. Shave any hairs from around your nipples (or have them permanently removed by electrolysis, see page 150), whenever they grow.

Alternatively, you could attempt to pull any hairs out with tweezers. Make sure that you pluck in the direction that the hair is growing, so as not to break it off. Waxing has proved to be a very efficient way of removing hair from the face and body.

Keep your hair soft and if you dye it, keep the colour subtle.

Retirement

For many people retirement is an important and rapid transitional period from an economically productive state to an economically non-productive and relatively dependent state. This raises all sorts of sociological, ethical, psychological and financial issues. Retirement means different things to different people, depending upon their sex, socio-economic status and psychological make-up. In general, however, we disengage from our main occupations and this brings about a number of changes in our lives in the spheres of daily activities, social contacts and standard of living.

Social disengagement

Very few of us keep up the pace and the diversity of social interaction into old age which we enjoyed in our late adulthood. Most of us begin to withdraw from the social whirl through choice. During our middle years, we live at the peak of our engagement with society because this is the time that many people depend on us and our time and energies are in great demand. We are, in essence, the establishment.

The transition we go through from adulthood to retirement age involves a natural withdrawal from the activities and obligations that had previously linked us and society closely together. To use an oft quoted metaphor – it is a kind of ritualistic dance. One partner, the person who is getting older, bows and steps back; the other partner, society, recognizes the cue, bows in return and also takes a step backwards.

The dance may continue but more slowly. The partners gradually move further and further apart. Soon society has found a new partner with a springy step. The old person sits down and takes a rest. They watch the dancers and smile, keeping time with fingers and feet. However, interest in the dance is waning; thoughts and feelings become subjective. The older person, by their own choice and that of society, has become a private person who is quite willing and happy to leave the whirl of the dance to youngsters. This metaphor describes very aptly the change from active participant to interested observer that most of us experience as we grow older.

Withdrawal from the mainstream of social activity is dramatically punctuated when we decide to retire.

For many people retirement brings the time and opportunity to catch up with the advance in technology by going to adult education classes.

185

With the ending of paid work, or a reduction in the time devoted to it, there are a number of consequences which automatically follow. For example, we no longer meet up with colleagues or workmates and have less to do with the social side of our jobs. Ties of friendship are weakened. Relatives and children are likely to be widely scattered, especially in communities where people move around a great deal and are therefore difficult to visit. It's a sensible attempt on our part to distribute our reduced energies and resources over fewer but more personal activities. Effort is conserved and we escape from demands which we don't wish to or cannot meet.

Methods of disengagement

We all disengage differently. Some of us stubbornly resist the pressures put upon us to reduce our commitments, shed responsibility and do less work. In such cases, we refuse to take advice if it means giving up activities which play a prominent part in our lives, such as running a small business, a cultural or scientific activity, or a social or civic responsibility. More of us resist the idea of giving up an independent life and our homes for residency in a nursing home. Some of us refuse to retire until we are forced to do so by ill health. Others of us die as we lived, active and involved in the world.

Although some of us fight all the way, some disengagement is bound to come. We have neither the physical nor the mental resources we had when we were younger. Disengagement, therefore, provides a solution to some of the problems of adjustment in old age and signifies a practical reappraisal of our position. Ideally, disengagement is graded to suit the declining biological and psychological capacities of the individual on the one hand and the needs of society on the other. The degree to which we can engage has as much to do with personality as it has with ageing.

It would be wrong to think of disengagement as a nearly always negative process. It involves the beginning of renewal of fresh engagements, especially those activities which involve family, friends and neighbours. The time made available by retirement from full-term employment may be easily employed through alternative activities and social relationships. Losses in social relationships following retirement, the departure of children, or the death of a spouse, may be made good by other relationships with friends, neighbours or kin. Furthermore, the activities and relationships of later life may be *more* important and absorbing because they are fewer in number and more personal in nature. There is, however, a natural inclination on the part of most of us to mix with others and participate in group and community affairs. This natural tendency is often blocked by present-day retirement practices, hence we should make arrangements to find worthwhile activities suited to our age, personal qualities and health.

However, the net effect is a shrinkage in the range of our activities and a lessening in the amount of contact we have with other people. Gradually, our lives become separated from the lives of others. We become less associated with other people, less emotionally involved and more absorbed in our own problems and circumstances.

Looking forward to retirement

Research obliges us to alter our ideas about the nature of retirement; it can no longer be thought of simply as a sudden, enforced dislocation of our working lives, almost inevitably resulting in feelings of rejection and physical or mental ill-health. A substantial proportion of us retire, or wish to retire, a few years before the usual age. After retirement age, an even larger proportion of us do not actively seek paid employment although lower levels of income are a strong inducement for us to continue to work for as long as possible.

For many of us the release from exacting, lengthy work in unsatisfactory conditions, is followed not by frustration and idleness but by more enjoyable leisure time, closer family ties and better physical health. With retirement come forty or more hours in the week that we need to account for, hours previously spent in connection with work. Many retired people say they miss nothing; some miss work itself and, of course, money. To a lesser extent, others also miss the feeling of being useful. Attitudes change fairly rapidly during retirement and it is not age, but the passage of time, that explains the differences between people.

Thoughts on retirement Working men over the age of sixty-five generally seem less lonely and better adjusted than retired men, but not *because* they are working. Physical health and personality underlie both morale and working capacity in later life. Over many decades there has been a gradual but absolute improvement in the health and welfare of retired people and in their standards of living. A high level of morale is only achievable when economic status is on the level of other working adults. The reduction in living standards and income subsequent upon retirement is of the greatest concern to most of us. When these are coupled with natural regrets on leaving close friends and familiar activities

187

they may bring about a temporary depression or anxiety.

However, it is often the *prospect* of retirement, rather than retirement itself, which leads to a morbid state of mind. Studies have shown that given reasonable physical health and financial resources, the average retired man or woman soon adapts to the changed circumstances and shows an improvement in physical health and outlook. It is not so much old age in retirement as the transition to old age and retirement that creates problems of adjustment. Retirement is rapidly becoming a normal and expected phase of the life path, to be looked for, prepared for, and enjoyed over a long period.

Planning retirement

Preparation for retirement is now a widely-recognized need. Many firms, voluntary organizations and centres for adult education cater for this. The financial and leisure problems of retirement can be met only by long-term planning. Many people do not face up to the problems soon enough and enter retirement inadequately prepared. Preparation means putting money aside, buying and disposing of personal property and assets, attending to health needs, getting information and advice about leisure time interests, and generally changing the balance between disengagement and activity.

Intelligence, education and social attitudes play a part in this preparation. We need to acquire new skills, new attitudes and interests, and new social relationships if we are to make the most of our retirement.

The most important areas to provide for would be:

● Income and assets to provide for our material well-being when we retire;
● Some continuation of earlier working activities or social relationships to promote a sense of belonging and participation;
● Attention to physical comforts and health to make for more activity and security;
● The proper use of leisure time to provide a kind of dividend in feelings of achievement, usefulness and happiness.

Men and retirement   Disengagement works best for people who have maintained some continuity of activity throughout their lives and have vocations rather than jobs. The professional man can pursue some aspects of his life's work and maintain his professional contacts right up to the end of his life. Moreover, he has the time, money and opportunity to prepare for his retirement and to cultivate interests and activities which carry on over into later years. This continuity of activity, relationships and attitudes provides a stable pattern of adjustment, which can carry him smoothly from his busy adult working life to a more leisurely but satisfying retirement.

Most men, however, spend a large part of their adult years in fairly routine jobs which earn them a living and retirement pension, but do little to provide activities and opportunities which extend beyond their jobs on into retirement. Some men in this situation find that retirement presents problems of adjustment, since it often occurs abruptly at the age of sixty-five, with neither the continuity, which is important for good adjustment, nor the time, money and opportunity to prepare for a satisfactory retirement.

Better provision for retirement and courses in preparing for retirement would enable many more men to use and enjoy their declining years. A shorter working week, longer holidays and a gradual retirement from paid work in years to come, will all give people ample opportunities to cultivate stable, long-term interests and personal activities throughout their working lives. These will carry them over into retirement. Increased opportunity for such personal outlets might do much to improve emotional stability and could lessen the social stigma attached to retirement.

Women and retirement Problems of adjustment in later life can be met by a similar process of disengagement. Women may find this task easier because, unless they are single, they are not faced with the problem of suddenly having to adjust to an abrupt retirement. A man depends on his job and his earning capacity for status, prestige and authority in the home and the transition from work to retirement may be difficult. His disengagement from work relationships is usually followed by the renewal of kinship ties and he becomes involved in domestic chores such as shopping and cleaning. Working women are more closely bound than men to family life. On account of their continued activities in the home and established social patterns, they have to cope with fewer demands for readjustment.

However, the departure of children from the home changes the environment of the middle-aged mother and a partner's retirement calls for a further readjustment. Additionally, most married women eventually become widows, which in turn creates problems of readjustment. Little research has been made into how these and other late-life problems of adjustment for women might be met more effectively through education, preparation and counselling.

Disengagement proceeds differently for most women as compared with men and some of the stages – loss of children, disability and bereavement – may occur relatively early. Apart from the differences in temperament and attitudes which are a result of sex, a man's absorption in his job and outside interests provide him with powerful supports and these can weaken his emotional involvement with his family. He may not react to family events with the same intensity as a woman. Women whose children have grown up or who have lost husbands may often find other women in similar circumstances, but retired men or widowers are less likely to have a large pool of friends and they may feel isolated unless they can turn to their families.

Planning our new found time

We must make the most of retirement by letting it make things easier for ourselves. We can choose to be by ourselves; we won't have to adjust our schedules to meet others' needs; we don't need to answer to anyone but ourselves; we can give priorities to spending our time, money and resources in ways that we prefer; we can decide exactly where and how to live. They are solely our decisions from now on.

It has been stated that success or failure in the second forty years of life, measured in terms of happiness, is determined more by how we use or abuse our leisure time than by any other factor. It is important, therefore, to learn how to enjoy leisure activities without any guilt feelings. Some people do have to learn not to work so that they can enjoy leisure. Just like work, leisure has to be planned and we have to stick to this plan to enjoy it. Now that we have so much time, leisure is not a second-rate activity, it is very important. Thus we should adapt to it in exactly the same way as we adapt to a new job. We have to be positive and enthusiastic about it and give it all we've got, devoting all our energy to enjoying ourselves.

Just because you have more leisure time, don't fall into the trap of feeling that all your leisure time has to be spent together as a couple. It doesn't. More leisure time can mean more time for private activities as well as those you do as a couple.

Although retirement may demand a good deal of flexibility and adaptation it can lead to a time of great happiness and contentment once negotiated. The critical period for adjustment is shortly before retirement. During this time people tend to become increasingly agitated about the consequences and problems. The problem is not so much being old as *becoming* old. Some interesting findings came out of research made in the USA, which shows that we come to terms with retirement in a number of different ways, depending upon our personality (see page 195).

TIPS FOR RETIREMENT

For both sexes

• Retirement, even pre-retirement, should be carefully planned several years in advance of it actually happening, certainly in terms of housing, financial arrangements, health care, cultivating hobbies, interests and activities that can be continued into retirement.

• Take the best advice you can to make your money work for you during your retirement years; take the best counsel on investments and insurance, mortgages and wills. An accountant or a bank manager will be happy to give you advice. Try to make a budget even if you have never made one before.

• As a practice run, it is a good idea to start living on your retirement income about six months before you or your partner retires. If you start to ease into retirement this way, before you are under the strain of the other changes that go along with retirement, financial adjustments may be easier to cope with. You will also have saved up the money that you didn't use in the previous six months which will give you a nest egg and a sense of security. You may get a pleasant surprise to find out that it isn't nearly as difficult as you thought it would be.

• If one partner retires and the other goes on working, you may find that your days get out of sync. Instead of both being up early in the morning, both getting home early in the evening and both wanting to go to bed at the same time, one may be exhausted when the other is raring to go. Sit down and talk about it. Examine the problem and find a solution which will work for both of you. Make a particular point of doing things together at weekends when your clocks become synchronized again.

• If you find yourself at home with lots of time on your hands, feel lost, lonely, unwanted and left out, then it is probably a sign that you haven't made the emotional transition to retirement. Your partner can help by sorting out with you how best to spend your leisure time together. Discuss a rota for the chores. Make a list of all your friends and relatives who are free during certain parts of the week whom you haven't seen for several years, and match up your interests with those people. What can be done with whom? A partner should be prepared to change his or her routine.

For men

• If you retire but your partner is still working, it is time for an egalitarian form of domestic arrangement. It is only fair that you should get on with some of the domestic chores while your partner is out at work.

• If you do start to take a pride in the home, you shouldn't become rigid and house proud. Men can be particularly prone to do this if they don't have interests outside of the home, and that is the best solution – to find important jobs to do which take you out of the house.

For women

• When your husband retires don't be a perfectionist. Don't keep your house spic and span with everything in its place, or always complain about newspapers or books on tables, unwashed dishes and a messy kitchen. Adjustments have to be made. If you can't relax, especially if you are working, you may have to consider premature retirement yourself.

• If you've retired while your partner is still working, start new projects and take up old interests; remember old passions and renew them. If you have got lots of spare time then spend some of the time pampering yourself. Sleep late, read in the afternoon, put your feet up whenever you feel like it.

• If your partner is retired and you are still working, don't resent their freedom, though you may have to get up early while they are still sleeping.

Deciding where to live

Some people do not want to live alone and run their own homes nor do they want to live with friends or a family, so they may opt to be a paying guest or a lodger in a boarding house. Before you take up residence in a boarding house there are various points that you should check before moving in.

• How will your room be furnished? Go and see it and inspect it carefully. Make sure that it is a bed-sitter. Also ask if you can bring your belongings into the room.

• What are the bathroom and lavatory arrangements? Is your room near them? How many people share the bathroom? Is there a separate lavatory? How about laundry and personal washing, are there facilities on the premises?

• What is the lighting like, particularly on the stairs and are the floor coverings in a good or bad condition?

• What amenities are shared? Are you meant to sit in your own room or with others any or all of the time? Can you use the telephone and receive calls? Is there a communal television set?

- Who else lives in the house? Are children and pets and other old people included?
- Do you join the household at mealtimes or eat in your room? Can you have a meal later or earlier than normal or on a particular occasion?
- What are the arrangements if you are ill, or you just want to stay in bed for the day?
- Are you expected to do any of the household chores, if so what and how often?
- What will happen when visitors come to see you? Where can you sit with them and make them a cup of tea or coffee or give them a drink? Can they go to your room?
- Are there any extra charges for heating or lighting or laundry, an early morning cup of tea, shoe cleaning, television, telephone?
- If you go away for a few days or take a couple of weeks holiday what will happen? How much will you have to pay as a retainer? Will your room be locked?

Following bereavement   This is exactly the kind of decision that you should not make quickly. Someone in a state of shock and grief after the death of a close companion is not in the best state of mind to make such an important decision about future needs. In practical terms it is better to wait several weeks or even months to see what actually happens; several unexpected things may arise which may make your decision a good deal easier.

Initially, for the sake of being taken care of, so that you won't be alone and so that you have the distraction of company, you may have decided to move in with your family or friends. Temporarily you will have escaped from your own empty home but it is unwise to give up your home irretrievably because you put yourself in a permanently dependent position. It is very important that you retain a base so that you have somewhere to go to when you feel yourself again. Nearly everyone who overcomes bereavement and grief feels strength returning and with it the desire to be independent once more and have a home of their own. Always leave this option open to yourself.

Quite a lot of people who are bereaved take the decision to live with friends or family rather than live alone. If the arrangement is anything other than on a temporary basis, then you have to take special care to make the right arrangements from the very beginning. Never forget that settling down in new surroundings means establishing a new pattern of living which has to be acceptable to everyone concerned. This means that you and the people you are living with must be honest and explain problems, difficulties, likes and dislikes as soon as they become evident. Everyone will have to make some personal

193

adjustments especially those who spend most of the time at home. You may have to work out timetables and job sharing. When is the most convenient time for getting up. How and when to have meals. Sharing the housework, etc.

An important aspect of this is that everyone in the household should be able to entertain friends without anyone feeling in the way. If it is going to be a room with family or friends then it should be furnished as a bed-sitting room so that you can get away from others without making it into a special issue. Have your television, radio and stereo in the room with you. Make sure that you are an equal member of the family group so that you can say how you feel about things.

Living with your children

This may seem a very tempting option immediately after your bereavement when you are grief stricken. Your children know and love you, you have been in close touch all your lives and you feel comfortable with them. Your children may even beg you to go and live with them, but there are several reasons as to why you should hesitate from doing this.

They may start seeing you as a parent all over again, and therefore as someone who will babysit regularly, cook big meals at weekends for many friends and do the odd bit of mending. This is obviously not the role that you want to play and you will almost certainly feel used, your feelings may get hurt and you and your children will start to get on each other's nerves. As a parent you will certainly have different ideas about how children should be brought up and you may even have rows with your own children about how they are bringing up theirs. If you still feel inclined to move in try it first on a trial basis.

Move in temporarily and leave somewhere to fall back on – your own home and your own furniture. Don't get rid of either of them. If you do this, remember that it is your children's house and they are the ones who lay down the ground rules. Don't interfere, don't make suggestions and don't offer advice. Never forget that you are the guest and you have to be sensitive to your children's needs. As far as you possibly can avoid asking favours. They soon become irksome if they are frequent. Whatever you do don't play the role of the critical parent. Look at your children as friends, not as your children. If you see them as friends they will *feel* more like friends and they will *act* more like friends. They will also be honest with you and not feel obligated to you. In other words you have to have the same sort of relationship with your children as you would with the rest of your friends. This is not always easy for parents so weigh up the options carefully before coming to any decision because you will have to live with your decision for a long time.

HOW WE ADJUST TO RETIREMENT

Research shows that most of us come to terms with life after retirement in several different set patterns. Some patterns bring more happiness and contentment than others and while none of us is ideal, seeing these personality profiles might encourage us to take up a more rewarding pattern. These are some of the personal attributes to be found.

Constructiveness
- Had a happy childhood, little emotional stress in adult life, and a stable occupational history.
- Free of financial worries, happily married, and has made uninterrupted progress through life.
- Satisfied with achievements, self-assertive without being aggressive, and is capable of expressing feelings.
- Intelligent, well-integrated, enjoys food, drink, work and recreation and is sexually active.
- Is humorous, tolerant, flexible, aware of achievements, failings and prospects.
- Interests are well developed and has continued to enjoy some interests from earlier part of life.
- Has close, warm, affectionate personal relationships and very few feelings of hostility, self-esteem is high and he feels he can count on the support of people around him at all times.
- Constructive and optimistic attitude towards the future, accepts old age including retirement and death.
- Tolerates deprivations and frustrations.

Dependency
- Married late and had a small family, a passively tolerant partner in relationships with other people.
- Unambitious, glad to retire, happy to be free of work.
- Well integrated but tends to rely on others for material well-being and emotional support.
- Glad to be free of responsibility and effort, gets little enjoyment from the work which has to be done now.
- Eats and drinks too much, gambles, tends to live beyond means.

Defensiveness
- Stable occupational history, well-adjusted at work.
- Emotionally over-controlled, habit-bound, conventional and compulsively active.
- Works hard, but seems to work for defensive reasons rather than because the work is interesting.
- Not easy to talk to, becomes anxious and evasive when discussing social and family relationships.
- Self-sufficient, refuses help to prove independence, afraid of dependency and inactivity of old age, puts off retirement.
- Actively engaged in social organizations, good long-term planning to meet financial problems of old age.

Hostility
- Life history has a pattern of minor incompetence and neurosis, now quite often anxious, pessimistic, depressed.
- Often has a submissive relationship with parents, has grown up giving and receiving little affection, in middle age becomes neurotically dependent on wife.
- Is aggressive, complaining, competitive and suspicious in dealings with other people, tends to be depressed.
- Lacks the capacity for making realistic adjustments in retirement.

Self-hate
- Ambivalent feelings towards mother and father, not interested in other people derives little satisfaction from heterosexual relationships, feels generally lonely and useless.
- Unhappily married or feels no warmth of affection for partner.
- Pessimistic, fatalistic, feels a victim.

195

Specialist help

Even though I was trained in the rather rigid school of orthodox medicine, I nonetheless believe in an eclectic approach to getting help from specialists like cosmetic surgeons and dentists, medical practitioners who give skin treatments, psychotherapists and certain branches of alternative medicine. Having visited many, however, I am extremely wary of health spas and beauty clinics that rely on expensive, glossy advertising and make claims which are untrue. Beware of any specialist help which promises you permanent changes in your appearance, your skin, your shape or your weight. Beware particularly of any clinic which claims to halt ageing. This claim is false, because science knows of no way to halt the ageing process. There is no "cure" for wrinkles and sagging skin other than surgical removal of them.

Most of these clinics are fairly expensive and to be fair to yourself you must have a clear understanding of what to expect from them and how well they will live up to their exaggerated claims. The truth is that no effect produced in a beauty clinic can be permanent. It lasts a few minutes, a few hours, but rarely even one day. All you can expect is to come out of a beauty clinic feeling pampered. Nothing, absolutely nothing, will have been done to change or correct any of your faults in any way at all.

Cosmetic surgery

Beware of beauty clinics' and also of beauticians' jargon. Pseudo-scientific words are created to give a false impression of medical or technical knowledge, but in nearly all cases this is artificial. In the first place the words are simply made up. They have no scientific meaning. Doctors don't understand them and are at a loss to figure out what their meanings may be. Many of the words are true nonsense, because for those people with a deep knowledge of the physiology of the skin, not only do they have no meaning, but they may even contradict themselves to such an extent that they may be dangerous.

At a consultation the surgeon assesses for himself and the patient possible changes by simulating the facelift with his fingers. This he does by pulling loose skin upwards and backwards.

I have included the various types of specialist help in the order in which I give them credence and so start with cosmetic surgery and cosmetic dentistry, medical skin treatment, psychotherapy and biofeedback. I have not found any scientific information to show that health spas, beauty treatment and beauty clinics are any better than a placebo. Oh yes, you may *feel* better but it will not necessarily be because you *are* better. You may feel better

197

because your attitude to yourself has changed, but you don't have to go along to a clinic to experience that kind of change. It can happen without a beauty clinic. It can happen because of your own will power.

Choosing a cosmetic surgeon

Before you even approach a cosmetic surgeon, examine yourself closely. It is important that your motives for having the operation are the right ones. For instance it is no good thinking that cosmetic surgery will be the cure-all for a disaster which has overtaken you. It is going to make you no better able to cope with divorce proceedings. Having your nose straightened will not be able to make you give up alcohol, so don't look at cosmetic surgery as an emotional crutch. It is important to give a lot of consideration to cosmetic surgery, so do weigh up the possible risks (page 204) before you make a final decision.

When trying to decide who should be your cosmetic surgeon, first see your own doctor for a professional, objective opinion; he or she is the one whom you should listen to. Next best is recommendation from a friend who can show you the results of cosmetic surgery and describe his or her own experiences. You will be able to make a "before and after" judgement if you have known your friend for some time. It is very inadvisable to take any notice of advertisements in newspapers or magazines. A good surgeon or a good treatment needs no advertising because he or she will have acquired a good reputation.

When you are in the process of choosing a surgeon look out for the following points. If you spot any of them move to another surgeon.

• A surgeon who is unrealistic about the possible results of the operation. No good surgeon will guarantee his or her operation to be 100 percent successful.

• A surgeon who will not explain in detail what the operation involves and what he is trying to achieve, with a realistic estimate of the chances of success.

• A surgeon who offers no professional opinion as to what you really need and is willing to perform exactly the operation you want. Any surgeon worth his salt will want to do the operation that has the best results for you and should offer his own suggestions about what he thinks should be done.

• A surgeon who will not answer your questions in detail with illustrations and photographs of other clients' surgery.

• A surgeon who is not prepared to take many and detailed photographs of the feature you require altering with surgery. Any good cosmetic surgeon will say that he needs many photographs to study in order to decide exactly how and what he has to do to make the correction.

COSMETIC SURGERY

Eyes
Blepharoplasty will improve puffy or drooping eyelids, remove the bags beneath eyes and reshape eyelids

Nose
Rhinoplasty will alter the size or shape of the nose, strengthen or straighten it

Cheeks
Cheekbone augmentation will make them more prominent

Ears
Otoplasty will pin back sticking-out ears

Chin
Remodelling will correct a receding or prominent chin and reduction will remove sagging skin beneath the jaw

Neck
A face lift pulls back loose skin, making the neck look healthier

The face　Cosmetic operations performed on the face are usually to remove signs of age or to improve features. Cosmetic surgeons will tell you that the classical patients are no longer the vain, rich women with nothing better to do with their money; they are more likely to be energetic, active women who are less interested in hiding their age than in looking as youthful as they feel. People in their fifties and onwards no longer resign themselves to be thought of as ageing. Many feel that growing older would be more comfortable if they could avoid looking old in the process. Many others justifiably feel that it is unjust that they should begin to show signs of deterioration when they are just reaching intellectual and emotional maturity. So when fine lines, wrinkles and sags appear on their faces they decide to fight back with cosmetic surgery.

199

The illustration on page 199 shows the facial features which you can have altered by a cosmetic surgeon. In the USA a new approach to face lifts has been developed for older patients, *total facial rejuvenation* (see chart, pages 202-203. The latest techniques can eliminate frown lines by a modification of the muscle structure under the skin.

The body Expense is not the only factor that should make you pause before contemplating body surgery. It should always be considered a last resort in the search for beauty – it's far better to exercise or diet your bulges away. From a medical standpoint, cosmetic surgery on your body will be more serious than on your face. The operations are lengthy; some involve a considerable spell of post-operative pain and immobility. All of them leave scars, though they vary in their degree of conspicuousness. Furthermore, the technology for these operations is confined to the main centres for cosmetic surgery in the USA and it is difficult to find good surgeons with all the best facilities elsewhere in the world.

Breast uplift or mastoplexy
This will correct drooping breasts. With age, the suspensory ligaments, the skin and the breast tissue itself will thin and become inelastic. Once this has happened nothing can make the breast regain its former shape. Not even exercises, no matter how much you are encouraged to do them. There is no muscle tissue in the breasts, and by strengthening the pectoralis major and minor you are doing nothing to improve the shape of your breasts. Occasionally breast uplift is combined with breast augmentation or breast reduction or the correction of a minor idiosyncracy like lopsidedness. A general anaesthetic is always needed. The length of stay in hospital is about three days, but in the USA clinics are offering breast uplift operations to outpatients. The technique used is virtually the same as for breast reduction, but only skin rather than skin fat and breast tissue is removed.

Breast augmentation is the most popular body operation in cosmetic surgery anywhere in the world. A request for surgery is usually made by someone who has tried every other conceivable method to improve her bust, including exercises, massage, bathing the breasts alternately in hot and cold water and hormone creams. None of these work. The only way to enlarge breasts successfully is through surgery. Before the operation, patient and surgeon should establish the shape and size of the breasts without being over-ambitious. Too large breasts make you look unnatural and top heavy. Study pictures of the various operations that the surgeon can perform and ask his advice about which will best suit you. Then ask to see a specimen of the implant material that the surgeon will use.

The operation is usually performed under an anaesthetic as an in-patient and your hospital stay will probably last a few days. An incision is made around the areola where it will heal without leaving any obvious scar. The implant is then placed *behind* the normal breast tissue so that it lies against the pectoral muscles. The deep layers of the wound are stitched together with soluble nylon which does not have to be removed and the stitches closing the incision around the areola come out a week after the operation. There is usually very little discomfort and any bruising disappears within a few weeks. There may be slight tingling or numbness around the nipple, but this will gradually wear off.

Start wearing a bra in your new size as soon as it is comfortable to do so. Make sure you buy one in advance to take into hospital when you go for the operation.

For about a month after a breast augmentation operation it is better to avoid very active sports like swimming, tennis and volley ball. Any movements which extend the arms high above the head and those which pull the elbows out at right angles should be avoided, but the operation should not interfere in any other way with your mobility. Your breasts should look and feel natural and they should not become hard after insertion. If they do, you may need further surgery, but this change is exceedingly rare with the new type of inflatable implant currently available.

Breast reduction
This operation is for women who are embarrassingly well endowed. Occasionally, some breasts are so pendulous that they hang down to the thighs and so heavy that the bra straps ulcerate the skin of the shoulder. Most cosmetic surgeons would agree that these breasts should be reduced for psychological if not medical reasons. You should first have photographs taken of your breasts from every angle, then agree with the surgeon on a new outline for them. An incision is made around the areola just as for breast augmentation and all the way down the front underside of the breast to where it meets the skin covering the chest wall. Skin fat and breast tissue are removed, leaving enough to fashion a breast of normal shape and size. The nipples have to be moved upwards to an appropriate position on the reshaped breasts, but this should not affect their sensitivity or rule out breast feeding later. Any scars can easily be hidden under cover-up make-up.

POPULAR COSMETIC OPERATIONS

Operation	In/Out-patient. Length of stay	Preconditions	Anaesthetic Time taken	Post-operative effects
Face lift Lifting skin of whole face	In-patient 3 days	None	General 2 hours +	Face red and swollen
Total facial rejuvenation Face lift, neck lift, eyelid repair, dermabrasion	In-patient 5 days minimum	None	General Up to 4 hours	Face red and swollen
Breast reconstruction Building new breast(s) after mastectomy	In-patient 3 days + for each stage	Psychological preparation. No indication that cancer has spread	General May be in 2 stages	Soreness, bruising
Breast augmentation Enlarging the breasts	In-patient; rarely out-patient. 3 days minimum	None	General; rarely local 2 hours	Occasionally soreness, bruising, tingling round nipple
Breast reduction Making breasts smaller	In-patient; rarely out-patient. 3 days	None	General Up to 3 hours	Bruising, tingling, soreness and numbness of nipple
Abdominoplasty Removal of folds of fat from lower abdomen	In-patient 7 days	First discuss operation with surgeon	General 2 hours	Drainage tubes in sound for 3-5 days
Buttocks, hips and thighs Recontouring of shape by removing fat and skin	In-patient 5 days if possible	Diet to lose fat first	General 2-3 hours depending on operation	Can move and sit same day but some discomfort likely for 2 weeks
Total body lift Removal of sagging skin from abdomen, buttocks, thighs, arms, neck and face	In-patient 5-7 days on each occasion	Diet to lose fat first	General 1-2 hours each session	Depends on operations
Hair transplants Transplanting skin from back of scalp to bald area	In-patient 7 days	None	General or local 1-2 hours each session	Swelling and crusting
Upper arms Removal of loose fat and skin	In-patient 48 hours	None	General 1 hour	Hardly any discomfort

Stitches removed	Care and dressing	Time fo full recovery	Possible complications	Results
Some at 5-7 days rest at 2 weeks	Can eat immediately, fully active in 3 days. Large dressing for 2 days	Superficial swelling subsides in a month	Feeling of tightness usually gone in a few months	Generally very good. Only fully apparent in 3 months.
Some at 5-7 days rest at 2 weeks	Can be fully active in 3 days. Bulky dressings for 48 hours	Swelling subsides in 3 weeks	Tightness round neck and numbness round ears, subsiding in few months	Good. May take up to 6 months to see best effect
5-7 days	As breast reduction	3 months	Visible scars. Rarely reduction in sensitivity of nipple	Good
1 week	No active sports or stretching for 1 month. Light dressing and antibiotic ointment	2 months	Hardening of implants. Any bruising and discomfort usually goes in a few weeks	Very good if up-to-date methods are used
1 week	No active sports or stretching for 1 month. Dressing for 3-5 days	2 months	Visible scars. Swelling, discoloration, infection possible	Very good
14 days	Keep body bent for 3-5 days. Mobility restricted for 4-6 weeks. Daily dressing	3 months	Scarcely visible scars	Good
7-10 days if non-soluble	Ordinary activities in 14 days. Sport in 1 month. Light gauze and antibiotic ointment	2 months	Significant scars	Very good if up-to-date methods are used
Depends on operations	Depends on operations	3-4 months after last operation	Significant scars	Good
7 days if used	Careful shampooing and combing. Bulky bandage for 7 days	1 year	None	Repeat may be needed. Better for men than women
5-7 days	No stretching for 2 weeks. Light gauze and antibiotic ointment	2 months	Visible scars	Very good

203

RISKS OF COSMETIC SURGERY

• Be aware that all surgery carries a risk. With any surgery there is risk of dying under general anaesthetic and a risk that the operation will give you a shock from which you will never recover. Both of these risks are very small.

• A proportion of patients over fifty undergoing cosmetic surgery can no longer be classified as young and are certainly less robust than people in their twenties and thirties, so it could be argued that the risks involved are higher.

• Remember that the period immediately after any operation can be unpleasant and cosmetic surgery is no different – the area involved may be uncomfortable and painful for days or weeks. You may have a period of complete immobility or at least severely restricted activity. With older people it is essential that you combine a régime of rest with activity, otherwise joints will stiffen and there is a possibility of pneumonia just from sitting in bed.

• Keep at the back of your mind that the operation may not turn out exactly as you had thought. Though it's very rare, they may be disastrous. You should be prepared for the results being not quite as you had expected. Occasionally, there are complications that delay recovery, and while these risks are slight in the hands of a good surgeon they must be taken into account when you consider the pros and cons of cosmetic surgery.

• Cosmetic surgery is not exempt from scars. They may be well hidden under the hairline or inside the mouth, but very occasionally a scar will be visible. If this is an aspect of cosmetic surgery which troubles you, try and talk to someone who has already had the operation so that you can get an idea of the probability of scarring. In my experience, the more expert the cosmetic surgeon, the more likely he is to take pride in leaving no scars, or only the faintest.

Cosmetic dentistry

Bridge | Missing tooth

Bridge in position

Fitting a bridge
This involves shaping the teeth on either side of the gap so that a bridge can be cemented to them.

As we get older our teeth tend to yellow with age and because of gum recession we might be described as being "long in the tooth". Both of these things can be mitigated by good dental hygiene and regular visits to the dentist. Avoid using toothpastes which claim to whiten your teeth, unless your dentist recommends otherwise, because this "whitening" is an optical illusion. The toothpaste contains a red pigment which turns our gums pink, making our teeth look whiter by comparison. Toothpaste which claims to give a white, polished smile makes the teeth shine by use of abrasives, including a very strong one known as "jewellers' rouge".

Avoid these toothpastes at all costs – they are much too harsh on teeth and work by scratching the surface enamel. Prolonged use of such toothpastes damages or wears away teeth. The safest and by far the most efficient way to give your teeth a new look is to visit a dental hygienist. When we were younger we should have gone every six months, now we should go every three months to remove plaques of calcium deposits.

Eventually these cause inflammation in the margin of the gum and pocketing which leads to loosening the teeth in their gums. The hygienist will also polish your teeth and make them several shades whiter, particularly if you smoke.

A good cosmetic dentist can alter the look of your teeth, your smile, the set of your mouth and therefore your facial expression. As we get older our teeth tend to be ground away simply by use or by having an especially-strong masticating muscle or perhaps by night grinding. Whatever the cause, our jawbones tend to become closer together and this accentuates the folds on either side of our mouths – and most of us would agree that this makes us look older. A cosmetic dentist can correct this by widening the distance between the jawbones by re-positioning the teeth and stretching out the skin in your laughter line. Even an increase as little as half a millimetre will make a substantial difference to our appearance.

Repositioning teeth

We think of cosmetic dentistry as involving complicated techniques with bridges, wires and crowns, but many dentists use commonsense and simple methods and materials to achieve their effect. For instance, it is quite possible to move the roots of the teeth within the jaw bone by anything up to a millimetre if they are pulled or pushed in one direction for any length of time. Even such tiny adjustments can make quite a difference to the overall effect.

Caps, crowns and bridges

Any badly positioned, ugly or broken tooth can be given a new cosmetic appearance by *capping* or *crowning*, terms which dentists use synonymously. Your dentist fits a cap by first filing away the tooth to form a peg, onto which the cap is cemented. This can still be done if your tooth is snapped off or has had to be removed right at the gum margin. Then, three or four posts are drilled into what is left of the tooth and the cap or crown can be fitted to them.

A bridge (page 204) is clear plastic moulded to fit over the hard pallet. The teeth required are fitted onto various parts of the bridge and this slips easily into place, held snugly in the mouth by wires which fit around your existing teeth. You should remove it and clean it in a sterilizing solution.

Shortening or lengthening teeth

If your teeth are too long they can soon be filed away and given caps that will make them look a little shorter than they were originally. The reverse problem is common too. The gums grow too high so that they make teeth appear to be too short. In this instance your gum margins can be cut away and your teeth lengthened with caps that are slightly longer.

MEDICAL SKIN TREATMENTS

These chemical and surgical techniques can be used to alter or repair the surface of the skin. I am very firmly of the opinion that they should be administered by medical specialists only, such as plastic surgeons or dermatologists; a non-medically qualified person cannot possibly judge how radical they can be with their treatment nor deal with side-effects.

Dermabrasion

Dermabrasion is used to remove or improve pitted acne scars on the face and to treat large, flat birth marks. It may even produce good results for stretch marks and fine lines around the mouth.
Great advances in dermabrasion have been made in the past twenty-five years largely due to high-speed rotary drills and better cooling techniques.

During the operation a strict procedure must be followed to avoid any accidents. The patient is sedated or tranquillized and then the area involved is chilled with cold packs. It is cleansed first with soap and water and then with spirit. Plugs of gauze, impregnated with ointment, are inserted into ears and nostrils whilst hair is carefully protected with towels. Eyes are covered with ointment and a lead shield. The area to be treated is frozen with a stream of cold gas and then the drill is used to abrase the skin to the required depth.

Crusts usually separate in seven to ten days and the wound heals more quickly if it is left open and dry. It is possible to treat the same areas again after a period of four weeks.

Chemical treatment

Skin peeling can be prevented for cosmetic or medical reasons by various chemicals. The area to be treated may be fairly extensive and so you may have to spend time in hospital. In the hands of an expert, skin peeling can make blemishes, fine lines, wrinkles and acne pit marks much less obvious and it can occasionally be used to treat discoloured areas of skin and freckles. It may soften the facial line temporarily, it will wear off within a year.

Curettage

In the right hands this procedure is straightforward. A curette, or a tiny spoon with a sharp cutting edge, is used to destroy or remove some skin conditions which are well circumscribed and embedded. The curette can enucleate small cysts and successfully remove warts and verrucae. The sharp edge is applied to the buried lesion at an angle and gradually separates it from the normal surrounding skin. It should shell out without any bleeding.

Electro-dessication/coagulation

These involve destroying tissue in two ways. By producing a spark which solidifies the skin or by heating it up to a temperature at which it coagulates. In the former, cells are shrivelled, while in the latter they simply solidify in the same way that the white of an egg does when it is boiled. By varying the current, the same apparatus can be used for both processes.

This treatment can be used to remove broken veins in the skin of the face and leg and it can also be used to treat warts that stand proudly above the surface of the skin. It is particularly useful for treating those little skin tags which appear as we get older and large numbers can be treated in one session.

Excision

Treating surface skin conditions involves complete surgical removal of a piece of full-thickness skin. Only a dermatologist or plastic surgeon can decide when this technique is necessary. A general rule is not to interfere in any way with pigmented skin such as a mole.

PSYCHOTHERAPY

Psychotherapy aims to help us acquire insight into ourselves and our behaviour so that we can learn to deal with our own difficulties. Therapy does not concentrate on symptoms only, nor does it seek to cure mental illness, more than that it seeks to explain the underlying reasons for them. The following forms of psychotherapy may bring useful insights.

Psychoanalysis
This is the best-known form of psychotherapy but it has certain disadvantages. It is expensive and it takes a very long time; sometimes the duration is five years at a rate of five days a week. Undoubtedly it has helped a lot of people, but friends and relatives are not always as enthusiastic about the results, finding that the person has not necessarily changed for the better.

Interpretive psychotherapy
This helps people to understand the causes of their difficulties and the symptoms which they are suffering. Psychotherapists cannot do this without understanding every aspect of a person's life, including childhood adolescence, family and personal relationships. They may interpret the significance of a person's symptoms as they relate to his or her present life, but quite often a special technique is employed involving the *transference* of relationships between a person and his or her therapist.

Suggestive psychotherapy
This relies on resolving a person's difficulties by making direct suggestions. Hypnosis is one of the most intense and dramatic suggestive therapies in which a person's state of consciousness is altered and active directions are given. Although hypnotherapy is often used to change patterns of behaviour, it can also be used to encourage a person to release repressed memory. This use is based on the theory that it is possible to make closer contact with the subconscious mind when someone is hypnotized.

Group therapy
This started after the second world war and quickly gained popularity. Small group therapy involves seven or eight people, usually strangers, who meet together with the therapist under strictly defined conditions. They all have in common the fact that they are unable to cope with the stress in their lives.

Group therapy aims to help a person to discover, rationalize, adjust and finally to cope with his or her problems. Talking gives a valuable insight into problems.

Thus it follows a logical, purposeful development with the end product a person who no longer depends on a group for inner confidence and social stability.

Behavioural therapy
This will greatly benefit phobias. A phobia is an overwhelming, unreasonable fear about certain situations – most people who suffer from a phobia are aware that they are behaving irrationally but are quite unable to control their fear. Very often a phobia can be the result of an earlier distressing event which has been forgotten. Phobic patients can be helped particularly by the different forms of behavioural therapy such as *aversion therapy, desensitization* or *modelling*.

Encounter group therapy
This gained prevalence in the early 1960s. It involves complete openness to any impulse, whether it is touching, caressing, undressing or cursing, and such is the variety of groups available that anything promoting this openness such as nudity or screaming will be used.

Hormone treatments

At any age, but usually around fifty when the levels of oestrogen decrease in our bodies, we frequently experience emotional and physical discomfort.

Men produce less testosterone as they get older – a hormone they need to function in all areas, particularly sexual, and testosterone replacement therapy (TRT) can correct this deficiency. Many doctors disagree with it because they believe it might cause prostatic pain during ejaculation and difficulty with orgasm.

Theory also has it that therapy relieves chronic fatigue and improves loss of memory. It has even been claimed that it can relieve muscular weakness. However, testosterone replacement therapy is never prescribed routinely and very little research has been done in this area and we should learn more in the future.

If you feel that TRT might be of use you should go to your doctor to talk it over. If he or she doesn't know a lot about TRT, ask to be referred to someone who does or get a second opinion. Don't be afraid. The more you find out about your body and the way your body changes and also the kind of treatment that is available to reverse these changes, the more you will benefit.

Gerovital therapy

This was introduced in 1956 by Dr Ana Aslan who was working in Rumania. She reported that treatment of ageing people with a substance known as procaine hydrochloride H_3 could improve memory, improve concentration and perception, raise the levels of oestrogen circulating in the blood, make the skin plumper, stimulate hair growth, relieve angina, high blood pressure and the stiffness that accompanies Parkinson's disease, and help sufferers from arthritis and certain skin diseases. Unfortunately, wide use hasn't proven successful and research in the USA produced disappointing findings so interest was quickly lost again in this form of therapy.

Regenerative cell therapy

This also made extravagant claims about rejuvenating or revitalizing the skin. Such are people's insecurities that these treatments often become widely used in the absence of any proof that they are effective. A currently popular treatment is one that was developed in the 1930s by Doctor Paul Niehans. It involves injecting patients with a mixture of cells from ten glands of freshly-slaughtered animals. Basic physiological factors do need to be considered. Our bodies have mechanisms to protect us from invasion by live foreign cells and also it is highly unlikely that an injected substance will reach a specific organ in any undiluted quantity.

Biofeedback

Biofeedback is a technique which teaches us to be aware of our bodies' inner workings through the use of machinery and it is presently the subject of research among scientists of all disciplines. It was initially the subject of much hostility but now that it has shown that we can achieve "mind over mattter", it has revolutionized many previous beliefs about the nature of nerve function. Some biofeedback enthusiasts would now go as far as to claim that this discipline is a way of eradicating all need for conventional medicine, by teaching people to gain complete control over their bodily functions, but this is absolute nonsense. By fewer people it is considered to be a means of reaching in a matter of hours a state of inner awareness and peace, spiritual and mental, which the practitioners of yoga, Zen, and other forms of meditation are only able to reach after many disciplined years.

Biofeedback suggests that information about our inner state is being relayed to us in the same way that information about our surroundings is fed back to us by our senses. This means that we can learn more about our environment and how to control behaviour in reaction to it. The sort of information gained by biofeedback concerns the structural activity of the heart, for instance rate of heart beat, and the blood pressure, the brain which indicates to us the way they function.

Various instruments such as an electro-encephalograph, which records brain waves, an electro-micrograph, which charts muscle tension and an electro-cardiograph, which records heart beats, can all make us aware of what is happening in our bodies and help us develop personal techniques to maintain physical and mental control. This way it may be possible to gradually feel the way our internal organs work.

Uses for biofeedback We can't all cart around an electro-encephalograph with us during our normal daily lives but there are much smaller and more convenient instruments which can monitor inner body functions. A small machine can be attached to one finger only and it will monitor and give a visual display of heart rate and blood pressure. What we can try to do is to relax, breathe regularly, clear our minds of anxiety (try the relaxation drills given on pages 80-81) and when heart rate and·blood pressure are back down to normal we must remember the kind of feelings that we have and then when blood pressure and heart rate have risen again attempt to recapture that feeling which accompanied our heart rates being slow and our blood pressure being normal.

209

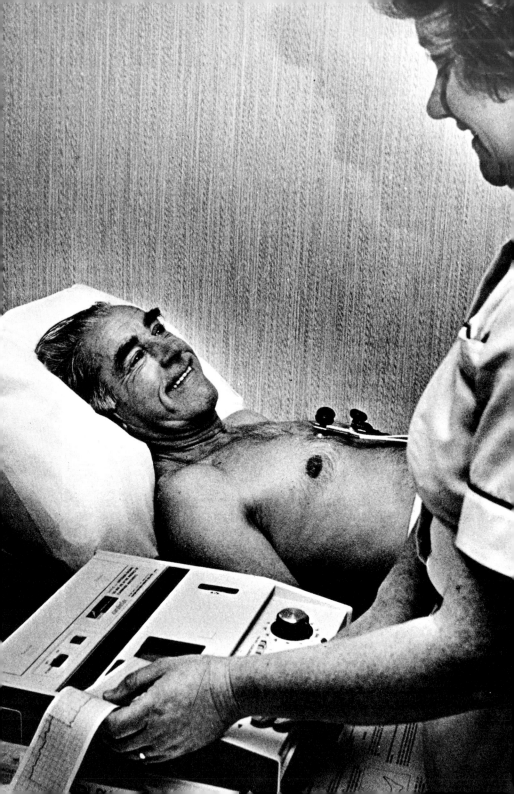

Special medical problems

Just as there are special diseases in infancy and childhood, so there are certain conditions which begin to show as we get older and become commoner as we age. Naturally enough, fear of these diseases also increases and the fear of getting heart disease or having cancer may grow to the point of irrationality, even to being a phobia. Medical conditions of age are largely those which occur because our bodies' machinery is changing down a gear and this alters the way it works.

Because the ageing process continues on through life, it is not as easy to identify a single malfunction in an older person as it is in a younger person. Many of the medical conditions of this age are those of wear and tear; and the ones that affect our vital organs are often dramatic, for instance heart disease, strokes and cancer. Most of the common medical problems of fifty-year-olds and upwards will be mentioned in this chapter. The accent will be on how to manage a medical problem yourself if you have it, what you can do to minimize its encroachment on your activity and enjoyment of life, how to slow its progress, how to deal with possible serious outcomes, and some tips on how others can help you. For the management of chronic illnesses in yourself and others see *Living with long-term ailments*.

There are certain signs and symptoms in medicine which indicate change: change from a normal bowel habit, change in the digestive pattern, a sudden bout of coughing up blood-specked sputum, severe headaches which strike out of the blue. In the majority of cases they are not serious, and whatever has gone wrong can easily be put right, but in some cases the underlying cause can be degenerative as in atheromatous arterial disease, or inflammatory as in rheumatoid arthritis, or cancerous as in a malignant tumour.

For this reason all the following warning signs represent something serious until proven otherwise when you take them along to your doctor. Please don't let them alarm you. They are described as warning signs and they are only a warning. In the majority of cases they will turn out to be easily explained and eminently treatable but any symptom or sign of change needs investigation, proper diagnosis and appropriate medical help. This list will help you to be alert to changes so that they need not be an unnecessary cause of worrying. To a doctor, change always represents a signal that the body is not functioning as it should. This doesn't necessarily mean danger.

211

Cancer

Cancer is not the worst problem facing us as we get older, but it causes a great deal of concern. It is common enough for almost every person to fear it as he or she gets older and to imagine that it is the cause of any symptoms he or she may have. Anyone who is aware of this should be sympathetic.

Growths account for about 15 percent of deaths as we grow older. In many organs such as the skin, the lungs and the digestive tract, the chance of cancer developing rises steadily with age, as do certain leukaemias. Cancer of the prostate gland is even more strikingly connected with the age of a man, but many other tumours such as those of the cervix and womb are more usually found in younger women.

There are some hereditary factors involved, so that your chances of developing cancer are greater if it runs in your family. Some cancers are caused by harmful agents like tobacco and industrial chemicals, most of which take a long time to show their effects. It is not surprising, therefore, that some cancers tend to appear latterly, as older people will have had more time for this to happen. Even though an ageing population will probably have more cancer than a youthful one, cancers in older people are often less malignant and grow much more slowly, and some even seem to get smaller.

While I will not discuss individual cancers in detail, there are certain facts about cancer in later life which are well worth mentioning. Cancer of the breast is fairly common and very often it is missed by the woman herself. Many of these cancers go undetected and we cannot avoid the conclusion that women know of lumps, more than suspect what they are, but decide to say nothing either because of embarrassment or because they are afraid to hear the truth and undergo treatment. Many tragedies result from this, from ignorance or fear. As most cancers in old age grow slowly, it is quite common for an older woman to have had one developing for many years.

Breast cancer Breast cancer is a curable disease. As the breast is almost a separate organ supported on the chest wall, it is easy to get at. This means that a small tumour of the breast which hasn't spread can be cured by surgical removal of the lump alone if it's small, or the breast or part of it.

Factors related to breast cancer

Many factors are known to affect the development of breast cancer. If you are white you run a higher risk than women of other races. If other members of your family have breast cancer then your chances are higher. Women who have no children are at a fairly high risk. Breast feeding also seems to have a protective effect, and there is an undoubted connection between a western diet and the development of breast cancer. It is generally agreed that the risk of developing breast cancer increases with age. Under the age of twenty-five it is very rare and up to the age of about thirty-five it is not so common, but then between the ages of thirty-five and fifty its incidence increases and after the age of fifty the risk is greatest.

If you fall into a high risk group you should examine your breasts monthly (see *Caring for a changing body*). You should go along to your doctor and have your breasts examined every three to six months and you might try having a mammography examination every year.

Discovering a lump
If you discover a lump in your breast it may feel clearly defined. It may feel hard and stony or it may feel round and cystic. It may or may not be associated with pain and the most malignant tumours are painless. It may involve the skin and send up constricting bands so that it is tethered to it pulling on a small area of skin making it dimpled. It may also tug at the nipple and alter its shape. All of these changes have important significance for your doctor, whose first concern is to exclude the possibility of your having a malignant tumour as rapidly as possible.

Your family physician will certainly refer you to a surgeon who specializes in treating breast cancer, and he or she will probably approach the lump in your breast as being malignant until able to prove otherwise. Your doctor will need to act with speed and efficiency, and will also try to find out if the tumour has spread and, if it has, to what extent. Ask your surgeon to keep you informed of the plan of action he or she has in mind for treating the lump in your breast and to give you reasons for why such a decision is made. You should be part of these decisions, and you need quite a lot of information to participate intelligently.

The surgeon may decide to perform some tests to confirm what the initial examination has already suggested. One of the most important which can be performed is a fine needle biopsy. It is a painless procedure where a fine needle is inserted into the lump and a little fluid is withdrawn. If the tumour is malignant, cancer cells will be found in the breast fluid in about 85 percent of cases. Some surgeons consider lumpectomy (removal of the lump alone) as an acceptable preoperative investigative procedure. Once the lump has been removed it will be examined in the pathology laboratory and a diagnosis can be confirmed. It

213

is also possible to do a breast biopsy where a little part of the lump is taken out to be examined for malignant cells.

In no case should you agree to surgical removal, partial removal or treatment of your breast until a diagnosis has been confirmed. Never go to the operating theatre having agreed to removal of your breast should the surgeon find it necessary when he or she gets you on the table. This is a brutal and heartless procedure not practised at the best centres.

Any of the preoperative investigative techniques which I have mentioned can and are performed in the most modern units so that women have time to adjust themselves to having a malignant tumour of the breast and also to the form of treatment that the surgeon wishes to follow.

Treatment for breast cancer

There are almost as many ways of treating cancer of the breast as there are surgeons but they usually involve one or any combination of three types of approach.

Surgery involves removing all or part of the breast and some of the underlying muscle, the lymph glands from the arm pit and lymph glands from the neck. All of these operations are given the general name "mastectomy" and then prefixes of "partial", "simple", "total", "modified", "radical", etc., which describes the extent of breast tissue removal. Naturally, the greater the extent of the operation, the greater amount of scarring.

MASTECTOMY OPERATIONS

There are seven different operations performed today for breast cancer. All require the removal of some, if not all, of the breast tissue, but they differ in the amount of tissue, muscle and lymph nodes removed.

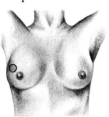

Lumpectomy
The whole lump is removed plus a little of the breast tissue. Your breast will not look very different.

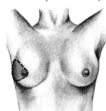

Partial mastectomy
Here, an amount of breast tissue, plus the overlying skin and underlying tissue are removed.

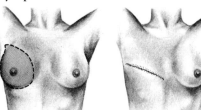

Total or simple mastectomy
In this operation the whole of the breast is removed, but the axillary nodes and the pectoral muscle are left untouched. The last lymph node in the breast is routinely taken out to see if the cancer has spread to the axilla.

Radiotherapy (deep X-ray therapy) is sometimes given before the operation, quite often it is given after the operation both to the breast itself and to the glands in the armpit or the neck. Further courses of radiotherapy may be necessary over a period of weekly visits to kill off any cancer cells which may remain in the area.

Hormone therapy has been found to diminish the size of breast tumours in a proportion of women if they are given courses of hormone therapy, usually oestrogens or anti-oestrogens (which have the reverse effect of oestrogens). This is because the normal growth of the breast is influenced by oestrogen levels, their sensitivity to oestrogen varying with age. Oestrogen-sensitive tumours will require treatment with anti-oestrogens.

In older women the approach to treatment of breast cancer is rather different from that in younger women. In younger women there are more mastectomies, and mastectomies plus X-ray therapy, whereas in older women, where tumours seem to have a closer dependency on oestrogens and anti-oestrogens, the tendency is to treat more often with hormone therapy with or without radiotherapy.

Hormone therapy takes various forms and in the best centres hormone therapy is tailor-made to suit each individual person's hormone profile. Endocrinologists, working closely with surgeons and radiotherapists, perform studies on an individual hormone balance and may even do tests on the tumour itself to see whether oestrogens or anti-oestrogens are more likely to be successful as a therapy.

Oestrogen is usually considered the treatment of choice for women who are more then five years beyond the menopause. Anti-oestrogens, often given in the form of androgens, are usually reserved for post-menopausal patients between two and five years beyond the menopause. Patients and doctors can usually see a response within six weeks from the beginning of treatment to hormone therapy of this kind.

The most popular form of treatment is di-ethyl-stilboestrol at a dose of five milligrams, three times a day. Tolerance to this régime is most easily achieved if the patient has a low dosage for a few weeks or takes a coated tablet. The commonest side effects are nausea and vomiting.

Anti-oestrogen therapy can be given by mouth, but if androgens themselves are used, injections may be necessary once- or twice-weekly. There are other hormones which can be used to promote appetite, increase in weight and remission of the tumour. Anabolic steriods are sometimes used along with corticosteroids and synthetic progesterone.

Women who are more than ten years beyond the menopause have an excellent chance of a cure. The older you are when the tumour is discovered and the more slowly it is growing, then the better your chances of a complete cure.

Cancer of the prostate

This is the most common cancer in men; it is not uncommon in forty-to-fifty-year-olds, and becomes marked in seventy-year-olds and over. As many as 20 percent of men over sixty have prostatic cancer. In its early stages it may be diagnosed by routine rectal examinations which can be supported by biopsies of suspected tissues. Treatment by surgery and irradiation is very successful when the cancer is detected in its early stages, but the prognosis is poor once it has spread outside the prostate. Therefore, routine rectal examinations every six months for men fifty and over are strongly advised.

This cancer usually develops in a normal gland, but it may also grow from a gland which is enlarged through benign prostatic hypertrophy (see page 217). No-one yet understands the cause of carcinoma of the prostate fully. At the moment it seems likely that an imbalance in the ratio of androgen which is oestrogens circulating in the blood plays an important part in its development. It is probably the amount of androgen which is critical because cancer of the prostate does occur in eunuchs. In addition, the tumour may lessen in size if oestrogens are given to a patient to restore the oestrogen-androgen balance.

It appears that androgens are responsible for inducing cancerous changes, while enlargement of the prostate may be under the influence of oestrogens. Carcinoma of the prostate is particularly common in Japanese men and this has been ascribed to the different sexual practices between them and men in the West.

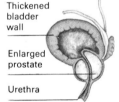

Thickened bladder wall

Enlarged prostate

Urethra

An enlarged prostate reduces the flow of urine by blocking the urethra. The bladder gradually thickens and strengthens as it works harder to force urine through the urethra.

When the prostate gland grows because of a cancerous tumour it obstructs the urethra so men suffer difficulty with passing urine, retention of urine and possibly urinary infection. Eventually any of these conditions may go on to chronic kidney failure if they are not treated to relieve the obstruction.

On the other hand, some men may have fewer urinary symptoms and mainly complain of pain in the lower back and sciatica going down the back of the leg. This happens when deposits of the cancer have spread from the prostate gland into the bone at the lower parts of the spine so they are pressing on the sciatic nerve.

When a doctor examines a cancerous gland through the rectum, the surface will feel hard, irregular and fixed. It may even be possible to feel an extension of the cancer out to the side walls of the pelvis, around the rectum and sometimes down to

CANCER OF THE PROSTATE

It is generally agreed by doctors that it is not necessary to attempt special treatment if the cancer remains confined to the prostate gland because it rarely spreads and removal is a radical operation with serious risks.

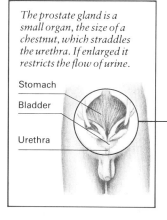

The prostate gland is a small organ, the size of a chestnut, which straddles the urethra. If enlarged it restricts the flow of urine.

Stomach

Bladder

Urethra

Cancer of the prostate does not spread in the same way as other cancers. Symptoms are indistinguishable from those of a benign enlarged prostate and this is a harmless result of ageing. If the cancer is not discovered it may spread to surrounding areas (left). Your doctor will advise you.

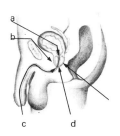

There are four kinds of prostate operation: a, suppubic, where the bladder is opened; b, supra pubic, where the bladder is bypassed; c, transurethral, where a slender tube is passed through the urethra into the bladder; and d, perineal, where an incision is made between the legs.

the bladder. When the blood is examined an enzyme, acid phosphatase, may be raised to confirm the diagnosis.

Unlike some other cancers, biopsy is rarely performed to confirm a diagnosis in a case which is difficult. A biopsy is usually done by passing a surgical knife through a fine tube by the urethra but it's risky. Sometimes, if the diagnosis is very doubtful, it may be attempted through one of the operative routes.

It is rare for a cancer of the prostate to cause symptoms until it has spread through its capsule into the surrounding areas. This means that there are few patients who are suitable for radical surgery. This kind of tumour is fairly resistant to deep X-ray therapy, and treatment is usually based on hormonal therapy. As the normal prostate gland depends on androgens for its proper growth and functions, hormonal therapy can be very successful against carcinoma of the prostate.

It is possible to reduce the secretion of the body's own androgens significantly by giving large doses of oestrogen, up to 30 milligrams of stilboestrol a day. The action of the oestrogen dampens testosterone production. Shrinkage of the cancer usually follows.

About 70 percent of patients will do well with this treatment but it may be necessary to give more than one course. A patient who continues to have difficulty with passing urine may have part of the prostate gland cut away by a small operation through the transurethral route.

217

Cancer of the lower bowel

This is quite common but very slow to develop and it is able to produce unusual symptoms to which you and your doctor should be alerted. It is not a very invasive kind of tumour and could be treated in its very early stages with a good chance of a cure.

Cancer of the rectum is also slow to develop but it may become inoperable because the patient is just too shy to mention rectal symptoms, or believes that rectal bleeding is just trouble with piles. The fault may be with some doctor or nurse who doesn't bother to make a rectal examination for symptoms of diarrhoea or constipation. Warning signs include constipation and/or diarrhoea; blood or pus in the stool; pain in the bowel; anaemia; loss of weight and general ill-health.

Cancer of the skin

This is very slow to develop in older people and it's not likely to spread very far or very fast. Usually, skin cancer occurs in those parts of the skin which have been exposed most to sunlight, and it's especially noticeable in older farmers. One kind of skin cancer which appears on the face, usually near the eyes, is called *rodent ulcer* and it is most commonly a small, raised area with a dark scab in the middle, which forms after bleeding. This cancer responds very well to treatment and will heal with scarcely a mark, so you should seek attention if you ever spot anything like this on your face. If it is not treated, it may cause considerable disfigurement.

Cancer treatment

In the older person, there is probably the greatest chance of a cure from cancer than in any other age group. Because cancers grow very slowly, they can be detected at an early stage and therefore the chances of successful treatment are greatly improved. As we get older we shrink from troubling nurses and doctors with little things, but little things may be the first sign of something which may develop into some serious illness.

The obvious treatment for cancer is surgery, but not all cancers in older people need surgical intervention. There are many groups of drugs which are effective against cancer. The full course of drugs may be long and they may make the patient feel unwell. Some cancers, for instance cancers of the prostate or breast, can be held in check for many months or years by using hormones which do not have a serious effect on the patient's general well-being. It is fair to say that most doctors feel heroic efforts to treat cancer are not usually advisable in the elderly because they are not worth the upsets they cause. Never think that cancer is the end of the world – do be alert for early symptoms and see your doctor. There's no need to feel intimidated by doctors and ultra-modern clinics with their high technology – they are there for the sole purpose of helping us.

Heart disease

One-half of all deaths in most Western countries is caused by *atherosclerosis*, which in turn is responsible for coronary heart disease, strokes and other blood vessel disorders. This condition, whereby fatty deposits cause vessel walls to thicken and narrow, is definitely related to age. It is rare before thirty, but by fifty most of us have some degree of atherosclerosis. It is more extensive in men up to fifty, after which women begin to draw even. The deposits in the blood vessels, or *atheroma*, restrict the blood supply flowing to the heart so that it becomes under strain. Additional burdens are added by physical and emotional stresses which may precipitate a heart attack because the heart is not being supplied with sufficient oxygen. Risk factors have been identified – heredity, diabetes, high levels of fatty substances (cholesterol and triglycerides) in the blood and high blood pressure and cigarette smoking, except for heredity, which cannot be altered, a change of lifestyle can protect everyone against heart disease.

Areas affected by heart disease
Hypertension can lead to a stroke, heart failure or kidney failure.
The tell-tale sign of angina is pain in the centre of your chest or, less commonly, in your arms.
The main symptom of a heart attack is a dull, heavy pain in the centre of your chest.

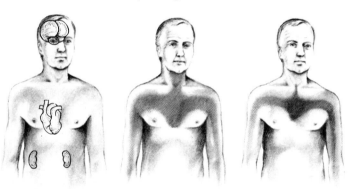

Hypertension   Angina   Heart attack

A heart attack When some of the blood supply to the heart muscle is cut off, a portion of the heart muscle dies from this lack. This incident may be small and never suspected by the person, or it may do significant damage which can be fatal. In the middle aged, the pain can be excruciating and crushing. Older people, however, often experience different symptoms such as shortness of breath and dizziness instead of chest pain. A heart attack is often caused by a thrombus in a coronary vessel, or a blood clot from elsewhere in the body (an embolus), which cuts off the blood supply causing the heart to be thrown out of gear.

Most deaths caused by heart attacks occur within minutes or hours of the attack so that if you show no sign of heart failure or heart rhythm disturbances six hours after the pain disappears, you have a 90 percent chance of recovery. Even after a severe attack, if you are alive one month afterwards, you have a 70 percent chance of surviving five years.

Heart failure A heart which is "tired out" and weakened so that it cannot pump blood around or provide sufficient circulation to the body tissues is said to be "failing". Untreated high blood pressure, coronary artery disease, chronic lung disease, anaemia, infection and alcoholism can be contributory factors.

Treatment is based on drugs which eliminate excess fluids in the body, thus relieving strain on the heart, which increases its pumping ability, and on those which strengthen the heart muscle. Heart failure does not necessarily mean you will be restricted for the rest of your life. You should reduce your physical activities, however, and get sufficient rest to conserve energy, but you should never let yourself become bedridden as this presents a good deal more problems.

Angina pectoris This condition, with classical, brief but severe pains over the mid-chest region which may radiate to one or both arms, the back, neck or jaw, is caused by a temporary inadequacy in the blood supply of the heart muscle. An attack is usually brought on by exertion, emotion, heavy meals or smoking. It goes away with rest, and can be difficult to distinguish from indigestion.

Angina can be relieved by medical treatment with drugs and certain operations. By-pass operations in which the blocked vessel can be replaced by a portion of a vein removed from another part of the body (see below) can be successful, but only if the person attempts to alter his or her lifestyle to avoid worsening the condition.

CORONARY ARTERY BYPASS

This operation relieves pain but it does not cure the underlying cause of the disease. You will be under a general anaesthetic, your breathing and circulation being taken over by a heart-lung machine. The surgeon then transfers a length of vein from your leg to bypass the blocked artery.

Afterwards, a few days in an intensive-care unit will be necessary to check your heart beat.

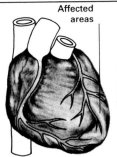
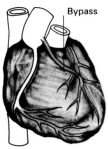

Affected areas — Bypass

Before operation — **After operation**

High blood pressure (hypertension) As we age our blood pressure increases and, if it is very high, it can complicate many other conditions, notably coronary artery disease, and kidney and brain disorders. About 75 percent of hypertensives are over the age of forty, but their condition is not often diagnosed until they are fifty or sixty. It is associated with excess weight, affects blacks more than whites, and men more than women, though after fifty women do complain of it.

The first signs of high blood pressure may be dizziness, headaches and lack of concentration or memory. Salt and stress have been found to be contributory factors as is being overweight. The treatment normally consists of drugs and rest.

Strokes

Diseases of the blood vessels of the brain (the commonest causes of strokes) rank high among our disabilities as we get older. Though not often fatal, they can deprive us of the pleasures of independence and the dignity of self-sufficiency. Responsible for about 12 percent of deaths in Western nations, cerebrovascular disease is exceeded only by heart disease and cancer. Most reports show clearly that there is an increase in the incidence of cerebrovascular disease with increasing age. Although this represents both haemorrhages and blood clots, the major cause is undoubtedly blood clots. The chances of dying as a result of a stroke is related to our age; even when other factors affecting survival are taken into account, the final outcome is worse the older we are and the poorer our physical condition.

Strokes are increasing in number every year, but so is the number of older people. Every year there are over two new strokes for every one thousand of the population. In the UK this means that there are between 100,000 and 120,000 new stroke patients every year.

Types of stroke Even in the acute stroke, the underlying abnormality is a narrowing of the cerebral blood vessels, either by atheroma or arteriosclerosis, which is insidious and progressive, long in advance of the stroke. Most of us think of a stroke as a debilitating illness which may paralyze half the body, disrupt speech, sight and hearing, and virtually leave its victim helpless. This is true of a very few cases, indeed. The term "stroke illness" covers a number of patterns. Below is a list of some of the more common ones.

• A transient and minor attack, say a drooping eyelid or paralyzed side of the mouth, which gets better within 24 hours.

221

- A transient attack of blindness in one eye which gets better very quickly.
- A stroke which is gradually evolving over a period of several days and getting worse.
- A very severe, sudden stroke affecting parts of the brain on both sides of the body so that there is loss of speech, difficulty in swallowing, an unsmiling and staring appearance because the eyelids cannot blink.
- An inability to make co-ordinated movements and a hesitant gait, a condition which does not get better without help.

Strokes are associated with certain illnesses such as anaemia, high blood pressure and a coronary thrombosis. It is always important to ask "Why has this stroke occurred?" If there is an underlying cause, treatment should be directed towards it and not to the stroke, which is only a symptom.

When a stroke develops it may be in an early part of its evolution, making diagnosis difficult. This may prevent urgent treatment and proper investigation and it may not be for several days that the full extent of the damage from a stroke can be clearly seen. Here are some of the grades of disability which can result from a stroke:

- Complete paralysis;
- A flicker of movement;
- Movement is possible when the force of gravity is removed;
- Unaided movement is possible against the force of gravity;
- Movement is possible but weak when it is resisted;
- Movement is normal when compared to the unaffected side.

The amount of damage which is done by a stroke will depend on two things. Firstly, which part of the brain is denied a healthy blood supply – only those functions controlled by that particular part will be affected. Secondly, the type of incident which caused the stroke – either a haemorrhage or a blood clot.

Hemiplegia is the commonest disorder. It is a paralysis down one side of the body, usually the arm and the leg together. The lower half of the face muscles may be affected, too.

Monoplegia is the paralysis of an arm or a leg on its own, meaning that only a small branch of an artery may be blocked.

Hemianaesthesia is a loss of sensation of various kinds down one side of the body. It is much less serious than loss of muscle power, and usually passes off quite quickly. In a straightforward stroke, hemianaesthesia usually occurs on the same side as the paralysis, but less than one in ten strokes has this kind of loss of sensation.

Hemianopia is loss of half the visual field, which is formed when both eyes see correctly. In strokes, it is the same side of the field of both eyes which becomes blind, and the same side as any loss of power or sensation. This is particularly important to know if you are looking after a stroke patient who is unable to see you approaching from the blind side and cannot be interested in anything if it's done on his or her blind side. Such a person is startled by someone unexpectedly appearing in front of him or her from this side, so as a general rule you should try to appear from the sighted side. Usually the central field of vision which is the part used in reading, writing and handwork is preserved and can be used as before.

Cerebral haemorrhage

A haemorrhage is usually more serious than a clot because if the blood pressure is high blood will pour into the substance of the brain doing a great deal of harm. This kind of stroke is usually dramatic, starting off with a violent headache and vomiting and then the person quickly falls unconscious with uneven "blowing" breathing. Usually his or her head and eyes are turned to one side and one cheek is "puffing". Often the neck is stiff and there may be limpness and paralysis down one side of the body.

An *embolus* causes a similarly sudden attack, but probably not as extensive in terms of body involvement. A thrombosis is usually a slower and gentler event.

Cerebral thrombosis

A cerebral thrombosis can come on at any time of day, but it is not unusual for someone to wake up, start to get out of bed, and fall down because his or her leg has lost its strength. Or he or she may be sitting at a table having a meal and suddenly drop a cup or a knife because his or her hand has lost its strength. So loss of conciousness is quite rare. It is fairly common for a stroke due to cerebral thrombosis to develop over several hours.

People suffering a cerebral thrombosis have the best outlook for recovery even though they may be completely paralyzed down one side. Legs usually recover better than arms, and often, at the end of several weeks of treatment, the person can walk without help but only has one effective arm.

It is important that the diagnosis is clear because as there is no haemorrhage taking place with a thrombosis, there is no need to keep the person quiet and in bed. Most physicians advocate a régime in which the person starts getting out of bed the very next day. There is no sense in wasting precious time.

As soon as possible, a physiotherapist should move the limbs through a full range of movement on both sides, affected and normal, to maintain joint mobility and preserve normal muscle

The physiotherapist will patiently teach a person how to move his or her limbs through a full range of movement.

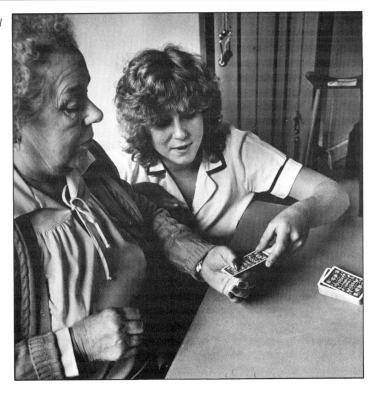

health. These passive movements are so important that they can be taught to husbands, wives, children, friends, neighbours, and anyone else who is interested so that they can be performed repeatedly during the day. They should be taught to the person so that they can be practised while he or she sits in a chair using the sound hand to manipulate the weak hand and arm.

Whenever somebody notices as much as a flicker of returning movement it should be reported to the physiotherapist who will devise exercises to encourage it.

Effects of a stroke   The side of the body which is damaged in a stroke lies opposite to the side of the brain which has been damaged. This is because all nerves controlling movement and sensation cross from one side of the brain to the other before they go into the spinal cord to travel to other parts of the body. It follows that damage in the left half of the brain produces most of its effects on the right side of the body and vice versa.

Dysarthria is a fairly common disturbance of speech which is not confined to stroke cases. It may consist of slurring of words, but the meaning is usually clear enough to us. In severe strokes, involving both sides of the brain, it may be so severe as to make communications extremely difficult.

Aphasia is a more complicated group of speech disorders and it is rarer than dysarthria, but basically there is a failure in the characteristic of certain strokes or other destruction of the brain. This can be exceedingly frustrating to a stroke victim; he or she may get very angry at any apparent stupidity, and that of anyone else in not understanding what is being said. Such a person may not understand that his or her speech may be nonsense to us, and relatives who do not understand the situation may think that this is a sign of mental derangement in the person. They have to be reassured that it is only part of the person's stroke problem. Many aphasic people are quite capable of understanding what is said to them, and it is a common and humiliating mistake to speak about them in their presence assuming that they do not understand. Aphasia is a great handicap. Sufferers have to be cured of it by being taught how to read and use words from scratch, as if they were children. This really is an area which should be tackled by an experienced speech therapist.

Dysphagia is a disturbance of swallowing, so that victims are in great danger of choking and inhaling food or drink. This is as terrifying for them as it may be for someone looking on, and when there is doubt about safety in swallowing, doctors may pass a tube into the stomach. The tube may have to be left in place for quite a long time. Usually, safe swallowing returns.

Emotionalism is a very common difficulty for patients who have suffered strokes. They tend to be emotional and to weep when people talk to them or try to help. A few do the reverse and burst out laughing. This is all part of the stroke illness and has occurred because the normal "brakes" which we apply to all our emotions to keep them hidden are released when the brain is damaged. Relatives quite wrongly suppose that these floods of tears are because they are doing something wrong.

Muscular difficulties   The state of the muscles, whether they are tense or floppy, is dependent on whether the nerves to opposing muscles, which bend and straighten joints, are paralyzed. However, when the nerves and muscles recover, they may not be in perfect balance, so the muscles which bend the joint may be stronger than those which straighten the joint. In this case the arm feels tense and may resist movement. When the opposite happens it stays floppy.

Brain failure

Brain failure, or dementia, has been described as "impairment of memory and personality but without impairment of consciousness". This kind of illness can be the result of a number of causes, with variable rates of progression. In the case of the two commonest forms of brain failure, there is a cause which is thought to be the cumulative effect of small strokes over a long period of time and another, the Alzheimer type, for which there is no known cause. It may run in families and be inherited through genes. A belief which is still commonly held, though quite wrongly, is that once a patient has been labelled as having a demented illness then deterioration is inevitable and early death unavoidable. This is untrue.

Brain failure is one of the greatly underdiagnosed conditions in older people. A survey in the UK has estimated that about 13 percent of the population over the age of seventy-five have a significant degree of brain failure. In a group over the age of eighty, the proportion rises to 22 percent. Cases of pre-senile dementia are not uncommon in the early fifties and there are some cases recorded prior to the age of fifty. Other than the Alzheimer type, there are many other causes of chronic brain failure which are eminently treatable, such as dehydration, drugs, renal failure, an underactive thyroid, diabetes, vitamin B12 deficiency, thiamine deficiency, lack of a good oxygen supply to the brain, sudden isolation, anaesthetics, epilepsy, stroke, chronic infections due to conditions like syphilis and poisons in the form of alcohol.

The symptoms of failure

A fairly typical picture of a person suffering from chronic brain failure would be a man between the ages of seventy and eighty. Everyone who is close to him has noted that he has a failure of memory, particularly an inability to deal with recently-given information. Sometimes worse than this decline in memory is a decline in initiative, and the quantity and quality of constructive activity. Speech may be difficult, there may be frequent repetitions, and favourite stories and anecdotes out of the long, distant past may recur. To personalize this picture even more, he might have been a proud gardener who has become totally apathetic about his favourite hobby. The garden is overgrown and disordered as the seasons go by unheeded, and the diasarray escalates. A lady who has been a proud housekeeper may have a very untidy kitchen where every surface seems cluttered. For her, life is limited to waking, drinking tea, eating bread and butter, and laying utensils aside unwashed until they have to be used again. Making plans for balanced and varied eating by organizing major shopping expeditions which take account of tomorrow and the rest of the week have become a thing of the past. Conversation hardly exists because an exchange with a neighbour about weather, chatting over recent happenings in the district, even discussing intimate details with a relative, will gradually deteriorate to nothing but monosyllables and nods.

One of the things which can be noticed frequently in a person with brain failure is that the mood which has predominated throughout his or her life tends to persist, but such a person has very little flexibility and cannot withstand changes which may be demanded in or outside the home. Sensitive people may therefore feel victimized; a timid person becomes patently fearful, and the life and soul of the party may lose all inhibitions and be bad-tempered and miserable to boot. Any kind of pressure in life which demands a rapid change cannot be dealt with and results in an explosion of hysterical behaviour.

Some unrelated conditions may be confused with brain failure. A patient who is very depressed, having been through a traumatic experience such as the loss of a partner, may give the appearance of being demented. Similarly, someone who is suffering from paranoia or any person who lives alone with no visitors, dim lighting and no other means of communication, may behave abnormally and even be diagnosed as demented, though there is immediate improvement when a social programme is organized and the person is given more psychological stimulation.

One of the best ways of assessing the amount of brain failure in a person is to ask him or her some very simple questions such as those in the questionnaire below. Any number of different questions could be included.

MENTAL QUESTIONNAIRE

This is useful for relatives who notice any strange behaviour in an older person in their family. Many doctors find that it is one of the best methods of assessing the amount of brain failure in somebody.

Name	Mr. John Brown	Name of town	Date of World War I
Age	42 West Street	Recognition of two	(year sufficient)
Time (to nearest hour)	Southsea	persons	Date of World War II
Time of day	Day of week	(doctor, nurse, etc)	(year sufficient)
Name and address for 5	Date (correct day of	Date of birth (day	Name of present
minutes recall:	month)	and month	Monarch
this should be	Month	sufficient)	Name of Prime Minister
repeated by the	Year	Place of birth (town)	Months of year
patient to ensure	Place:	School attended	backwards
that it has been	Type of place (i.e.	Former occupation	Count 1-20
heard correctly:	hospital)	Name of next of kin	Count 20-1

227

Arthritis

This is one of the oldest diseases known. Paintings done by the Neanderthals more than 40,000 years ago illustrate an arthritic relative who is stooped and walks with bent knees. Arthritis occurs in all races at all ages. Just as most functions in the body begin to show measurable decline around the age of thirty so does joint degeneration. All of us over thirty-five and possibly over twenty-five have some degree of osteoarthritis. It also occurs in animals. The diplodocans of the Natural History Museum in London has arthritis in its tail!

Osteoarthritis is a thinning, wearing down or roughening of the cartilage which covers the ends of the bones at the joints. This damage may also be complicated by chemical changes in the cartilage which can cause a joint to become inflamed.

Nobody knows exactly why osteoarthritis occurs, but it does become more frequent as we get older and has been described as part of the ageing process which affects us all. It is unusual for it to show before middle age, except if there is previous injury or prolonged stress to a joint. Other factors, such as being over-weight and having bad posture, are implicated as causes of the condition. It occurs most frequently in those joints which are subjected to the most stress: knees, hips, ankles, feet and hands.

The main symptoms of arthritis are painful, creaky joints. The small joints of the fingers and toes are affected as well as the bigger, weight-bearing joints which take the most wear and tear during life. One of the most familiar places to see osteoarthritis is the final joints of the fingers and thumb. As a sort of defence to the arthritis, the body quite often builds up little pieces of bone around the joints and so you often can see pea-sized swellings at the side of the joints and these are characteristic of osteoarthritis. They are called Heberden's nodes after the man who first described them.

Far and away the commonest weight-bearing joints to be involved are the knees and hips. In the knee you often can hear a grating sound as the rough cartilages grind together. Later on there may be so much pain that the range of movement of the knee is limited. Then there may be loss of stability in the knee joint. I have often heard people say that "their knee lets them down", and this causes them to fall. Just as the joints build bone to form Heberden's nodes in the fingers, they do in the knee, and it may become swollen and deformed and fluid may collect.

The cause of arthritis is not clear. The synovial membrane of a joint gradually becomes inflamed and swollen, eventually leading to inflammation of other parts of the joint. The result can be severe disfigurement as shown here.

Osteoarthritis

Osteoarthritis of the hip is probably the most disabling type of arthritis because the pain and stiffness interfere so crucially with everyday life. It makes getting out of a chair very difficult, climbing on and off a bus very slow, walking up and down the stairs an act of endurance and getting in and out of the bath quite hazardous.

Sometimes it is difficult to pinpoint osteoarthritis in the hip because pain doesn't always occur there – it is often referred down to the knee. The arthritis progresses in exactly the same way as in the knee. There is, however, one ray of hope for anyone suffering from osteoarthritis of the hip. When the joint becomes very stiff and painful, unable to bear weight and causes disability when walking, an orthopaedic surgeon will consider replacing the joint with an artificial one and this can be done whatever your age.

There is no known cure for osteoarthritis. Relief is achieved through the judicious use of analgesics and anti-inflammatory agents. Quite often the initial changes in osteoarthritis cause no symptoms whatsoever, so it is essential that you embark on a life-long programme, certainly from your twenties onwards, of looking after your joints.

If your osteoarthritis is going to be a long-term condition, then your treatment and management should also be viewed in the long term. The mainstay of treatment is pain-killing drugs. Some of the newer ones need not be taken more than once or twice a day, are very effective in relieving pain and help to

HIP REPLACEMENT

Replacing a damaged hip is very common nowadays – the majority of operations are successful. This is a constantly improving form of treatment, the joints being made of metal or a combination of metal and plastic.

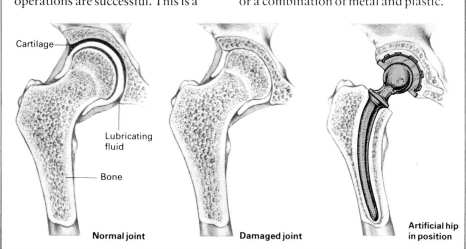

Cartilage

Lubricating fluid

Bone

Normal joint

Damaged joint

Artificial hip in position

increase mobility and strength. Physiotherapy is also extremely important in encouraging full movement of the joints thereby increasing the muscle strength in the limbs, leading to greater stability and mobility. A wider range of movements, particularly for the hip and knee joints, helps to distribute forces such as weight-bearing over a larger area of the joint's surface and this helps prevent the gradual deterioration.

Occasionally, shoulders are affected by osteoarthritis so that they become less manoeuvrable and people suffering from this kind of arthritis are unable to raise their hands up to their head and neck. This means that they lose the ability to dress, to do their hair and to feed themselves.

Rheumatoid arthritis

This is quite different from osteoarthritis. It affects small joints like the fingers, hands, toes, ankles, wrists, shoulders and elbows, whereas osteoarthritis mainly affects large joints. The pain is worse in the morning – the oppposite of osteoarthritis. It's common in women and may appear early in life. Not so with osteoarthritis. There is active inflammation of the lining of the joints (causing them to become inflamed and swollen) and other tissues such as the tendons. It also affects organs other than joints such as the lungs, kidney and heart. It often starts at around forty to fifty years of age, and it is not uncommon for older people to be attacked. Unlike osteoarthritis, we know it is caused by an allergic reaction in the joints. Why some of us develop this allergy is only partly understood.

Rheumatoid arthritis can start slowly, or it may be very abrupt, even explosive. Very often the first joints to be affected are the finger joints but not the same as those in osteoarthritis. In the case of rheumatoid arthritis, it is the middle joint of the finger which is affected and it may become very tender, swollen and "spindle-shaped". Later, the arthritis may affect the wrists, the ankles, the knees, the elbows and the shoulders. The main symptoms are pain, stiffness, swelling, and a loss of the full range of movement. During the early stages pain is usually aggravated by movement and lessened by rest. Stiffness is a problem of the disease as it progresses. It is usually worst in the morning (morning stiffness) and following periods of rest. It usually gets better with exercise. In the long term, people with rheumatoid arthritis may suffer loss of appetite, depression, weight loss and a slowly-developing anaemia. Round, yellowish nodules may develop on the elbow joints and the surfaces of the limbs that are rubbed most.

The aim of treatment is to dispel pain and try to halt inflammation. There are many anti-inflammatory agents now available for the treatment of rheumatoid arthritis. There is a menu for your doctor to choose from and he or she is therefore able to select a medication which is particularly suitable for you. It is generally agreed amongst physicians that steroids are hardly ever used for the treatment of rheumatoid arthritis, though they were used to a great extent in the USA in the past.

The main guiding principle for the treatment of arthritis is a very careful balance between rest and activity to keep joints mobile and in shape. If a joint is immobilized for any length of time, especially if it is in a faulty position, severe disability and crippling can occur. In the active phase, however, rest is essential and the joint should always be placed in the optimum position of rest and function. It is fairly essential to wear light PVC splints which are moulded to the limb, especially for the wrists and knees, partly for comfort and partly also to prevent deformities. Sometimes the joints are so sore that the patient may feel that the weight of the bedclothes is too much and you can relieve this by using a bed cradle.

As the active phase wanes, this may be anything from a few weeks to several months, the physiotherapist will teach you how to carry out a wide variety of exercises to keep you mobile and agile. Generally, your physiotherapist will make sure that the exercises are related to the various activities that you perform during your daily living. They won't only help you when you get home, they will improve joint function and keep your muscles up to strength for a very long time if you keep doing them at your own steady pace.

Gout

Gout is caused by a higher-than-normal level of uric acid in the blood. The first attack of gout usually occurs in middle age, but the kind of gout or arthritis which leads to deformities in the joint is usually seen in older people. The joints which are affected are the big toes, the ankles, fingers, knees, elbows and wrists, the big toe being by far the commonest. An acute attack of gout or arthritis is extremely painful, sometimes described as "exquisitely"painful. It usually lasts about four or five days and then eventually subsides completely, leaving the joint apparently normal. Sometimes, several joints are involved at the same time or in sequence.

Avoid rich foods high in protein and eat carbohydrates.

If you have a number of episodes of this kind of arthritis, it becomes chronic and may deform the joints and limit their movement. It may also damage your kidneys. The treatment of an acute attack is with a strong anti-inflammatory agent such as

231

phenylbutazone or with special gout medication such as *colchicine.* There are other drugs which can reduce the amount of uric acid in the blood, and they are well tolerated in older people. Long-term management of gout will require a special diet from your doctor which is low in proteins and fortified wines, and possibly a maintenance dose of an anti-gout agent, or a uricosuric agent, to keep the level of uric acid in the blood and joints down to a low level.

Osteoporosis

As a person grows older, this condition – the thinning of the bone substance – becomes increasingly common. It is found more often and earlier in women than men: 1 out of 5 post-menopausal women will experience this gradual softening of the bones caused by loss of calcium and protein. This condition is sometimes also linked to the thinning and flattening of the spine's vertebral discs, its gradual curvature and loss of height. Colloquially, this condition is known as "dowager's hump" in women.

Prevention lies in taking calcium and vitamin D supplements; women should do this both before and after menopause, and they may also require a course of hormone replacement therapy (see *Specialist help*) during the menopause. Such treatment can stop any weakening of the skeleton but it will not restore it to its previous condition.

Dowager's hump
Collapsing vertebrae leaves a rounded back.

Osteomalacia

This is a change in the bone which occurs with increasing age due to insufficient calcium being deposited around the architecture of the bone. While it is not confined to any age group, during old age there are many predisposing conditions which can give rise to it and therefore it is not uncommon. Osteomalacia is more common in women than in men and in one study the ages of patients ranged from thirty-nine to eighty-nine, so you can have it while you are still young.

The management of osteoporosis and osteomalacia is well worthwhile in that it may prevent some kinds of arthritis and alleviate others. The most effective treatment for menopausal osteoporosis is sex hormones which restore calcium balance and therefore the health of the bones. In women a régime of female sex hormones will reduce the number of fractures that they suffer on falling and will prevent any further loss in height due to softening and flattening of the vertebral bones. It is also necessary to back this up with a high calcium intake and moderate doses of vitamin D.

Anaemia

As we get older there are remarkably few changes in the blood. For instance, the normal range of haemoglobin is unaltered by age. As it should be 12.0g/100ml in a younger person, it should be exactly the same in someone older and a low reading should never be thought of as simply due to ageing. There are two types of anaemia which are commonly seen as people get older.

Iron deficiency anaemia
This accounts for nearly half of all older anaemic patients. The blood becomes deficient in iron mainly due to blood loss from the stomach or intestine due to a hiatus hernia, peptic ulceration, diverticulosis and haemorrhoids. Sometimes it is due to minute ulceration of the stomach wall caused by drugs such as aspirin, and other medications used for the treatment of arthritis. As ulceration may be symptomless you should always take a specimen of your stool to your doctor. If you are anaemic, he or she can test it for hidden blood which, if found, suggests that you are losing small quantities from the stomach or intestines. If you have had a partial gastrectomy for the treatment of a peptic ulcer this may contribute to your becoming anaemic because of inefficient absorption of iron.

Pernicious anaemia
This is due to the poor absorption of vitamin B12 from your food, it is found in 1 in 10 patients who go to their doctors with anaemia. There is a 1 in 5 chance of someone in their older years suffering from pernicious anaemia without having any symptoms at all.

Treatment
Living with your anaemia means living with fairly long-term treatment or a treatment which has to be repeated on several occasions. Many patients with iron deficiency anaemia relapse after treatment and this is mainly because people forget to or won't take iron tablets by mouth. Make sure that you are not one of these people. A course of six-to-eight weeks on iron tablets should bring your blood back to normal. However, it may be necessary to continue therapy with iron for another three months so that your body can replenish its iron stores.

Iron medication is sometimes complicated by nausea, slight diarrhoea, mild discomfort at the top of the abdomen and some constipation, though these side-effects can be contained by always taking the iron tablet after a meal. There is no harm in halving the dose for a little while until discomfort subsides. Occasionally it may be necessary for you to get iron by injection as this gives a faster rise in your haemoglobin level.

Pernicious anaemia may be quite severe and you may have to go into hospital to have a special blood transfusion. You are committed to having injections of vitamin B12 for the rest of your life. When you start the treatment you have an injection every other day for two weeks which will correct the anaemia and replenish your body's stores of the vitamin. After that you will only need one smaller injection every three months. Supportive therapy for both of these kinds of anaemia is obviously to take plenty of food which is rich in iron.

Parkinson's disease

About 1 percent of the population over the age of sixty has Parkinson's disease to one degree or another. It is due to biochemical and structural changes in certain parts of the brain which control our movements so that they flow smoothly and are well co-ordinated.

A person with Parkinsonism has a combination of tremor, muscle stiffness and a noticeable slowness of movement. The tremor is always worst when he or she is relaxed, and improves when he or she is engaged in some kind of activity. The tremor of Parkinsonism can be controlled by carrying a newspaper or glasses in the hand which trembles most. Such a person's face is often expressionless, arms motionless, and they walk with shuffling gaits without swinging their arms. Their bodies are bent forward with their arms held rigidly at their sides, they rush along with small, shuffling steps – a kind of battle to keep up with themselves. There may be excessive production of saliva, and the skin may be oily due to overactivity of the sebaceous glands.

The treatment of Parkinsonism was revolutionized by the introduction of L-dopa which relieves some of the biochemical abnormalities in the brain. It is very effective in controlling tremor, rigidity and difficulties with movement. L-dopa does not cure Parkinsonism, it only alleviates it. Nor should it blind you to the importance of good physiotherapy and occupational therapy. Walking has to be practised and lost skills re-learned.

Hypothermia

This is a mysterious condition in which the body loses heat and is unable to maintain the temperature balance necessary for normal working. It has been known for many years that even young men exposed to intense cold for long periods experience a severe fall of body-core temperature (the temperature of the vital organs such as the heart, the lungs, the kidneys, the liver and the brain), but it is only in the last fifteen years that it has become clear how widespread this condition is amongst the elderly. Instead of the usual 37°C (98.6°F) temperatures have been recorded as low as 21°C (78.5°F) and there have been many cases in the range between 24° and 32°C (75°-90°F).

At one time it was thought that hypothermia was the result of falls and lying in the cold, and of course these cases do occur, especially if an older person breaks a limb when falling and has to lie there because he or she cannot move. The same thing can happen after falling at night in a cold bedroom, if the victim doesn't think to pull the bedclothes on top of him or herself.

However, recent research has revealed that there are other circumstances in which hypothermia appears. At first there may be a serious illness which, instead of raising the temperature, lowers it, as in sudden pneumonia, and this usually means that the outlook is grave. It can also happen after a heart attack, after using certain drugs, and during strokes. But a very old person sitting quite still in a chair for several hours is sometimes found to have severe hypothermia, as if the heat-regulating mechanisms in the body are suddenly thrown out of action totally without warning.

Symptoms of hypothermia

Hypothermia can cause deaths and is more dangerous than the fall in temperature would suggest. A small drop can be a danger sign in an old person. It is therefore imperative that anyone who deals with older people should know of it and be wary in suspicious circumstances. As a relative of an older person you should be aware of the signs: a cold room and lack of activity, slow and slurred speech, a slow pulse, a small amount of confusion but no shivering. A victim may be drowsy but he or she does not look cold. The face and hands may often look warm and red or purple-red, which tends to throw everyone off the scent. The extremities feel cold but so do the hands of many people in cold weather. A crucial point is that the places which are normally always warm, like the abdominal wall or the insides of the thighs, are as cold as marble.

An ordinary clinical thermometer will read as low as 35°C (90.5°F) at its lowest mark. It doesn't, however, give a reading

235

of the body temperature if it is less than this so it may give a false impression that there is no urgency. If you have an older person living in the house, or even for yourself, you should make sure that you have a thermometer covering the range of 24° to 40°C (75° to 104°F). The best way to check a low reading is to place a low-reading thermometer in the rectum for five minutes.

Emergency treatment for hypothermia is still not satisfactory. Young people can be warmed up fairly quickly without coming to harm, but rapid warming is still dangerous for older people and they may suddenly die as a result. Warming should be carefully controlled at no more than 1°F rise an hour, simply by putting a few blankets on the victim and keeping the room warm but not applying any heat directly.

However, the real answer to hypothermia is practical. Firstly, we must do all we can to help older people keep warm by good housing, good clothes, enough money for fuel, plenty of hot food and, above all, by encouraging them, even bullying them, to move about and generate some of their own internal heat. Secondly, by always being on the alert for the condition which comes on slowly and takes us unawares, and which is so very dangerous. Then it is possible that we might catch the temperature before it falls too low. If the temperature drops no lower than 32°C it may be possible to warm the person up at home, but ask your doctor's advice in any case. At any lower temperature the person should be taken into hospital as quickly as possible where he or she can be treated by experts.

Preventing hypothermia
It's possible to become dangerously cold without realizing it – living environment should have a minimum temperature of 20°C (68°F). This wrap is ideal for long winter evenings.

Diabetes (diabetes mellitus)

There are two main forms of diabetes: one which comes on at any age and is due to a failure to produce insulin in the pancreas; the other is more common as we get older and is due to a "relative" lack of insulin (not a true deficiency) made worse by a high carbohydrate diet, obesity and increasing age. As with other glands in the body, the pancreas becomes less efficient as we age. The amount of insulin it produces, therefore, can become insufficient to cope with the amount of sugar in the blood and diabetes can result. This is especially likely to happen if you are overweight. There is a school of thought which believes that diabetes is the only disease related to excess weight. Heredity, too, plays an important part as nearly a third of diabetics over forty have a family history of the disease.

The symptoms of diabetes are increased thirst, passing large quantities of urine, loss of weight and weakness, but these are rarely present in the more elderly cases and occasionally diabetes is confused with some other conditions such as cholecystitis, kidney failure and heart failure.

There are several serious complications of diabetes if it is not treated properly and kept under good control. High blood pressure, coronary artery disease, cerebrovascular disease and narrowing of the blood vessels to the legs preventing walking from any distance are all commoner in diabetics than in the average population. So are damage to the retina of the eye, glaucoma and damage to nerves in the limbs and face which cause blunting of sensation and weakening of muscle strength. Atherosclerosis develops twice as fast in diabetics as in the rest of the population; and coronary artery disease is twice as common in diabetic men and five times as common in diabetic women. If diabetes is well controlled, a great deal of these complications need not supervene.

Not all diabetics need treatment with insulin. Diabetes which begins in middle or older age can often be controlled simply by restricting the amount of carbohydrates to 100 grams per day. For many others, diabetes can be controlled by taking tablets orally. If you are a diabetic always consult your doctor about cuts, abrasions and bruises on your extremities, and about any serious damage. You should visit the chiropodist regularly and have annual examinations (or more frequent checks if your eyesight is deteriorating) by an ophthalmologist.

If you are sensible you can expect to continue leading a full and healthy life. Do have regular medical check-ups to see that everything is fine and follow the timetable of meals and snacks which doctor advises. Self-discipline is vital.

Do-it-yourself tests
Twice a day you should test your urine for glucose levels. Drop a tablet into a sample of your urine and match it to the colour chart.

237

Thyrotoxicosis and myxoedema

These are the two most common disorders of the thyroid gland: thyrotoxicosis describes an overactive thyroid and myxoedema an underactive gland. Overproduction of thyroid hormones is commonest between the ages of twenty and fifty. It hardly ever occurs in those who are over seventy. Very often the disease goes undiagnosed because its symptoms may be different from normal with ageing, and in the elderly, thyrotoxicosis by no means conforms to the picture drawn in medical textbooks.

Symptoms in the elderly primarily affect the heart and give rise to things like palpitations and insufficient heart function. Mental symptoms such as depression and confusion are fairly common and so is weight loss. Sometimes the most outstanding symptom is a feeling of weakness and fatigue. Contrary to the way it affects younger people, the basal metabolic rate need not be raised and the eyes certainly don't swell and bulge.

Myxoedema is a lot less common than thyrotoxicosis. Mild cases probably go unnoticed, as the sufferers and the people around them think the symptoms are the result of normal ageing. The symptoms are the same in younger and older patients. Most victims suffer from feeling the cold; their voices become lower and croaky; their faces may appear puffy; they suffer from physical and mental sluggishness; they are constipated and probably deaf.

One of the reasons why this condition is missed is that the full picture may take a very long time to develop and therefore gradual change is accepted. It is essential that you take vague symptoms which worry you to your doctor, and if he or she doesn't mention it, ask about the possibility of an underactive thyroid. Only in this way will you help to prevent serious complications developing.

Diverticulosis

This, the presence of diverticula, and diverticulitis, inflammation in the diverticula, are rare in young adults and tend to increase from age forty onwards. If you are prone to diverticular disease, the overall number may increase with age. Women are affected more often than men.

Diverticula are tiny balloons of intestinal lining which burst through the muscular wall of the intestine. They are usually about 1 or 2 centimetres long. Faecal material can collect either in or at the mouth of the tiny diverticulum and block it off and then it may become infected and ulcerate. The commonest symptoms are bouts of bleeding with constipation, diarrhoea and left-sided lower abdominal pain in between. Most complications are rare.

To look after diverticular disease, you should go on a high residue diet and possibly obtain antibiotics from you doctor. You can bulk up your diet by using bran on food and in cooking, and eating some stringy vegetables like cabbage or parsnip each day. The skins of peas and beans are good too, and have some fresh fruit with the skin still on, say an apple or a pear, every day. This is exactly the opposite kind of a diet recommended when I was a student, but it's absolutely correct.

Ulcers

Duodenal and gastric ulcers reach their peak in middle age. In younger people pain can be the predominating symptom, but as we get older there may be no symptoms at all, or they may be unexpected, like weight loss, anaemia and painless vomiting. The first symptoms of an ulcer, at say sixty, may be due to a chronic ulcer developed at forty. If an ulcer appears for the first time when you are sixty, the outlook for a complete cure is very good. Very often the symptoms of an ulcer are very mild such as a loss of appetite, a general feeling of malaise and some slight discomfort at the lower end of the breastbone. The temptation is to treat yourself with antacids, which can lead to a dangerous delay in an accurate diagnosis.

The most serious complication of a long-standing peptic ulcer is haemorrhage. If you have a peptic ulcer you should watch more and more carefully as you grow older for a black, tarry stool which almost certainly means that you had a bleed from your stomach. If you ever vomit blood, be it bright red or very dark red, you should contact your doctor immediately. A haemorrhage from a peptic ulcer in an older person should be considered an indication for immediate surgery. Very small haemorrhages over the long term can lead to quite a severe iron deficiency anaemia (see page 233). If you are becoming anaemic, a peptic ulcer is slightly different in older patients than in younger people. Bed-rest and a special "gastric diet" have been shown to be fairly ineffective in older people. In the long term, smoking should be avoided; antacids can be used to relieve the pain, but not freely – only in the quantities prescribed.

Nowadays there are some newer treatments which promote healing. One is *carbenoxalone* and the other is a very new, highly effective medication called *cimetidine*. Both of these treatments are only available on prescription and when you are on them you should be carefully monitored by your doctor with regular check-ups.

Hiatus hernia

This becomes more common as we get older because the tissues inside our bodies become slack. When the opening in the diaphragm, which lets the gullet (oesophagus) pass through from the chest into the abdomen, becomes slightly enlarged, it is possible for a small part of the stomach to slide up through into the chest. This encourages reflux of the acid contents of the stomach which in turn may cause some soreness, inflammation and ulceration at the end of the gullet. Hiatus hernia is usually a long-term complaint and sufferers are going to have to get used to a fairly long régime of medical treatment.

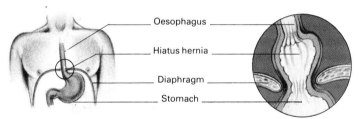

Oesophagus

Hiatus hernia

Diaphragm

Stomach

Hiatus hernia occurs when the abdominal portion of the oesophagus protrudes upwards through the hiatus into the chest-cavity.

It's quite common as we get older, especially if we are overweight. The main symptom is usually heartburn or perhaps regurgitation of acid fluid.

You should sleep with the head of your bed raised and avoid stooping. Reduce the size of your meals, especially those which you eat late in the evening. If you are overweight you should diet. Other than these things, you can get drug treatment from your doctor, cimetidine, which is also used for the treatment of peptic ulceration. You should take antacids prescribed by your doctor four times a day after meals. This will relieve many of the symptoms due to a reflux of oesophagus. These measures usually cure hiatus hernia, but if it persists your doctor may advise surgery to repair it. This involves a relatively simple operation after which you will be able to return to work and continue with everyday activities within a few days.

Mouth disorders

It is not uncommon for older people to complain of a sore tongue or mouth ulcers. These may be due to trauma from sharp or irregular broken teeth as well as other causes such as a vitamin deficiency, anaemia and possibly other blood diseases, as well as plain ordinary aphthous ulceration and infection. Treatment should be directed towards the cause of the ulcers.

Aphthous ulceration, which can be quite extensive as we get older, will respond to pellets containing hydrocortisone which can be sucked. These are very effective in relieving pain.

Sometimes a sore tongue is due to drug therapy or to an infection in the mouth. The commonest infection by far is monilia (candida albicans) which is known to most people as thrush. It is quite common if antibiotics have been taken for long periods by mouth. If you can see white patches on your tongue, throat or on the inside of your cheeks, it should make you suspicious. Ask your doctor to confirm the diagnosis and he or she will take small specimens for culture from the mouth and throat and give you nystatin as pills or lozenges.

Jaundice

Not an affliction found particularly in older people, jaundice is a fairly common sign of liver disease. It can be part of an inflammation of the liver such as occurs with infective hepatitis; it can be due to the effect of toxic drugs, or cirrhosis. Jaundice is not necessarily a sinister sign. More than half of its sufferers will get completely free of their liver complaints.

Jaundice is nearly always due to a gall stone blocking the exit from the gall bladder. An older person who has one or more attacks of jaundice due to this cause, and confirmed by special X-ray tests, should be considered for surgery to remove the blockage. A newer method of treatment is to try to dissolve gall stones of the cholesterol type by giving medication in the form of bile salts. Treatment is continued for about six months.

Cirrhosis

This is the terminal state of liver injury and decay. The liver becomes very small, hard and lumpy, and is unable to function properly. It is irreversible. Alcoholism (see page 61) with its long-term dietary deficiencies is far and away the most important and serious cause of cirrhosis. The liver can be rested and further damage halted by giving up drinking. Continued assault to the liver will inevitably lead to liver failure, coma and death.

Gall stones

Gall stones are responsible for about a quarter of all attacks of abdominal pain. In the fifties and sixties gall stones are more common in women than in men, but after seventy there is no difference in the sexes.

The most common symptoms of gall stones are nausea, indigestion, a feeling of queeziness after eating fatty meals, vomiting and bouts of cholecystitis. Gall stone pain usually occurs just below the edge of the rib cage on the right hand side and it may go up to the point of the right shoulder.

Gall stones can be removed by surgery, but for patients over the age of sixty doctors prefer a more conservative approach. If you are overweight you will be asked to lose weight. Then you should avoid all fatty foods and you should take antacids. You can eat carbohydrates and a lot of protein, however. Surgical removal of the gall bladder, with the gall stones, is only considered when the condition is acute, very severe or life-threatening.

Antacids Antacids neutralize acid in the stomach and so relieve indigestion and heartburn. They also control the pain from a duodenal ulcer. We all have a tendency to over-use them.

● Read the constituents on the packet before purchasing. Avoid anything which contains more than 115 milligrams of sodium in the maximum daily dose.

● Don't take anything which contains aspirin, phenacetin, or caffeine as these may irritate the stomach; phenacetin damages the kidneys when taken in the long term.

● Antacids which contain calcium carbonate can cause constipation and raise the calcium levels too high. They can also promote production of acid in the stomach.

● The two safest antacids are aluminium hydroxide and magnesium hydroxide. Aluminium hydroxide has no limits on dosage and it is slow in its action, but it usually gives prolonged relief. Its major undesirable effect is constipation. Magnesium hydroxide is efficient and it is safe but it does cause diarrhoea.

● Anyone with a kidney problem should not take more than three teaspoons of milk of magnesia a day.

Constipation

This can be a common accompaniment of ageing, but it doesn't have to be. The causes are many and varied: an unbalanced diet with lack of fibre and bulk; lack of exercise; overusing aperients and ignoring the emptying reflex. Another problem is the psychological attitude of many people today that a daily bowel movement is essential for health. This, of course, is not true, but as people become older and more self-absorbed in their bodies, this preoccupation with constipation increases so it seems that nearly every elderly person complains about it.

No laxative, aperient or cathartic is perfect or harmless and it is generally thought that their regular use can do little good and a lot of harm. One of the dangerous effects of laxatives is to prevent absorption of important vitamins from the diet. The body's mineral balance can also be seriously affected by laxatives. Most over-the-counter preparations containing kaolin and pectin should be left on the shelf because their effectiveness is questionable. They could be said to be a waste of money because they do very little good.

Occasionally, constipation in older people results in faecal impaction. The faeces become hard and relatively immobile due to the slow passage of bowel contents and the excessive absorption of fluids in the large bowel. Then the hardened faeces becomes moulded by the movements of the bowel and stay firmly in one place. As we get older we become more unaware of the bowel reflex when the rectum becomes full. Sometimes the faeces become round and pebble-like so that they may even resemble gall stones. In almost 100 percent of cases the faeces impact in the rectum.

Treatment for constipation

As far as managing your long-term constipation is concerned you should be reassured that a regular bowel action can be achieved with the appropriate treatment. First of all you must drink quite a lot of fluid to keep the motions soft. You must add additional dietary fibre to your daily diet if it mostly contains refined carbohydrates like bread, cake and chocolate biscuits. You can do this by simply adding bran to semi-liquid dishes such as porridge and cereal, and you might even try putting bran into your cake mixes. Alert your doctor that you have a tendency to be constipated as there are certain drugs which are known to make it worse and these should be avoided. Only very gentle laxatives should be used for the treatment of long-term constipation, but if the faeces have become impacted it may be necessary to use suppositories or an enema, repeated if this is needed, to dislodge the hardened stool.

243

Haemorrhoids

These are present in the majority of people over the age of fifty. They can be internal, inside the anus, or external, projecting from the anus. Haemorrhoids are really varicose veins of the rectum and they are caused by prolonged over-use of laxatives or enemas, having to strain at stool, chronic coughing, or, in women, by pregnancy.

There are many preparations on the market which claim to treat itching, swollen tissues and promote healing. However, there is very little evidence that these products actually do what the advertisements say they do. Always get a specific treatment from your doctor prior to using over-the-counter preparation.

Treatment for haemorrhoids This comes in two forms: suppositories and ointments. Nearly all suppositories contain local anaesthetics such as *lignocaine* or *benzocaine*. These should never be applied to the skin as they may cause an allergy. Chemicals which shrink the swollen tissue are also available, one such is *ephedrine*, and there are also antiseptics. Suppositories frequently move up the rectum after they have been inserted, and therefore away from the area which they are supposed to be treating.

One of the best ways to treat haemorrhoids is to get at the root cause, for instance a chronic chest cough, and at chronic constipation or laziness of the bowel by bulking and softening the stool. Doing this is far more effective.

Cataracts

All of us, it has been said, would develop cataracts if we lived long enough. The stage beyond yellowing is the formation of opacities in the lens so that it is no longer transparent. This interferes with the passage of light to the back of the eye, the

A cataract is the progressive clouding up of the jelly-like substance which forms the lens of the eye. In severe cases, the total lens may be affected, making the pupil in front white. Effects on vision differ depending on the extent and location of the cataract but they can blur direct vision.

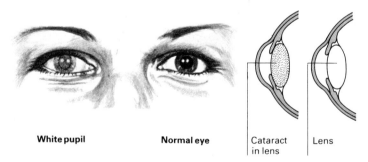

White pupil   **Normal eye**   Cataract in lens   Lens

retina. Depending on the number and severity of the opacities, a person will find his or her vision blurred and dim. From the age of forty onwards, nearly all of us find that we need a brighter and brighter light to read in.

Lens opacities cannot be dissolved away, but surgical treatment is extremely effective and safe. The lens with the cataract is removed. This is an operation normally performed under local anaesthetic but fearful patients may require a general anaesthetic. Such an eye becomes very far-sighted and lenses are required to correct the vision; these may be glasses, contact lenses or plastic lens implants.

As cataracts are eminently treatable and will not lead to blindness, there is no need for anyone to be needlessly frightened by the entirely false belief that cataracts will be severely disabling. Though your vision will not be completely restored to normal – cataract glasses have quite thick lenses so that objects appear magnified and seem closer than they really are – it is just a question of you adjusting.

Glaucoma

The second most common disorder of the eyes as we grow older is glaucoma. This is a condition of an abnormally high fluid pressure within the eye. It has nothing to do with cancer or high blood pressure and so it need not spell doom. Go immediately to your doctor when you suffer symptoms so that they are recognized and given proper care, attention and treatment. If you are alert to the first symptoms of glaucoma, even the smallest loss of vision can be prevented.

The symptoms of glaucoma include blurred vision, dull pain in the eye, watering of the eyes, nausea and headache. Another early warning sign is the appearance of "haloes" around electric lights. Glaucoma usually starts after forty, and leads

When the eye is normal (right) fluid, aqueous humour circulates in order to drain it via a drainage channel. If the channel becomes blocked (centre) there is a build-up of fluid. An iridectomy can be performed on the eye to produce an artificial channel (far right) through which the fluid can drain.

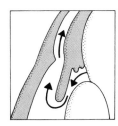
Drainage channel

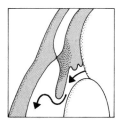
Obstruction

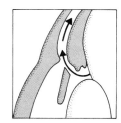
Artificial channel

245

to the gradual loss of peripheral vision if it goes untreated. This means that we find ourselves bumping into things or not seeing things on either side of us; not seeing a passing car is a common complaint. All this results in "tunnel vision". If glaucoma is left untreated, the peripheral vision gets less and less until we can only see what is directly in front of us. This can eventually lead to total blindness.

Acute (angle-closure) glaucoma is treated by surgery which removes part of the iris to allow pressure to be equalized; chronic (wide-angle) glaucoma is treated medically with eye-drops or tablets which reduce the secretion into the eye.

Since glaucoma is easily detected, it is very important that from our forties onwards we have annual eye examinations to check the angle between the iris and the cornea and the internal position of the eye. You should ask your doctor which is the nearest hospital with a special eye clinic.

Varicose veins

This condition is not restricted to a particular age group, but it is quite common in older women who have borne children. Varicose veins are aggravated by occupations which involve a lot of standing. Such veins are raised and twisted and stand out from the back of the leg between the knee and ankle. They have very thin walls and contain a large volume of blood so that they can be easily damaged and may cause haemorrhaging.

If you have varicose veins, you should wear elastic stockings or support hose, especially if you are doing a lot of standing. Take them off when you go to bed or sit down with your feet up, or when you go out for a walk. These stockings help to keep blood from pooling in the legs.

Varicose veins can be treated with injections containing irritating solutions which produce inflammation. The body responds to such inflammation by creating scar tissue which stops the high-pressure backflow of blood through the vein and reduces swelling. Seriously overweight patients, and those with extensive varicose veins or ones which extend to the groin, should be treated surgically. Two procedures – stripping and tying off – are available. Stripping involves passing a wire along the length of the vein, and tying off involves cutting out the vein.

Irritating dry brown patches may appear on the lower part of the leg which can form into an ulcer. These ulcers must be treated immediately by a medically-qualified person before they develop into something more dangerous.

PUTTING ON SUPPORT STOCKINGS

It is important that you see your doctor before using elastic stockings or support hose because in some instances they can be dangerous. They should have open toes – to allow your toes to breathe comfortably.

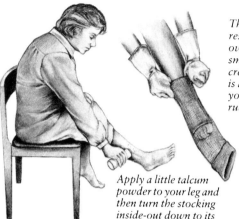

Then, slowly draw the rest of the stocking over your leg, smoothing out all the creases as you go. This is a good deal easier if you wear pimply rubber gloves.

Apply a little talcum powder to your leg and then turn the stocking inside-out down to its foot and pull the foot portion over your toes.

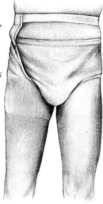

A thigh-length elastic stocking with a waist attachment for a man.

Shingles

Shingles, caused by herpes zoster, can bring real disability as we get older. It is an infection of the nerve roots by a virus which is linked to childhood chickenpox. It is remarkably common among late middle-aged and older people and it can make them quite ill over a long period.

It causes intense pain in the area which has been affected. This is then followed by a severely blistered rash which takes 10 to 14 days to disappear. The rash is distributed in a sharply marked band over the area of the affected nerve.

In the elderly the head and face, including the eye, are quite often affected and the pain can be intense. Worse still, the pain or acute tenderness may persist for many months or even years after the rash has gone. This causes great misery and depression almost to the point of suicide. To make things worse, treatment of this post-herpetic pain is notoriously difficult.

One of the things which can be done is to make sure you avoid going near small children suffering from chickenpox – even your grandchildren. If your eye is affected by shingles, seek expert advice from an ophthalmologist urgently.

247

Falls or drop attacks

Falls become more common as we get older. The following are some of the causes:
- Accidents (about a third of all falls);
- Insufficient bloodflow to the brain;
- Drop attacks;
- Heart and blood vessel disorders (such as high blood pressure, irregular heart beats, coronary thrombosis);
- Dehydration;
- Anaemia;
- Osteoarthrosis;
- Any disorder which makes the gait shuffling and stumbling. (e.g Parkinsonism).

Accidental falls

Cervical neck collar
This is comfortable to wear and it will prevent any sudden neck movement.

These may be caused by minor paralysis or stiff joints, but more often they are due to poor home conditions such as worn-out floor coverings, trailing wires, and insecure stair carpets and rods. All these, coupled with failing vision and poor lighting, increase the risk of our falling, especially if we are inclined to wander. As we get older, our control of swaying gets less, and this means that we find it more difficult to correct a false movement once we have committed ourselves to it.

Insufficient blood supply to the brain occurs as the result of an osteoarthritic change in the vertebral bones of the neck. The blood vessels supplying the part of the brain which controls many of our movements is filled from an artery which runs through a canal between the bones. Any degree of osteoarthritis in the neck vertebrae causes narrowing of the bony canal. As it occurs in nearly all old people, it's not surprising that the supply to the brain is diminished in all of us as we age. Classically, it causes a sudden loss of balance directly following rapid neck movements, and one of the ways of controlling attacks is to limit the amount of movement of the head and neck. This is best achieved by wearing a full cervical collar during the day and at night substituting it for a soft collar.

Drop attacks

These can occur in anyone, including the young, but the kind experienced by people as they get older is a specific entity. First of all the falls are sudden – there is no loss of consciousness or any other symptom. Some older people will simply say that they found themselves on the ground, and they may have had considerable difficulty in getting up although they seem to be able to move all their limbs perfectly well. Once they are standing, however, they can walk away as if nothing had happened. Doctors think that this kind of drop attack is caused by temporary loss of the mechanism which keeps us standing up straight. The reflexes can be restored fairly rapidly if we can press the soles of our feet against a wall.

One of the most serious side-effects of a drop attack is that it destroys confidence and prevents going out, even locally to the shops. Occasionally, following a drop attack, a person is unable to get back onto his or her feet. This is risky if a person lives alone, so he or she should know how to get up from the floor without help. In a cold environment there is the added risk if someone has to stay in this position for a length of time.

Trigeminal neuralgia

This excessively painful condition is almost unknown under the age of fifty. It is a condition causing severe "lightning" flashes of pain in parts of the face supplied by the trigeminal nerve, namely the cheeks, nose and mouth. Attacks are typically brought on by cold, wind, movement, eating and touching the trigger area during shaving, etc. Quite often a victim feels in real dread at the possibility of firing off an attack. He or she may even not wash his or her face, or eat, lest it starts off the pain.

This is a difficult condition to treat but one new drug, *carbamazepine*, is sometimes helpful. If the pain is unremitting, it is possible, under general anaesthesia, to inject a small amount of an anaesthetic into the nerve root which may keep the person completely free of pain for about two years. Then the injection has to be repeated.

Headaches

Older people are not commonly headache sufferers so any kind of new headache must be carefully investigated. It is not always true, as some people say, that migraine sufferers improve and have fewer attacks as they grow older. A headache could be symptomatic of several things: that a stroke is about to occur; or depression which needs treatment; or renal failure; or as a side effect of certain drugs. Most important of all, a persistent headache in the forehead or temples raises the possibility of an inflammation of the blood vessel which runs up the side of the face and often looks a bit lumpy and tortuous as we get older. This can be treated very effectively with new drugs, so help from doctors should be sought.

Special hazards and unexpected happenings

One of the things that happens to our bodies as we get older is an inability to cope with change and debility. So a severe fall which puts us to bed may be complicated by a chest infection if we get a minor cold. In our younger days our lungs would have been capable of putting up a stronger defence.

Leg vein thrombosis

Clotting of the blood in the deep veins of the legs is a well-known risk of general and gynaecological surgery, but recent research has shown that it occurs so often as to be frightening and it is worthwhile doing anything we can to prevent it from happening in the first place.

Basically, thrombosis (clotting) is caused by a lessening of the pumping action of the leg muscles which normally send the venous blood back to the heart. The blood becomes static. This is more likely to happen as we get older because we may lie quite still for a long time. In addition, existing heart disease may have reduced our blood circulation – a contributing cause of a leg vein thrombosis.

Such a condition is bad in itself, but one of its worst complications is that the clot may become detached from the leg, so that it passes to the heart, and thence immediately to the lungs where it will cause failure of the blood supply there. This condition, *pulmonary embolus*, will cause a sudden urgent attack of breathlessness, blueness of the skin and chest pain. These attacks can be fatal in people of any age, but the older we are, the greater the danger, and it is one of the most common causes of sudden death as we go from middle into older age.

The warning signs that a thrombosis may be occurring in one of our legs is that there will be swelling and the legs will be of disparate sizes. There may be a blue discoloration of the skin, and coldness. Another common symptom is pain in the calf and along the inner side of the thigh. You should know what to look for and to pick up early signs and keep a watch out for them. At the same time, you can keep your legs moving – bending and straightening your knees for say, ten or fifteen times every hour, though only a little exercise can be enough. You can also do leg and foot movements of all kinds while you are in bed and leg swinging over the edge of the bed. A bed cradle will help because your legs will then not be restricted, but pillows should not be put under your knees or thighs. Breathing exercises and taking plenty of fluids also help.

A bed cradle will prevent your bedclothes pressing on any painful areas on your legs.

Thrombo-phlebitis This is quite a different condition. It is an inflammation of the veins near the surface of the skin, and such an area becomes swollen, tender, red and warm. It does not carry the risk of embolism and for this reason is much less serious.

Pneumonia

Almost everyone knows that older people who lie down for any length of time are prone to get pneumonia. This is due to a combination of pooling of the secretions in the lung, the possibility of infection, and poor ventilation because of shallow breathing. It is a very good reason for trying to keep older people out of hospital and at home because it can spread round a ward of frail people like an infectious disease, especially in the winter when there is an enclosed atmosphere.

Pneumonia can occur quite severely in a matter of hours and your doctor may advise that you go into hospital for a while but he will certainly advise cough medicines and antibiotics.

Dehydration

This is one of the diseases of deprivation. It is also one of the hazards of being ill. We have seen already that the older we get the smaller the reserves in our kidneys and they need ample water to work. Many older people get into a habit of drinking very little, especially women. This may be for domestic reasons, if there is an outside lavatory or garden privy, they may be reluctant to use it in bad weather. Some people with a tendency to be incontinent imagine that they will lessen the problem by drinking less. In fact, the reverse is true. If there is very little urine flushing out the bladder, there is a tendency for it to become infected and for cystitis to develop.

Older people who go to bed feeling ill may not feel like getting up to make themselves a drink. The danger of dehydration is much worse if there is diarrhoea and vomiting. In an older person, dehydration will come on all the more quickly and there may be a very serious deficiency of water and salt. Both invalids, and those who care for them, often do not understand the need for fluids. Fears and instincts about incontinence may suggest cutting down fluid intake. When you are ill you may have a constant battle with yourself to drink enough but both you and the people who look after you must win it.

Epileptic attacks

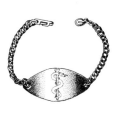

Most people suffering from epileptic attacks have fits through all of their lives and still go on having them in old age. However, fits can come for the first time as we get older, and they must be fully investigated. Most often these fits turn out to be the result of narrowing of the blood vessels in the brain but other things have to be ruled out. One must always be on the alert for a stroke or a heart attack that first appears as a fit.

It's a good idea if you are an epileptic to wear a bracelet with the condition printed on the back. This will alert people if you have a sudden attack.

The epilepsy may take two forms: *grand mal* and *petit mal*. The major epileptic attacks usually start with sudden unconsciousness, rigid muscles, breath holding and a bluish-grey colour of the skin, and then jerking movements which gradually subside. It is essential to keep the airways clear. Minor epilepsy is momentary. The person may stop what he or she is doing, look vacant and then carry on. This kind of epilepsy is not very common in older people but when it does occur the absences can last much longer than in younger people.

Hysterical fits

These are quite different and easy to distinguish from epilepsy. Sometimes they may be a way for an older person to register a protest against something which displeases him or her, but it is not put on just for show. An hysterical person does not consciously understand the reasons behind the attack. He or she is quite likely to be noisy, dramatic, make strange movements or writhe on the floor. However, the person never hurts him or herself. These dramatic turns can be likened to temper tantrums in children and they are best treated in much the same way – by walking away.

Simple fainting

Fainting happens quite commonly in older people as a result of pain, oppressive heat, psychological stress, severe anaemia or unexpected internal bleeding. If none of these conditions are at the root of the problem, recovery is usually quick, though not as quick as in younger people. Fainting should never be dismissed lightly in later life, because it usually has a specific reason and treatment may be needed, so you should ask your doctor's advice as soon as you possibly can.

Little strokes

People with narrowing of the arteries of the brain are sometimes liable to have attacks where they may feel a weakness of a limb or loss of vision, lose their speech, or perhaps feel giddy and faint, but the attack passes away very quickly. They are alarming for everyone and they may be an early sign of a more serious and lasting stroke.

Abnormal hypoglycaemic attacks

These attacks are due to a *serious* fall in blood sugar and when they occur the victim feels cold, sweats and becomes unconscious very rapidly. Attacks occur in diabetics (see page 237) who have been given too much insulin or who are not eating the full diet which has been prescribed for them. Hypoglycaemic attacks can, of course, occur in diabetics of any age, but they are of special importance in later life because often heart attacks and strokes come on at the same time. Hypoglycaemia must be carefully avoided and it is better for older diabetics to show just a little sugar when their urine is tested to stay on the safe side.

It has become fashionable, particularly in America, to suffer a hypoglycaemic attack whenever one feels dizzy, lightheaded and weak. Physiological hypoglycaemia, that is when we are hungry, needs no treatment. It is self-correcting and should not be interfered with. Medically correctable hypoglycaemia is very rare, and should only be treated by a physician.

Giddiness

Giddiness, or vertigo, is one of the most common of all our symptoms as we get older and very often the feelings are difficult to describe. The older we are, the greater the chance of our experiencing vertigo. Women are more likely affected by this condition than men.

There are many possible causes and often we never get to the root of the matter. Wax in the ears, ear disease, high and low blood pressure and also certain drugs are amongst the commonest and there are links between vertigo and deafness, and one particular type called *Ménière's disease*, which has a preponderency in people, particularly men, over the age of

253

about forty-five or fifty. Ménière's disease is an acute and violent type of giddiness of deaf people in which the patient has a sensation of spinning and vomiting and every movement is a nightmare. It is due to disease in the balancing organ of the inner ear, and can be treated successfully with certain new drugs from your doctor.

Accidents

Accidents are an increasingly important cause of death and disability among the older population. In 1974 nearly a quarter of the total accidents occurred in only 10 percent of the population who were sixty-five or over. Furthermore, approximately 70 percent of all fatal falls, 30 percent of all deaths due to fires and 25 percent of all pedestrian deaths caused by motor vehicles, occurred in the same 10 percent of the population. For people aged sixty-five to seventy-five accidents were the fifth most common cause of death at a rate of 77 per 100,000 population, which is just ahead of the 75 per 100,000, the death rate for pneumonia.

However, there is a silver lining to these statistics; the death rate from accidents among those in the sixty-five-and-over age group has fallen more than 30 percent since 1964. This is due, at least in part, to the fact that as we get older we do pay more attention to staying fit, mobile and alert. Of all fatal accidents which occur in the UK, 43 percent occur in our own homes; 25 percent occur as motor vehicle or pedestrian accidents; and a further 31 percent occur in public places or hospitals.

Deteriorating vision, hearing and balance, combined with dizziness, the possibility of drop attacks, unsteady gait, less mobile joints and stiff muscles, all contribute to accidents. Drugs, of course, may also disturb our balance, bring on symptoms of Parkinsonism, affect our hearing and make us unsteady on our feet. Some medications have been attributed to causing accidents.

Accidents involving older people seem to occur at a particular time of day – most of them between 6 a.m. and 12 noon. This corresponds to getting up and out of bed, dressing, and the period of greatest activity for most people. Accidents then decrease during the afternoon hours when many of us will be taking a rest and there is a moderate increase between 5 and 9 p.m. which corresponds to dinner and going to bed. Very few accidents are reported between 9 p.m. and 6 a.m., when we are probably in bed. Of those that do occur during the night, about

30 percent are due to falls when the person tries to get out of bed. Of these, 15 percent were when the person reached for an object on the bedside table and more than half while the person was walking in the room or to the bathroom.

This emphasizes the importance of vigilantly taking precautions to prevent accidents.

Burns and scalds

Burns and scalds are so frequent in older people living at home that everyone should be taught about preventive measures. Here are some potentially dangerous situations:

• Smoking in bed or in an easy chair, especially after drinking alcohol, may cause fire and death;
• Forgetting to turn off the hot water or a gas jet;
• Fire spreading rapidly from the kitchen to the bedroom of a split-level house;
• Having casement windows which are often too small for escape if there is an emergency;
• Ovens in wall units frequently don't have adjacent counter space on which to place hot and heavy utensils which are being removed when cooked;
• Loose clothing may be caught in the flames of a gas jet;
• Hot kettles may be touched or dropped;
• A modern stove with complex dials and controls may be confusing to many people (see *Adapting your environment*).

Fractures

These are markedly different in older people. Usually it takes a considerable amount of violence and a direct injury to break the bone of a younger person. In contrast, fractures in the elderly result from minimum or moderate violence and the site of the fracture is usually right next to a joint rather than the shaft of a bone. Fractures of this kind are more likely in women than in men, especially fractures of the hip, the lower end of the forearm and the vertebrae in the spine.

Research has shown that fracture of the neck of the femur (the thighbone) is dependent on the amount of bone present in it. It can decrease below a critical level with osteoporosis (see page 232). In addition, 20 percent of women and about 40 percent of men who fracture the neck of the femur are also suffering from osteomalacia (see page 232). This, in turn, varies with the season of the year, it being highest in February to April and lowest in October to December in the Western hemisphere. The obvious conclusion is that the variation in the hours of sunshine is responsible for the seasonal change, and this makes vitamin D deficiency a very important factor. As we get older, it is not hormones which we need to keep our bones healthy, it is vitamin D and calcium, both of which can be prescribed for us by a doctor.

Fractures of the wrist are affected by age and sex; they are common in young boys and girls but uncommon in adults. There is then a steep rise in women as they get older, but this is not the case with men. This is thought to be due to a hormone deficiency syndrome related to the menopause and it can be corrected with hormone supplements (see *Specialist help*). In older age, crush fractures of the vertebrae become more and more common. This fracture causes a compression of the softened spinal bones and most authorities believe the primary cause is osteoporosis.

Surgical treatment

It's not surprising that most of us are afraid of surgery, after all, most of us are squeamish at the sight of blood. There are always risks with surgery, but they are getting lower and lower for everyone. Surgery in older people is a matter of balancing risks, and yet many older people themselves are convinced that surgery has a doubtful chance of success, and feel that operations will be dangerous "at any age". Of course, no-one can operate on a patient without consent, and no-one should try to put pressure on a person to accept surgery if he or she is against it. But it is important to realize what surgery can and cannot do and not be unduly afraid of it. In fact, nearly 1 in 10 older people who enter hospital benefit from surgical treatment.

Our aim is to arrive at the age of retirement in the best possible health, and it is true that some surgical correction is better done in our forties and fifties when problems are much smaller, rather than our having something done much later in life as an emergency. Examples might include abnormalities of the feet, hernias or arthritis of the hip. Of course, we have to have the courage and foresight when younger to appreciate what the disability might mean in later life.

There has been a tendency in the past for many doctors to be conservative in their treatment of older patients. A major operation was thought inadvisable except if there was a real emergency and surgery was the only answer. Even now we do not advise operations for trivial conditions, and very rarely simply for cosmetic purposes. Nevertheless there have been notable advances in anaesthetics, in surgical techniques and especially in the pre-operative preparation of patients and their post-operative care. The hazards are, therefore, much less serious than they were. Now, it often happens that a new operation is devised and used for younger, resilient patients successfully, after which its use is extended to help older people.

The aims of surgery for older people are not quite the same as for people who are younger, nor for that matter are the aims of rehabilitation. A young person wants a total cure so that he or she can appear normal and as inconspicuous as possible. On the other hand, many an older patient's main purpose is to have restored to him or her as much capability and comfort as possible in the circumstances, and the result may be a long way from perfection. It must not be despised for all that. Doctors who have a broad, humane outlook give countless benefits to older people, but the surgeons who are perfectionists look upon an older body as already past being able to benefit from their skills. These doctors are not of much use to the elderly.

Fractures and surgical wounds

These heal very well in older people if the circumstances are right; the main one is having a well-nourished body. Anaesthetics these days have much smaller risks than they did even a couple of decades ago. As an older person is most at risk if he or she is inactive and confined to bed, it is important to get the person into an upright position as soon as possible.

The patient's viewpoint

This, our viewpoint, should be considered at all times. It is not surprising that we are very cautious about radical treatments. When we were younger the risks of surgery were very much higher than they are today, and many of the operations which we now consider to be simple did not even exist. Often we cannot be expected to judge these chances and we have to be advised. Certainly we have a right to know how bad the risks of operation are, and it is only fair that we know. In an emergency state, the sort of thing we need to be told is "the risks are so-and-so, but if the operation is not done the likelihood is such and such". It is also necessary to be told what will happen after the operation, and as some doctors neglect to do this, it is as well to have another, maybe a younger person, to go with us to see doctors, so that they can insist that we be given information which is our right. There is nothing more annoying and worrying than not knowing what is going on around us.

257

Here are some reasons why operations are performed for older patients:
• Real emergencies where immediate life-saving is the object.
• An operation to save life but which does not necessarily have to happen immediately – it could be delayed and a good moment chosen for us to have it.
• An operation which might cure the condition and also might not – and only time will show.
• An operation which will not cure, but which would help with the very severe symptoms, e.g. pain.
• An operation which might make a patient more mobile, speed up recovery or reduce the risk of complications.
• Planned operation simply for comfort.

What surgery can do for older people

It used to be that people beyond a certain age were virtually disqualified from having surgery. With improvements in anaesthetics and surgical procedures this is no longer so. At any age being able to have surgery is more dependent on your fitness than anything else. So keep fit, don't deny yourself surgery.

Abdominal surgery Almost any known catastophe in the abdomen can strike as we get older. Emergency operations are quite common and quite serious when they are performed on unhealthy people.

Some conditions are quite common, like the perforation of a diverticulum in a patient suffering from diverticulitis (see page 238), or twisting of the bowel so that the blood supply is cut off. As I have already mentioned, many of the classical signs of these illnesses and conditions, like perforation of the stomach from a peptic ulcer, or acute appendicitis, or strangulation of a hernia, are often not present and the diagnosis can be misled. This means that it is very important for you to take all complaints about abdominal pain seriously, and have a medical opinion.

Many of the abdominal operations can be planned ahead and carried out with safety and success. These include operations for gastric ulcers, for narrowing the outlet of the stomach, for removal of the gall bladder due to repeated attacks of infections or gall stones, and operations for slow-growing tumours in the colon or rectum. Colostomy is feasible for an obstruction of the lower bowel (see page 259) and it also helps in the treatment of diverticulitis, after which a diet with bran is advisable.

COLOSTOMY

A colostomy is a surgical opening made in the front of the abdominal wall. Through this, material from the colon, or large intestine, is passed.

One performed on the left side of the colon, shown here, passes solid material, because more liquid has been absorbed from the food during digestion. A colostomy on the right side of the abdomen discharges liquid faeces which is passed through the stoma into a bag.

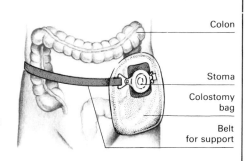

Colon

Stoma

Colostomy bag

Belt for support

In the area of gynaecology Apart from dealing with cancer of the uterus and ovarian cysts, surgeons are often asked to help women with less serious conditions such as stress incontinence. This is the trickling loss of urine which only happens with coughing or straining. Because of increased pressure in the abdomen, there may be complete prolapse of the uterus which is distressing and also comparatively common (see page 170). As women get older, elaborate repair operations are often not feasible, but there are very simple procedures which can give complete relief from a uterine prolapse to make a woman more comfortable.

One small and simple operation involves inserting a silver wire into the wall of the rectum to prevent a prolapse which "comes down" repeatedly. This symptom causes a great deal of distress, particularly to the frail, older woman, who is the most likely victim. Such a simple operation entirely cures a rectal prolapse when she would otherwise have to stay in hospital, and perhaps even in bed, because sitting up caused the prolapse always to be "down" and therefore uncomfortable.

Hysterectomy

Hysterectomy involves surgical removal of the uterus. In some forms of hysterectomy other reproductive organs may be removed at the same time, such as the cervix and the fallopian tubes. When a complete hysterectomy is performed the ovaries are removed too, an important fact for you to know before you have your operation because it means that your monthly cycle of female hormones will stop forever. This means that you are going to need replacements of those hormones, hormone replacement therapy.

About 25 percent of all women fifty and over have had hysterectomies in the USA. Quite often, and particularly in the USA, hysterectomy is performed for comparatively trivial reasons such as the removal of small fibroids. There are even some American doctors who advocate routine hysterectomy once child bearing is over and now there is a growing fashion for prophylactic hysterectomy to prevent a cancer developing. I see no good reason for this last operation unless there is clear medical indication that this is necessary such as very heavy and frequent periods or suspected cancer. Removal of the uterus is one of the greatest losses that a woman can suffer both physically and, more importantly, psychologically.

Reasons for hysterectomy
There are several reasons why hysterectomy may be advocated by your gynaecologist: to remove cancer in the vagina, cervix, uterus, fallopian tubes and ovary; or to treat severe and uncontrollable pelvic infections. Under some circumstances a hysterectomy has to be performed to stop severe and uncontrolled bleeding. These are the kinds of life-threatening diseases where hysterectomy is absolutely necessary.

There are some other pelvic conditions which affect women where a hysterectomy is one of the treatments to be considered. These would be extensive and very painful endometrioses, large or multiple fibroid tumours, injuries to the pelvic musculature at childbirth which are severe enough to interfere with bowel or bladder function, recurrent and severe attacks of pelvic infection and vaginal bleeding which is so heavy that anaemia results. These cannot be controlled with hormone treatment so your doctor may recommend hysterectomy.

HYSTERECTOMY OPERATIONS

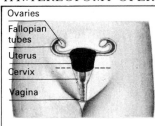

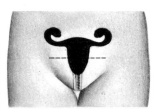

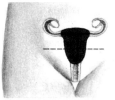

Ovaries
Fallopian tubes
Uterus
Cervix
Vagina

Total abdominal hysterectomy and vaginal hysterectomy
This is removal of the uterus and the cervix through a horizontal incision in the lower abdomen. Alternatively, an incision is made in the vagina.

Complete hysterectomy
This involves removal of the uterus, cervix, fallopian tubes and ovaries through a transverse incision in the lower abdomen.

Sub-total hysterectomy
This operation is not done very often because the cervix on its own has no essential function. The uterus is removed but not the cervix, ovaries or fallopian tubes.

TIMETABLE OF RECOVERY AFTER HYSTERECTOMY

WEEK 1	WEEK 2	WEEKS 3-4	WEEK 5
You'll be encouraged to get out of bed in one or two days. You may have pain and discomfort from wound. You may find urination difficult (tell the nursing staff), you may need an I.V. drip for 24/36 hours until you take solid food, then minor wind pains.	Home at 7 to 10 days. Don't stay in bed but take it easy. No moderate activity, e.g. walking ½ mile for three more weeks. Can walk up-stairs, sit in garden. Don't carry any weights or lift anything heavy.	Gradually increase activi-ties and take rest periods rather than rest most of the time and being active occasionally. Go to bed early. Try slowly making the bed to see if you can stretch a little (STOP IF ANY PAIN).	Start moderate activity – going to the shops and doing light shopping, do light housework, walk the dog. Go to the hair-dressers. Do gentle exercises. Stop if you feel tired.

WEEK 6	WEEK 7	WEEK 8	WEEKS 9-10
Do mobility exercises every day plus some strengthening exercises. You may still feel tired at end of day so rest with feet up for 15-20 minutes. Start bending gently but not to floor.	You should be back to full normal activity. Con-tinue exercises. Sexual intercourse safe and possible. Rest once a day with feet up.	You can go back to work if it's sedentary. The rest of your life should be entirely normal. Don't bend to floor. Don't lift.	You can safely bend fully and lift.

You should talk to a gynaecologist in some detail about the need for your hysterectomy and ensure that you are satisfied. in your own mind that it is absolutely necessary, that you want to have it done and that your partner agrees with you. Never forget that hysterectomy is an irrevocable step. Once it is done you are sterile. If ovaries are removed you will have an artificial menopause after the operation and you may well suffer menopausal symptoms. Some women fear that they may put on weight after hysterectomy but this is absolutely untrue. You will only put on weight if you eat too many of the wrong things; a diet rich in protein, fresh vegetables and fruit will help you to recover and give you sufficient energy to undertake exercises.

Sex after hysterectomy Quite a few women are concerned about their sex drive and how much enjoyment they will derive from sex. Research has shown that neither need be affected if the operation is done well and if a woman *wants* to have the operation. Just as many women experience an increased sexual drive as experience a lessening. If you find after a hysterectomy that anatomically you are not able to have intercourse, you should consult your gynaecologist immediately and ask for rectification. Another effect that women are scared about is depression. Hysterectomy is notoriously connected with post-operative depression. Research has also shown that this is not true. Only women reluctant in the first place get depressed.

Orthopaedic surgery

This branch of surgery offers great possibilities because it can correct deformities, relieve pain, and improve a person's chance of walking. Successful replacement of diseased hip joints has been done for twenty-five years or more, and now artificial replacements of the knee joints are becoming more and more feasible. They are likely to be suggested for older people who are crippled by a type of osteoarthritis which causes great deformity, pain and a limitation on activity. Broken hip bones – a very common injury, especially in women as they get older – can either be "fixed" with nails and plates, or replaced entirely so that the patient can be walking again in a fraction of the time it took formerly. The old days of full-scale hospital nursing for broken legs extending over many weeks, patients strung up with a network of suspension and traction apparatus, risking innumerable life-threatening complications, are virtually over.

Other helpful orthopaedic operations include corrections of foot faults of all kinds. There is help for patients whose limbs are crippled and distorted from rheumatoid arthritis. Usually, contractures and tendons are severed to correct foot drop and to allow permanently bent legs to be straightened, so that a fresh start in walking can be made.

Neurosurgery

As we get older we may be prone to tumours and other abnormalities within the brain or spinal column which need surgical treatment. Most of these tumours are *not* malignant, but nearly all of them require detailed investigation. Other important areas in which neurosurgery can help older people are the treatment of the severe pain of trigeminal neuralgia (see page 248) and the cure of blood clots in Parkinson's disease (see page 234) which grow larger and may prove fatal if they are not surgically removed.

Genito-urinary surgery

Even in quite old people it is possible, indeed it might be essential, to remove a kidney which has been destroyed by stones or riddled with infection. After all, it may have ceased to be an effective kidney some time ago, so the remaining kidney is presumably keeping pace with the extra load, and its capacity is really quite easy to test. Surgery is possible, too, for bladder abnormalities and cancer. Otherwise it is the prostate gland which offers the surgeon a full field for action.

Surgery of the blood vessels

This part of surgical work is making great strides forward and opportunities are opening up for older people, in whom artery disease is widespread. It is possible to replace parts of diseased blood vessels with artificial grafts. Large arteries like those of the leg can have grafts or by-pass operations done at low risk.

Surgery has a lot to contribute to preventive medicine in the older patient. For instance, certain sorts of strokes can be treated with grafts or by-pass operations, thereby preventing further strokes. If special X-ray techniques show that there is obstruction to the arteries in just one place, the obstruction can be removed by opening the vessel and "coring it out" just as one might core out an apple.

Plastic surgery No doubt older people consult plastic surgeons in order to give themselves an appearance of youth (see *Specialist help*). Apart from this use of surgery, there are many other ways in which plastic surgeons will save lives and correct gross deformities for instance, by treating serious burns, by removing skin tumours, by correcting eyelid deformities which become commoner as we grow older, and by removing obviously disfiguring or painful blemishes like sebaceous cysts or fatty tumours. Plastic surgeons are often needed to help in treating some varicose leg ulcers or for providing covering skin grafts for large pressure sores.

Pain relief Research into pain pathways and the setting up of pain clinics have resulted in a number of effective treatments for relieving intractable pain, especially in older people. Some older patients can benefit from these advances and the possibility should always be kept in mind.

In the past, surgeons cut pain-conducting tracts in the spinal cord. Now it is quite common for injections of alcohol or other drugs to be made into the spinal cord so that immediate and, we hope, permanent pain relief can be given. These techniques are most often studied and perfected by anaesthetists.

Amputation Most of us would see the necessity to have a part or a whole of a limb amputated as being the end of the world but there are many examples which show that it is not the case. A large number of patients who have suffered the misfortune of an amputation walk again with help, thanks to a good artificial limb and plenty of encouragement. Even double amputation need not be a total disaster. There was a case reported of a splendid lady who, at the age of ninety-one, had her two legs amputated, and was taught to walk again on two full length artificial limbs with no-one supporting her.

Everyone deserves the chance to adjust psychologically and emotionally to the prospect of losing a part or all of a limb, and to build up a positive approach to post-operative rehabilitation. Therefore, I feel that every person should be given sound psychiatric counselling so that he or she can get used to the idea.

Living with long-term ailments

When you, or someone close to you, is chronically sick or disabled you have to adapt your lifestyle to cope with it. This can be difficult. We all have to learn to live with our bodies when they are no longer as young as they were; only unhappiness can result from unrealistic expectations and placing heavier burdens on our physical and mental resources than they can bear. On the other hand, there is no reason why you shouldn't look ahead positively; there are ways to prevent a chronic ailment from completely dominating your life – no ailment need do this if you take care of it thoughtfully.

Chronic ailments not only affect the person involved, they also have a significant effect on offspring – often themselves middle-aged adults, who may be suddenly confronted with financial, emotional and moral problems. Deciding whether to keep, and then look after, an older person in our own home, or to try and support them in theirs or in an institution, is difficult. Institutionalization is stressful for both the person and the relatives. Grandchildren can be affected by stressed parents, and by reduced family finances. An incapacitated, sometimes disorientated, incontinent and crotchety grandparent in the home, instead of a loving and generous one, is particularly disturbing for children.

Fifty onwards is a significant stage in all our lives and our state of health can be at its most divergent. You may or may not be quite fit and healthy; you may have a partner or parent to care for who is less than fit; you may be interested to find out how to cope better with a chronic ailment should it occur. Therefore, where appropriate, I have addressed myself directly to the reader as the concerned party. However, where I feel the information is more likely to be of use to you as a "caretaker" of others, I have worded it more generally.

Chronic heart disease

Heart attacks   If you are recovering from a heart attack you will need to rest and possibly reorganize your usual activities until your heart muscle is healed. Several weeks of strict rest may be ordered. However, many physicians now mobilize heart patients sooner than was customary in the past. Your doctor may order chair

265

rest if you need long periods of relaxation; while you cannot be more active in a chair than in bed, sometimes the upright position is more comfortable. It allows for easier breathing, it prevents pooling of blood in the lungs and it may improve the efficiency of your breathing. These measures will considerably ease the workload on the heart.

Although rest is important for a person who has had a heart attack, you should never allow yourself to be labelled as an invalid. You should be encouraged to join in physical and social activity as soon as recuperation is complete, even though it may be somewhat limited. The degree of mobility you have will be an important way of measuring your improvement, both to you and your family, doctors and nurses. Prolonged bed rest is dangerous in that you may begin to feel hopeless, and more importantly, it can lead to complications such as weakness of the muscle, the formation of blood clots, particularly in the legs and lungs, and bed sores.

After the acute phase of a coronary thrombosis you will probably be looked after at home unless home care is impossible. You and your family should be told clearly that you have had a heart attack, and be reassured that home care is best. In this instance, your family doctor and the community nurse and health visitor have an important role to play in keeping up your morale. If you do have to stay in hospital then the most comfortable place is a ward of the district general hospital where you will find the pace slower, and where routines are geared to the needs of others of your age. In a busy general hospital you may get a bit depressed and even frightened at all the activity which is going on twenty-four hours a day. We all feel vulnerable when we are unwell.

Whether you are at home or in hospital you should be encouraged to become mobile as soon as possible. From the beginning you should sit up in a chair and use a commode. Doctors now feel that early mobilization decreases, rather than increases, complications after a coronary thrombosis. For instance, if you pass a stool into a bed pan you put a great strain on your heart, thus you should not be allowed to use one unless you find that it is absolutely necessary.

If, after your heart attack, you are suffering from a recalcitrantly slow heart rate and it doesn't respond to drug therapy, then the treatment of choice for you may be an electronic pacemaker. Most doctors agree that age and ill health are not contra-indications to having one fitted, and you should only be denied a pacemaker if your general mental and physical health is so poor that you would not enjoy the benefits of having one. Your doctor will advise you on this.

PACEMAKERS

Pacemaker operations are relatively common these days. In Britain each year, one person in every 20,000 has one implanted and in the USA, one person in every 4,000, so if your doctor recommends one it is no cause for alarm.

A pacemaker is a device which sends a stimulating current to electrodes in contact with the heart muscle. It has a small generating unit powered by a battery which lasts three to four years, though nuclear-powered pacemakers are now being tested which will last a great deal longer.

If it is not intended for long-term use then the generating unit can be attached to a belt. Alternatively, it can be implanted under the large muscle on the left of the chest.

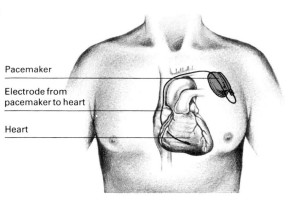

Pacemaker

Electrode from pacemaker to heart

Heart

Angina Angina pectoris, or chest pain associated with heart disease, becomes less of a problem as we grow older. Quite a lot of people who are troubled with angina in their fifties lose it as they age further. It is unusual for people who get chest pain to feel incapacitated, probably because they take little exercise. The symptoms can be controlled, and to a certain extent pre-empted, by putting a tablet of glyceryl trinitrate under your tongue whenever you feel the angina coming on or if you intend to do something strenuous in about a half-hour's time. This occasionally may reduce your blood pressure and you may feel a bit dizzy. Certain new drugs called *beta-blocking agents* will reduce the workload on your heart but they may also cause dizziness. It is far better, however, to rely on sensible advice and support from your family, doctors and nurses than from tablets. For example, a home help can be used to do the shopping, the heavier housework and the cooking for you, rather than you doing it and needing a tablet to manage.

Hypotension Sometimes, as we get older, we become hesitant, rather confused and shaky when we stand up even though we are bright and co-operative and alert when sitting in a chair. The reason is that blood pressure is normal when we are sitting down and falls as soon as we stand up. This is called postural hypotension. There are several practical things which can be done

267

to prevent this fall in blood pressure: you can lessen the risk by getting up very slowly from a chair or bed; your doctor or physiotherapist can give you a set of exercises which will help you to prevent your blood pressure falling suddenly; elastic stockings and corsets will prevent pooling of blood in the lower legs or abdomen, and your doctor may consider salt-retaining drugs which are sometimes helpful.

Hypertension Treatment for hypertension must relate to your own problems and the effect that high blood pressure has on you. There is no blanket solution. Treatment has to be tailor-made for you, and any drugs should be carefully and slowly adjusted according to *your* particular response. There are a variety of drugs which can be used with the aim of keeping your blood pressure down, and not causing side effects. One of the commonest is a diuretic agent which makes you pass quite a lot of fluid and gets rid of excess liquid in the body, thus giving your heart and lungs an easier job to do. Bear in mind, however, the possibility that you may have some pre-existing urinary incontinence (see pages 291-293). A diuretic may make this worse and your doctor should take this into consideration. There is very little point in treating one condition if it is going to make another any worse.

Treatment All patients with chronic heart disease will have to cope with
régimes three main types of treatment.

Drugs
If you suffer from such conditions as hypertension and angina pectoris you will be on long-term drugs; you will probably have to live with them for the rest of your life. If you are suffering from angina pectoris, for instance, you will have to carry around with you a supply of glyceryl trinitrate. You may also have to go on long-term anti-coagulant drugs which thin down the blood and lower the risk of a clot forming. This will require not only taking medication, but going to hospital for regular blood tests to make sure that your blood is just the correct thinness to allow your heart to function properly.

Diet
If you have heart disease, be it arteriosclerosis, atherosclerosis, high blood pressure or angina pectoris, you will probably be put on some form of diet, one which mainly restricts foods containing cholesterol (cheese, eggs, smoked salmon, etc.) animal fats, and the amount of salt you take. You will have to live with this diet for the rest of your life. It is not so bad, you can still have treats, though stopping cigarette smoking in one fell

swoop can do more to ensure that you don't have another coronary thrombosis than any other single thing. Alcohol, on the other hand, in moderate quantities, is quite good for you. Any man will live longer for taking six glasses of wine a day, a woman three glasses, rather than remaining abstemious.

Exercise

The modern approach to treating heart disease is to make sure that your body has plenty of exercise – exercise that raises the pulse rate to 120 beats per minute for two minutes a day and puts all your joints through their full range of movements. Being over-protective about yourself, considering yourself an invalid and moving only short distances slowly will do you more harm than good. Don't be over-cautious!

Strokes

People with strokes probably do best at home. A person having a stroke is nearly always insecure and therefore it is vital to adopt positive attitudes to counteract natural fears. Hospital admission will depend on the severity of the stroke and the availability of help and rehabilitation in the home or at a nearby hospital outpatients' department.

The people who have looked after the victim in hospital should be in close touch with all those who will care for him or her at home. There should be a medical assessment of the person in your home. The need for any structural adaptations to the home (see *Adapting your environment*) can be requested from the appropriate department of the Local Authority. To be of maximum benefit, adaptations must be carried out quickly, ideally before the patient goes home, and of course with his or her agreement. You should make certain that any health visitors and therapists continue visiting all stroke patients returning home. Problems can then be highlighted at an early stage, and measures taken. Some people may be unable to take care of themselves, and accommodation in private or Local Authority residential homes or continuing care hospitals may be necessary for their own security and peace of mind.

Recovering from a stroke

Almost two-thirds of people who have had a stroke will recover spontaneously: half within the first week or two and the remainder somewhat later, but still to a point where they are capable of independent self-care and return to home. It is worth having a very positive attitude in looking after a patient with a stroke, encouraging him or her to have an optimistic outlook, to be determined and to practise exercise – both physical and intellectual – as often as possible. Even a proportion of those people who seem severely disabled can progress to self-care and a degree of independence.

It is important that someone who's had a stroke is set realistic goals; these should be reviewed frequently to make sure that they are being achieved. If they are not, the situation may be reassessed. A simple grading system may be used, but it is probably better to describe goals in terms of what activities can be done, such as turning over in bed, sitting up alone, standing up with help, etc. A stroke victim must be encouraged to do things for him or herself rather than to have them done for him or her. Try to resist the temptation to help. It's better to encourage a person to achieve a goal – which may be to feed him or herself – even though this may be a rather messy and protracted procedure.

Initially, movements are developed in bed, followed by exercises out of bed aimed at retraining lost balance and function of the body. When these are developed, the person should be able to stand unaided and then to progress to walking. Once the person is able to walk it is important that he or she should walk to the lavatory. This small achievement confers disproportionate self-confidence.

People who are suffering great difficulty with their speech and pronunciation should have an assessment by a speech therapist as soon as possible, and speech therapy should be started. It is quite important that we test to see whether a person can communicate by writing or using a typewriter as this is a separate skill, though closely related to reading and speaking.

Some stroke victims appear to be unco-operative and a bit awkward. This may be only apparent to us, not intentional. It is the understandable result of someone's inability to hear and co-ordinate movements. A common defect after a stroke is loss of position sense, so while the person may have remarkable muscle power in, say, making a punching movement into your open hand, this is of little help if he or she doesn't know how to use it and control it. Also, the brain can receive false messages so that a paralyzed limb does not appear paralyzed to the person who has had a stroke, and he or she is unable to recognize the paralysis without being told. Another strange situation is when a person with a stroke can only receive information on the side which is not paralyzed. If you wish to speak you have to walk from the affected side to the unaffected side, as though you had gone through a door to get to the person's consciousness in order to be understood.

Exercise therapy

At first, occupational therapy may have to be confined to, say, only the good arm, but as some activity starts to reappear in the other hand and arm, effort has to be concentrated on encouraging their activities, however small they may be. The weak hand, in particular, should work at squeezing a soft rubber ball, a roll of plastic foam, or a piece of plastic putty. Only at a later stage, supposing hand/arm recovery is proven to be unlikely, should occupational therapy be concentrated on making it possible for a person to live, dress, cook and manage generally with the remaining normal hand. At an early stage the person should be fully dressed in his or her own clothes and good shoes. He or she can now do no end of bed drills by placing the feet against a board and pulling him or herself up and down from a chair, by using the bed rail or a specially-raised T bar. This is one of the first steps to independence and it is vitally important for morale. Even more important are the first steps in walking after doing trunk and leg extension exercises on the bed to strengthen those "lazy" muscles.

Patients with strokes can benefit from, and enjoy, organized class work. They can take part in competitive activity, perform group exercises, play indoor ball games and indulge in other activities which encourage particular muscle movements in a cheerful, competitive team spirit. Nursing staff, relatives and family, and possibly even neighbours, should be involved in this activity, encouraging, congratulating, showing sympathy but remaining equally optimistic, and seeing that the types of activities which patients are taught are continued in the ward, in the bathroom, at the wash basin and, of course, when the patient is rehabilitated at home.

Once at home, the patient should be helped through a range of normal daily activities with the physiotherapist and the occupational therapist, so that performance can be recorded. If any aids such as sticks or gadgets are necessary, they should be provided. There is a great variety of aids for eating, cleaning teeth, putting on clothes, stockings and shoes, lifting, cutting bread, reaching for distant objects, and generally making independent life possible for people whose recovery may only be partial, a selection of which can be seen on page 272.

Any remaining needs that are required in the home, and gadgets that the patient may require in order to lead a semi-active life at home, should be supplied by the Local Authority. Many adaptations can be made to the house to make it more comfortable (again, see *Adapting your environment*).

Each person has to capitalize on existing abilities so that useful movements can be developed. Being satisfied with impaired function of "what's left" must be rejected.

A specially-raised T-bar enables exercise in bed.

271

AIDS FOR THE STROKE SUFFERER

This is a small selection of some of the aids which can be bought easily to help day-to-day living or perhaps adapted from existing things you already own.

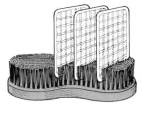

Tray
A handle on a tray will prevent spillage.

Rolling pin
A one-handed rolling pin can be easily adapted from one more conventional.

Cards
An inverted kitchen brush allows all playing cards to be visible at a glance.

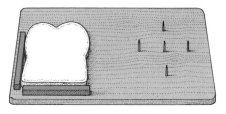

Cutlery
A deep bowl or a plate guard prevents food from sliding off the plate and it should be used with either a combined knife and fork or a pusher-spoon.

Breadboard
A spiked board is useful for cutting and buttering bread and for peeling potatoes. It should have a non-slip base.

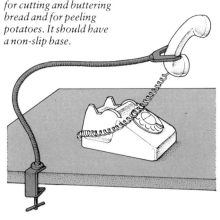

Telephone arm
This clamps on to the edge of the table (right) to hold the receiver.

Bookmark
This will keep the pages flat for reading.

Helping with recovery

Anyone who's had a stroke, even if he or she has made a good recovery, is still "at risk" from accidents, further strokes, and other problems associated with hardening of the arteries such as hypothermia (see page 235). Regular follow-ups and visits will be essential. As a relative you should consider short-term or intermittent hospital admission as a method of management, not only to relieve yourself of excessive burdens of care, but also to ensure that optimum performance is being achieved.

The treatment of stroke illness in the elderly is one of the most demanding and challenging aspects of medical care, both by the professions and families and friends. The attitudes to the disease by the patient, his or her relatives and therapists, play a vital part in recovery. Greater success will be achieved if everyone shows realistic optimism. Complete recovery for a stroke is not instantaneous – full rehabilitation is usually only achieved after a period of two or three months or even longer. For this reason, the admission of a stroke patient to an acute medical ward with a rapid tempo is often inappropriate. Several hospitals have special units specifically designed for the management of strokes. With the concentration of everyone's skills, the results have been most encouraging. With the development of new aids the future looks more promising.

TIPS TO HELP SOMEONE RECOVERING FROM A STROKE

- Adopt an encouraging, positive approach, but avoid artificial praise. If you are relaxed and unhurried this, in turn, will reduce the person's apprehension and tension considerably.
- Keep your own speech simple and slow, but never childish. Unless the person was deaf before his or her stroke, there is no need to raise your voice.
- Encourage the person to talk and give plenty of time for response. Do not put words into the person's mouth.
- Let the person know when attempts at speech are successful and encourage the person to continue. Minimize correction and criticism at all times.
- Difficulty with speech does not mean that the stroke sufferer has lost any basic intelligence. If speech is difficult, try showing objects and pictures and encourage the person to point to the things that are wanted.

- Place clothing where the person can easily see it. Later, if there is a partial loss of vision, you may try to help the person and learn to compensate by moving the clothes slightly out of their range of vision and getting them to turn their head.
- Start dressing on the bed and progress to the sitting position on the side of the bed or chair. Be sure that the person has plenty of support.
- Put a full-length mirror in the person's room so that they have an opportunity to observe mistakes made in dressing and to note improvements.
- Try to get the patient to dress themselves so that they are satisfied with their appearance.
- Keep background music to a minimum, for instance, from the television or radio. Watch out for minor distractions that preoccupy the stroke sufferer.

CLOTHING AIDS

Selecting clothing is a very personal process and there is no reason why this should change for somebody who is suffering from a stroke.

Clothing aids encourage a person to accept much independence.

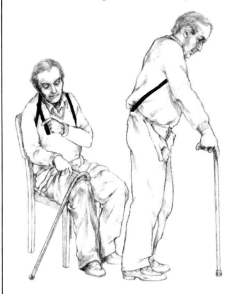

Velcro can be used to adapt buttons, cuffs and, as shown here, ties. Remember to choose clothes in light-weight and stretch fabrics.

Use braces to pull up trousers or put loops on to underwear. This is often the most difficult stage of dressing.

Make sure that shoes support your feet well. Elastic shoe laces may be bought or the one-handed method learnt.

Cancer

It seems presumptuous to suggest how a person might cope with the task of facing life with cancer and come to terms with the possibility of imminent death. Living with cancer is surely more about living with oneself than anything else, and it would be wrong of me to interfere with that personal process. Doctors are often of help in spiritual matters but not, I think, in illnesses of this kind. You will find much greater strength and warmth from religious and spiritual cousellors, who have had a great deal of experience, than from anything I can possibly say.

If one considers practicalities, I would refer you to page 282 where I suggest quite a lot on making confinement to bed as comfortable as possible.

There are several other ways that we can provide assistance to a person who is dying from cancer.

• Never pretend the patient isn't dying. Always make conversations open and honest. Try to share the responsibility if the patient sees dying as a crisis.

• Always make sure the patient has contact with other people. Concentrate on making these times as rewarding and as fulfilling as you possibly can under the circumstances.

• Help the patient to suffer grief at the loss of family and friends but make sure good relationships are retained with a clear idea of what the days hold.

• Encourage the person to accept the situation with dignity and integrity in this immensely difficult time, something that will become increasingly difficult as time goes by.

• Try not to let negative views creep in. Keep up the person's self-respect. Try to avoid personal shame and deprecation. The important thing is to help a person towards death as they would wish. Everyone's death will be different, but it can be appropriate to them, and this should be borne in mind at all times.

It is important, however, that the patient understands the truth about his or her condition and its implications. Though there will be worries about the pain and discomfort that lie in the future the person can be reassured that much can be done.

Chronic arthritis

How well you learn to live with chronic arthritis and get the best out of life has as much to do with your attitude of mind as anything else. The same amount of joint disease can cause complete disablement in one person and hardly any in another. We all know people with chronic arthritis who are agile and sprightly, do their own shopping, ride bicycles, and do all their own housework. The people who succumb to arthritis and let it rule their lives are self-pitying, are using their condition to appear helpless and to gain sympathy from others, and feel negative towards themselves, the arthritis and to the world around them. If you try to be the other kind of person you will feel that life improves almost immediately, and you are capable of doing a great deal more than you ever thought.

Some of us can lead quite normal lives without having to make any alterations to our homes. Sometimes, simple things like making use of duvets or electric blankets, instead of heavy comforters, can make a great deal of difference. There are also many specially-designed gadgets available (see page 276).

275

AIDS FOR THE ARTHRITIC

It is quite possible to lead a normal life no matter how chronic our arthritis. Below is a selection of some of the many specially-designed gadgets.

Cutlery
This is just one of the many existing aids to eating available. There are many other designs for thick-handled cutlery.

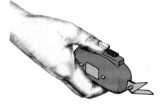

Dress-making scissors
These electric scissors will make it easy to continue sewing and dressmaking.

Can opener
A hand-held electric can opener is often easier to use than one mounted on the wall.

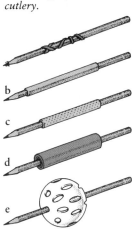

b

c

d

e

f

Scissors
Self-opening scissors with extra wide loops are made to accommodate swollen fingers.

Cutting bread
Hold the bread down with a flat hand and cut across. This way there is less strain on the fingers and wrists.

Writing
Increasing the diameter of a pencil or pen aids writing so use the following: a, rubber band; b, rubber sleeve; c, pimple rubber sleeve; d, adhesive tape; e, plastic ball; and f, sponge.

Dressing aid
A dressing stick made from an old wooden coat-hanger will pull straps over the shoulder by the V-notch.

Keys
A toggle device attached to a key helps a weak grip as well as arthritis.

TIPS FOR LIVING WITH OSTEOARTHROSIS

These guidelines will help you to live with osteoarthrosis.

• Do not make any wrenching, heaving movements on rigid door knobs and tight screw-topped jars. Use the whole of your hand to lift any heavy objects from below, certainly not with first finger and thumb.
• Exercise and walking are fine, but beware of standing and walking on hard surfaces for prolonged periods.
• Sitting in cramped seats becomes painful after half an hour or so. When this happens it is helpful if you stand up, walk around or massage your knees.
• Sitting with your legs crossed (like Buddha) is not good for your knees.

• Hips stiffen quickly if not exercised. Sitting like Buddha, though bad for your knees, is good for your hips. An important exercise is for you to flex your knees to a right angle.
• Backs stiffen with age so it's a good thing if you exercise your spine after a hot bath or shower. Swimming is also good.
• Necks stiffen if not exercised, so regular relaxation exercises keep your neck supple.
• Sensible footwear is essential. Don't wear pointed shoes because they push your big toe out of line.
• When lifting heavy objects bend your knees and straighten your spine.
• Stay trim. Extra weight means less exercise and immobile joints.

TIPS FOR LIVING WITH RHEUMATOID ARTHRITIS

These guidelines will help you to live with rheumatoid arthritis.

• Energy is important so make certain you preserve it.
• Full range of movement exercises are necessary. Keep supple; exercise after a bath or shower. Not doing enough will lead to stiffness; doing too much will increase pain and swelling in the joints.
• Eat like any other healthy person. Diet does not influence rheumatoid arthritis.

• Alcohol can be good in moderation.
• Maintain hobbies and interests. Lead as full a life as you are able. A good general rule to follow is if any exertion makes you ache badly for more than two hours afterwards or makes you feel bad next day, then you have taken too much.
• Take drugs as prescribed; if any medicines cause symptoms then tell your doctor about them.
• Don't expect any miracle cure. Great tolerance and patience are most needed.

Pain relievers Hot baths or showers are often helpful in easing pains, as are hot water bottles and heating pads and lamps. However don't overdo the latter and burn your skin.

Your doctor can supply you with painkillers and other drugs to ease your condition but often keeping yourself busy and active can be the best medicine. Anxiety and depression, coupled with uncertainty and fears of the future, definitely aggravate pain. A positive and hopeful approach to life and enjoyment of hobbies and other interests can make life full and interesting and increase your pain threshold. You should get out of the house as much as possible and try keeping a job – even a part-time one – and develop interests.

EXERCISES FOR ARTHRITIS

You should make certain you put all your joints through a full range of motion every day – though don't over-exercise.

The movements below will help you to keep up muscle strength and joints moving properly (5-20 times daily).

Wrists
Rest your arms on a table or arm of a chair without supporting your hand. Bend your hand down towards the floor and then lift it up.

Shoulders and arms
Hold your arms straight down but across your body, then lift them upwards and outwards uncrossing them as you go. With your arms in this position, clasp your hands behind your head.

Next, move your hand to the left and then to the right. When you are doing this make sure your hand rests in the mid-position and is in line with your forearm and does not fall downwards.

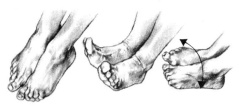

Feet
Push your toes and feet down and then pull them up towards you. Move your toes and ankles round in a large circle.

Hands and fingers
Bend your fingers and grip tightly, then stretch and spread your fingers. Touch the tip of each finger in turn with your thumb.

Quadriceps exercises can be done by just tightening the thigh muscles and pulling the knee-cap up. Some people find it easier to pull the foot up from the ankle while lying down, and this tightens the thigh muscles, others let their legs dangle over a chair, then bring their knee up straight and hold it there for ten seconds before letting it go down slowly.

Hips and knees
Lie down, preferably on the floor, and exercise one leg at a time. In turn, bend each leg up on to your chest towards the opposite shoulder.

Brain failure

In many senses brain failure is like failure of any other organ in the body, such as the heart or the kidneys, simply a gradual decline. Most doctors would agree that brain failure has occurred in a person where there is failing mental capacity and an inability to cope with everyday life unless he or she gets help and support. Furthermore, the person may be a danger to him or herself and to others, by behaving in an inappropriate way.

There are drugs which claim to cure brain failure. Of course, they don't. This has given them a bad name and has spread the belief that nothing can be done. This is not true – there is a good deal that *can* be done. Drugs can alter moods, improve depression and paranoia; mild sleeping pills can prevent wandering and embarrassing behaviour at night. Sometimes older people have inverted sleep rhythms and mild sleeping pills will give a good night's sleep and cut out the nocturnal noise and activity which is common.

Both family and neighbours are often concerned about the danger when such a person wanders around, leaves the gas unlit, or uses matches and lighters, etc. But many of these problems are easy to overcome; for example, you can fit a lock to the front and back doors to keep an affected person inside a supervised house; the local gas board can fit fail-safe gas taps.

Many of the accompaniments of brain failure such as incontinence (see pages 291-3) may not be due to brain failure *per se* and should always be thoroughly investigated.

There are social aspects to the care of a demented patient which are very important, and if you are concerned in this kind of situation you need support and help, too.

The role of partners in brain failure The majority of people suffering from brain failure live at home either with a partner or child, or with some kind of regular supervision. Probably the most happy situation is when there is a loving partner of longstanding. Such couples have lived through life sharing a great deal, and will go on to share and cope with one of them having brain failure. Many people are strengthened by having shared a world war; they remember hunger marches; they remember times before the motor car, air travel and space travel. Even if they have had a marriage which is tinged with "hatred", long-standing familiarity goes hand in hand with a preparedness to care for a partner in distress. Such a partner may find it fairly easy to cope with the escalating demands of the other. The "queer turns" and "dizzy spells" may worsen so slowly that the partner is given time to adjust. Furthermore, the calm and tranquillity of long and

279

complementary pairing makes anxiety, depression or paranoid thoughts and attitudes very much less likely to happen.

There is no question that the "husband and wife team" has many ingredients for success. Other caring groups have to develop the same trick, while providing help without invading self-sufficiency. This conflict, of what a person needs to live a normal life and what he or she actually wants, can be a source of great unhappiness and contribute to the development of paranoia and depression. It makes dementia appear worse than it really is.

Other family members can be similarly good. Sisters and brothers often come together again in later life and opposite or same sex siblings provide care for each other which is usually very impressive, even though it may fall short of the the quality and quantity of the kind of care that exists between married partners. The most frequent support system is daughter/parent or daughter/parent-in-law.

Help with care People who are suffering from brain failure need to be visited regularly so that you can anticipate problems and look for solutions. Many people feel a lot better if they attend a day centre or a luncheon club, or receive voluntary visiting. If you can arrange this regularly then it will provide great relief for yourself and others in your family. Health visitors, social workers and psychiatric nurses can be consulted to reassure you and make you feel that you are not alone. Most local authorities have a service by which they arrange for periods of relief with holiday admissions or to an appropriate residential home or hospital to give you and your family a rest. One of the most important aspects of the continuing care of a person with brain failure is that there has to be an atmosphere of trust between everyone who is concerned. When there is a crisis, relief should be immediately available and no-one should have to wait until tomorrow, even worse next week. Agreements and contracts must be honoured, so that you as a family must see, as well as feel, that you are being supported.

In many cases the family can be augmented by nurses, visitors and workers in order to be able to help an older person to have a well-supported life at home. There are medicines, walking-sticks, nursing expertise, modifications to the house, home help, meals-on-wheels and neighbourhood wardens.

Inevitably, some patients will require institutional care when attempts to maintain them in the community fail. Entry into a special residential home should be planned well ahead. If possible, strict custodial care should be replaced by methods which encourage independence so raising the morale of patients.

TIPS FOR ENVIRONMENT AND MEDICATION

Drugs help your internal environment, but possibly more important is the help that you can get in adjusting to your external environment – the world about you. The following will act as guidelines for both.

- You should try to keep up a close liaison with your doctor, social worker and physiotherapist.
- To live an active, mobile life you are going to have to encourage yourself to *get* dressed rather than *be* dressed, go to the lavatory rather than use a bed pan or a commode, and spend as much time as you possibly can practising walking whether with a walking aid or without.
- With active exercises physiotherapists can increase the range of movement both of your joints and limbs and give you greater mobility.
- You can also increase your mobility by using a variety of walking aids.
- If you are unable to walk at all you will almost certainly still be capable of leading an independent life in a wheelchair.
- You may find that you are not quite capable of overcoming obstacles such as the steps and stairs in your home, but you can ask the physiotherapist to visit your home to make a first-hand assessment of the sort of obstacles that may interfere with everyday living, and improve them.
- An occupational therapist can have a vital role to play in helping you to get back to normal activities. The occupational therapist working with the physiotherapist will ensure that you are able to get in and out of bed, to get dressed and undressed, to walk, and to use the lavatory. If you can do all of these things without help then there is absolutely no need for you to stay in hospital a moment longer.
- Doctors and social workers consider skills such as cooking, housekeeping and shopping as luxuries which should never prevent your discharge from hospital, since you can get help from meals-on-wheels, a home help, a laundry service, or from the Social Services Department.

- Drugs prescribed by your doctor will help to make your body well and they will be an aid in carrying out the acts of everyday life. Below are some basic guidelines and principles you need to know before taking drugs.
- As we get older our reaction to drugs can change. We may become more sensitive to them and therefore need a smaller dose than before, or become insensitive to them and require more than before. It is therefore necessary for doctors to treat every patient individually, and adjust the dose of a drug according to your response. Doses of drugs should be increased or decreased by very small amounts, slowly.
- Many drugs hitherto harmless may not remain so. A good working rule is that all drugs should be considered potentially risky as you grow older. If your doctor has decided that a drug is essential then it is his or her duty to monitor the effects of the drug very carefully.
- The drugs you are taking must be kept constantly under review. Older people frequently have more than one condition and this may mean that you have to take more than one drug. Doctors have also to be aware of how many drugs you are taking (including aspirin or antacid) and you yourself should be on the lookout for possible interactions between the drugs.
- For younger people and children, doctors sometimes give a large *loading* to start off a treatment with rapid response. In older people this is very rarely necessary and the maintenance dose is often lower than in younger people.
- Always be suspicious of routine repeat prescriptions for a long-term complaint. They should never be given to the older patient for longer than a period of two to three months, depending on the complaint.

281

Confinement to chairs and beds

Choosing chairs

Inevitably, as we get older we spend a good deal of time sitting, and chairs become perhaps the most important part of our furniture. Few of us give any thought to chairs. The worst ones for older people are the modern, low, sloping-backed chairs with thick upholstery and broad arms. We need chairs in which we can sit up well with our backs straight, hips and knees at an angle of 90°, or certainly as near to this as possible (see page 38).

It is important for us to keep our backs straight even while sitting and to distribute our weight evenly over our buttocks and thighs. Chairs should have arms because these help us to get in and out, but the arms should be slender at their ends so that they can be grasped by hands which may we weak or arthritic. Most people agree that a partly upholstered wooden arm is best. The really critical measurement is the height of the seat to the floor, which should be the same measurement as the sole of the foot to the knee. It is much better to have a chair too high than too low.

Different chairs may be needed during the course of an illness. Firm, high armchairs with wings and built-in trays and foot rests are good if the person is very frail and disabled, but light, modern, dining-style chairs will do if he or she is convalescent or usually spends time fairly actively in day rooms. It is possible to get specially-designed chairs which have extra long legs. Not all people need high-backed chairs. Some less able ones will hold a better sitting position and keep more alert if they have lower backs to their chairs.

Ageing relatives may fall forward out of very high chairs. However, the modern geriatric chair in its various versions can correct this. Its swivelling but fastenable tray table will lessen the risk (though some people will manage to slide down even this). Otherwise it is possible to place a person in the chair facing towards the side of the bed so that the risks of falling forward are very much less.

Getting out of and into a chair

Getting out of chairs is very difficult when one knee is stiff. With two stiff or straight-splinted knees, the chair might even have to be made twenty-six or more inches from the floor. Yet even this can be done. There could be no better example of how necessary it is to match furniture to people and their physical problems to make life comfortable.

The design of a chair is very important. It should be stable and strong because we put all our weight on one side when we get up and we may fall back heavily when we sit down. This latter is inadvisable and should be avoided (see opposite). Padding at the front of the seat allows circulation in the legs.

GETTING OUT OF AND INTO A CHAIR

Unfortunately, few people understand how to get off a chair safely. You might find it necessary to demonstrate the correct technique time and time again for a forgetful relative. This, however, will be well worth the effort.

When getting out of a chair, your feet should be brought back underneath with your hands placed forward on the arms of the chair.

Lean forward until the point of overbalancing and thrust forward and upward with your arms and thigh muscles.

Still holding the arms of the chair wait until you are perfectly balanced. Sitting down should always involve the reverse process.

The correct bed Your bed should be suitable in height; nursing in low beds is impossible, and trying to get out of beds which are too high is dangerous. Bed heights, like chair heights, are critical for elderly people who are learning to be independent. A good back rest and an overbed chain and handle are necessary, so are castors on the bed; these must be of the locking type.

Safety sides should be used, not to restrain but to prevent ill or restless people rolling out of bed. Modern, telescopic, temporary safety slides are clamped down onto the frame. They are silent in action, safe, and fold down unobtrusively to bed level when not in use. They remain below mattress level so that it is simple to make the bed. Vertical spaces are not wide enough for a confused person to get his or her head stuck.

Bed cradles, which hold bedclothes off the legs, ankles and feet, should be a rule of nursing an older person. They are usually made of tubular steel and are of the cantilevered type. They should be obligatory for any person who could possibly develop a foot drop; all stroke cases; and anyone who is immobilized, as they can help in the prevention of pressure sores. Having the correct bed is an investment.

Exercising in bed

People who are confined to bed also need regular exercise sessions so that muscles are not allowed to become disused, joints don't become stiff and mobility and strength are retained. Exercises can be devised where the therapist resists pushing or pulling arm movements and kicking or leg-raising movements while the person is attempting to make them.

It is possible to exercise the arms, shoulders and hip girdle by pulling on weights and pulleys, punching at suspended punch balls and exercising in suspension. Suspension means that the effect of gravity is counteracted. The limb is held from an overhead frame with ropes, slings and springs so that little muscle power can produce large ranges of movement; these special suspension techniques help a lot of people. It is possible to make muscle groups work harder and harder by working against more and more powerful springs. Home nurses with the help of relatives who are 'handymen' can often set up simple suspension exercises by attaching pulleys and hooks to ring bolts in the ceiling.

Problems of movement

As we get older our walking slows down. Many older people can walk very well, but seldom very fast. We walk more and more deliberately as if concentrating on what always has been a complex activity. Failure to concentrate may lead to disaster. If we begin to stand with our bodies bent and stooped, the way we walk soon suffers and we tend to lean forward, sliding our feet without swinging our arms. Arm swinging helps greatly in keeping our balance, and it is well worth encouraging. Most of us could take longer paces if we swung our arms and lifted our feet higher. Some of us who walk very badly on the flat can still walk upstairs quite well. If we walk poorly without having any abnormality, it is mainly because of bad habits and our not making demands on ourselves. However, if we have painful feet or don't possess shoes with a good enough support or wear our bedroom slippers (which give no support or firm basis for walking) all day, we can make walking more difficult than it need be which makes life uncomfortable.

Overweight people characteristically waddle in an attempt to distribute their weight safely, but waddling can also indicate a joint disease like arthritis (see page 275).

Aids to walking As we get older, we become especially afraid of falling over backwards, so it helps to push something in front like a stable walking aid. (This can also be a help if we are frightened of having a walking stick, or a giddy stick.) When frightened, we instinctively lean forward and any stick is held far out in front. If we've lost all confidence or have been lying in bed for a long time we tend to totter forwards with tiny steps and look absolutely terrified. This kind of walking represents a great fear of falling and it is difficult to overcome. Sometimes we have to be put on an inclined board to help us get a more normal balance. Or we may start to walk normally as long as there is someone there to help us, but revert to our faltering steps as soon as the support is gone.

Some of us need sticks but will not use them because we think it is a sign of decrepitude. This is a bad mistake. We should ignore what other people might think and use this simple tool, which could make the difference between activity and being confined to a chair. The stick is surely a sight of seniority – not a hint of one foot in the grave. All sticks should be rubber tipped, stout enough to bear our weight and long enough so that when we hold them by our sides our elbows are just bent.

If we are learning to walk again we should try to look up – not at our feet. Some of us may have lost the sense of knowing where our feet are, but this is rare. When starting out, the way should be quite free of obstacles and we should have a target to watch at eye level. Sometimes it's a good idea to stamp our feet down and practice stepping over things. Slippery floors, or those that appear slippery because of reflections, are frightening, so it's best trying to walk on carpets or on floors that are patterned with coloured tiles to split up the appearance of uniform, polished surfaces. It is regrettable that there will never be enough physiotherapists to help us all, therefore we should ask for help from everyone we can. More people want to help than you may think. These include our relatives, social workers, home-helps, and neighbours.

Despite severe disabilities most of us retain a tenacious desire to remain mobile and would rather slide downstairs in the morning. If you hang on to this determination and gather up your courage you will never stay confined. It does take a lot of strength and effort to be this positive but it can be done.

Walking frames are stable and rubber tips prevent sliding.

285

Taking care of feet

Many older feet are deformed and painful and this is bound to interfere with comfortable walking and mobility generally. If we want to keep moving, regular foot attention is a most crucial matter. Orthopaedic abnormalities such as bunions should be put right, nails should be cut and other faults like corns should be dealt with somehow or other through a chiropody service available to all of us who need it, *every four to eight weeks.*

If you are a diabetic, special risks are involved see *Special medical problems.* You should never attempt to cut your nails or corns. You must wear good, stout shoes with no rough parts inside and be careful to avoid any kind of injury, however slight, to your feet. Wash your feet regularly in warm water, dry them and powder them carefully. These are good rules, too, for any older or not-so-old feet whose owners want them to be healthy for life-long use. Ask your doctor and chiropodist for more tips to keep your feet healthy and comfortable.

Wash your feet regularly in warm water to minimize the risk of fungal infection.

Dry your feet carefully, paying special attention to the spaces between your toes.

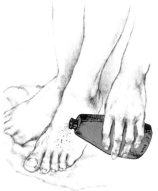

Powder them carefully to dry out those wrinkly areas that are difficult to get to with a towel.

Nursing an older person

The nursing of older people can be problematical. Here are some practical tips which may help you if you are a relative or even if you are the older patient.

Practical nursing

To make a good approach to a person you are nursing, you should do so face-to-face at the right height. The best position for doing this if the person is in a bed or chair is to kneel on one knee. This position is hard on the stockings and trousers, not to say the knees, but is, by far, the best for making real contact. Speak clearly but not necessarily loudly, and look into his or her eyes. Give the person time to consider the answer he or she wishes to make. Use plain, adult language with a touch of humour, adding the reassuring pressure of your hand when things are difficult. Talking down to elderly people as if they were children is deplorable. Tying up an older woman's hair in girlish ribbons is equally unacceptable. The key is to be kind and sympathetic always, and always to allow the person to do what he or she is able without any help. This will require self-discipline on your part.

If you are nursing an older person you should introduce yourself by name and do as much as possible to help the person orientate him or herself. When people are confused you may have to introduce yourself several times until all the information sinks in. Older people do not naturally pick up simple ideas about where they are, what time lunch is, even which way the lavatory is, as younger people do.

When you approach a blind person, you should also introduce yourself very clearly to relieve any anxiety or alarm: "Hello mum, it's Mary". If you approach a deaf person, you should be clearly in the line of vision when it is straight ahead, and you must make every effort to communicate with the deaf person by careful articulation of words, not shouting, offering the chance to lip read and writing words down and making signs. This will make communication a great deal easier.

Here is a list of the sort of things you should be on the lookout for if you are a patient or if you are nursing one.

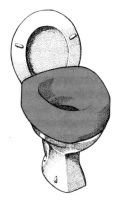

Raised toilet seat

- It is far safer for the person to be up than confined to bed. The rule should be, every patient up unless the doctor says otherwise.
- For beds, see page 283.
- Tables are best if they are of the cantilevered type which can go over the bed or chair and still better if they will tilt back as a book rest or writing desk.
- For chairs, see page 282.
- Commodes are much better than bed pans if the person is confined to bed. Almost anything is better than a bed pan.
- A sanitary chair is one with a lavatory seat in which a frail person can be taken from his or her bedside to the lavatory itself and is clearly better than anything except making the actual journey, walking. These chairs require that the doorways and lavatories should be large enough to accommodate them.
- Lavatories should be of the ordinary height, but some should have raised seats for special patients. It is helpful if the lavatory is constructed with rails to assist the person to get up and down,

Commode

287

and these rails must allow a sanitary chair to go over the lavatory. The lavatory, if possible, should be off-centre in the room so that a helper can comfortably get round to one side to help with clothing.

• For practical purposes, baths should be accessible on all sides, and contain aids like the widely-used bath seat, bath board, hand rail or upright pole. There should be a non-slip mat of special material, and a non-slip surface in each bath. Many people are frightened of drowning in an ordinary long bath and prefer a sitting type bath. There are many kinds of sitting type baths such as the "medic" and the "ladywell".

• To most people a shower bath suggests something under which they stand controlling the taps themselves. Many older patients can be *given* a shower and enjoy it. They can sit in a shower sink or on a waterproof stool holding onto a grab handle while they are bathed by another person who holds a flexible shower pipe and sponge.

• Devices such as hoists for lifting patients are very useful, especially if they are obese or frightened of being handled. There are many types of hoist – hydraulic, wall-mounted and electric; the latter being mounted on a gantry so that an intelligent but very disabled person could take him or herself from the bath to lavatory to wheelchair.

It is helpful to make a list, such as the one below, to remind yourself of the stages of progress that are being made.

CHECKLIST FOR DAILY LIVING

Using this checklist you will be able to assess the everyday improvement that your "patient" makes.

Feeding	**Ambulation**
Self	Weight bearing
With help	With help
Adaptive equipment	Use of cane, crutch, brace
Use of knife, fork, spoon, cup	Wheelchair

Exercise	**Dressing and hygiene**	**Transfer activities**
Passive	Self	Bed to wheelchair
Active	With help	Wheelchair to bed
Passive resistant	Adaptive equipment	Commode
Active resistant	Teeth, hair, shaving etc.	Lock wheelchair
		Use of chair

Bath	**Positioning**	**Writing, reading etc.**
Self	Bed	Self
With help	In wheelchair	With help
Adaptive equipment	In chair	Adaptive equipment
Tub shower room	Dependent	

A word about privacy

One of the difficult parts of getting older is that we may find it necessary, though no less difficult, to surrender the privacy of our homes and lives because home helps, meals-on-wheels, health visitors and nurses may become necessary to live a normal life. Even if we are only indirectly concerned, for instance when caring for an older relative, we should be aware that taking privacy and independence away can be a shocking and shameful experience. Self-reliance is one of the few sources of pride left to a person as he or she grows older.

Privacy is one of the aspects of living which most of us jealously guard and take great care to protect. In a social sense, there are times when it seems acceptable to let strangers in: if, for instance, we are ill and need the care of a doctor; if we are in legal trouble and have to allow the lawyers to share our secrets. But when you think about it, we do most of the important things in our lives away from the eyes of the world. Even if we do share with someone, it is usually a partner or a person who is very close to us through family links. At any rate, most of us decide when, and with whom, we share our lives. Any violation of this right to privacy can make us fight fiercely to cling to any last vestiges of it. This fight can become violent as we grow older because privacy becomes more important.

People who are self-possessed can find it crushing to realize that they are unable to look after themselves and give care to others. For such people, words, medicine and medical investigations seem futile and irrelevant. What is needed is time and old-fashioned care by creative people in the proper surroundings. However, these are nearly always scarce, expensive and undervalued.

Coping with sexual feelings The sexual feelings of people who are learning to live with long-term complaints are often ignored; worse, they are judged by moralistic doctors, nurses, and even family. Many studies have shown that sexual behaviour continues into old age (see *A lifetime of loving*).

Nursing experience and long-term facilities have shown that the frail older person, although not able to participate in overt sexual behaviour, will still demonstrate that he or she has sexual feelings and needs. An example would be the seventy-year-old man, who, despite being frail and suffering from Parkinsonism, suddenly makes a suggestive remark or pinches a nurse. Another example might be the older woman who insists on holding the doctor's hand at each visit for a long period of time. It is not uncommon for visitors to encounter masturbation or exposing behaviour in long-term care patients.

The elderly person should be provided the opportunity to pursue sexual outlets which have been his or her right throughout the years prior to that time. It is not the place of relatives or health professionals to judge what is normal and what is abnormal.

Families may need help and counselling concerning the sexuality of parents, grandparents and other relatives. Many family members have great difficulty accepting that their parents were, and still are, sexual human beings. Also all of us must appreciate the effect of the mass media on the image of the older person as perceived by others and by the older generation themselves. Older people in many cases have internalized the attitude that they are not attractive to others and that they are sexually diminished.

In addition to the fact that sex continues to be an important part of the lives of most older people, other factors such as closeness, a feeling of being valued, intimacy and the psychological effects of touch are very important. Research has shown that older people are helped a great deal simply by warm human gestures such as touching or holding hands, and maintaining direct eye contact face to face. This appears not only to be true in patients who have had strokes, but in older people in general. The person does better and communication appears to be tremendously improved by touching and keeping good visual contact whenever this is possible.

Incontinence

Incontinence is something we meet more and more often as we grow older – from the stress incontinence that is quite often experienced by women in their late forties and fifties, generally due to disturbance of the pelvic floor muscles during delivery, to the frank urinary incontinence and faecal incontinence which may be experienced by people in their late sixties and seventies. This affects approximately forty percent of people in the very old age group. It may be due to restriction in bed or a change from familiar surroundings. Incontinence which starts during any acute illness usually disappears when the illness is cured.

Easing the problem Incontinence may be made worse or even brought on when a person has to face ill-health and a strange environment like a hospital or home. Mobility is extremely important. Many older people have difficulty in going to the lavatory quickly enough.

291

INCONTINENCE AIDS

There are several factors to be considered when choosing aids to help incontinent people; individual needs are of prime importance. Age and condition, both physical and mental, should be taken into account.

Urinal
This is valuable when a person cannot move.

Female urinal
This is small and light, easy to use in bed.

Feminal
This is a polythene bag inserted in a plastic holder.

Fitted pants
These are made of soft material with a water-proof outside pouch.

Stretch pants
These are light, open-stretch pants designed to fit any person.

French knickers
These have a wide leg opening for convenience.

Dress
The flaps at the back can be moved of this wrap-over back.

Kylie bed sheet
This combines a drawsheet with an underpad.

This is particularly significant after a stroke, where disability is complicated by over-activity of the bladder. Drugs which increase the output of urine (diuretics) also make incontinence worse. The design and layout of accommodation and the amount of supporting care have a direct bearing on the extent to which these factors create problems for older people.

Where immobility is a problem, care must be taken to ensure that the patient has ready access to a lavatory. This may mean getting a commode at home. Wherever possible, however, attempts should be made to adapt the lavatory to the person's needs. If it is inaccessible you may even have to think about moving it to a more suitable situation.

Toilet training plays an important part in helping to care for an incontinent person. It is particularly important when the capacity of the bladder is kept low by irritability of its walls or weakness of the sphincter. In this case people should be encouraged to visit the lavatory once every two hours. You may have to wake the person during the course of the night. This is less distressing than for him or her to awake in a urine-soaked bed in the middle of the night or the morning.

Bed pans should be avoided because they make emptying the bladder and the bowel physiologically and psychologically difficult. They also cause increased dependence on other people. Commodes have a limited value in the management of severely disabled people at home. In most other situations, they should be avoided, because patients begin to consider themselves permanent invalids and this discourages them from trying to be mobile and independent.

Whenever severe and embarrassing incontinence is due to prostatic enlargement, surgery should be considered now that prostatectomy can be performed by an internal cutting knife which is passed up a very fine tube inside the urethra (see page 217). Surgical repair should also be considered when stress incontinence in a woman is due to a relaxed pelvic floor.

For an incontinent woman, nothing of a practical nature has been developed, except more water-absorbent materials which can be of value in reducing the amount of laundry necessary for sheet of water-absorbent paper with a waterproof backing. Although this pad only absorbs a limited quantity of urine, it can be of value in recucing the amount of laundry necessary for bedfast patients with relatively mild incontinence.

Loss of bowel control Faecal incontinence or loss of bowel control is much less common than that of bladder control. Some of the causes would include hard, stone-like faeces, diarrhoea, leakage of liquid paraffin, damage to the pelvic floor, and loss of the inhibition

293

reflex which stops the bowel from emptying itself all the time. Faecal incontinence due to hardening of faeces in the rectum and large bowel is really the result of leakage of liquid faeces from the anus. The large intestine secretes excess mucus in response to the presence of hard faeces. It can usually be treated by using an enema. Once the colon has been emptied of faeces, it is essential that regular bowel movements be maintained. This can be helped by choosing the right diet.

Pressure sores

Pressure, or bed sores are better prevented than treated. A.N. Exton-Smith, a professor of geriatrics at University College Hospital, London, has shown that it is possible to predict which people will be most endangered by giving them a score related to certain of their abilities.

PRONE TO PRESSURE SORES?

The scoring is best done in the first place by a doctor, but a rough score can be achieved by an observant relative. It will vary according to progress and so it needs to be repeated.

General Condition	Score
Good	0
Fair	1
Poor	2
Bad	3

Mental State	Score		Activity	Score
Alert	0		Ambulant	0
Confused	1		Walks with help	1
Apathetic	2		Chairfast	2
Stuporose	3		In bed all day	3

Mobility in Bed			Incontinence	
Full	0		Continent	0
Slight limitation	1		Occasional incontinence	1
Very limited	2		Usually incontinent of urine	2
Immobile	3		Doubly incontinent	3

Total =

The interpretation of the test is as follows:
1. The higher the score the greater the risk of pressure sores. The best score is 0, the worst 15.

2. Scores of 7 and upwards indicate a severe risk. Preventive measures should be concentrated most on patients with high scores.

Causes of bed sores

Bed sores are due to pressure causing loss of blood flow, death of cells, then ulceration of the part which is being pressed. The most commonly-injured place is in the lower part of the back and buttocks when the patient is lying down on the back, and on the hip prominence when the person is lying on the side. Other commonly-injured areas will be the heels (especially the backs), the ankles, the knees, the backs of the elbows, and the ribs as illustrated below.

In the sitting position, half of our body weight is supported on eight percent of the sitting surface and pressures can exceed 300 millimetres of mercury. The inevitable result of sitting or lying immobile for any length of time will lead to the development of pressure sores over the bony prominences.

In a well person, sitting or lying still will be uncomfortable and we automatically shift our weight. However, in the older person with diminished sensation, debilitation or disablement, shifting weight may not happen and ulceration will result. In order for the wound to heal, pressure has to be eliminated, and anything which prevents the wound healing should be minimized. These factors would be anaemia, dehydration, any chronic illness and some medications such as steroids.

The tinted areas indicate the areas of the body most vulnerable to pressure in somebody lying or sitting for long periods of time.

It is important to avoid those other factors which irritate the condition, namely moisture next to the skin, friction, or even crumbs in the bed.

Treatment of bed sores

The main part of treatment is frequent changes in position at least very two hours to minimize the development of ulcers in other areas. Proper skin care is important, and the area should be washed three times a day with a very mild soap and then a thin layer of ointment should be applied to lubricate the skin. Only if the ulcer is becoming infected should anti-bacterial ointments be used on the sore itself.

Gentle massage of the area is beneficial on the basis that it stimulates blood circulation and increases blood flow there. Other treatment can be aimed at preventing pressure ulcers elsewhere – the elbows, knees and heels should be padded. A water mattress and sponge rubber or gel-filled cushions are also helpful in distributing the pressure more easily when in a sitting position. All areas which are commonly affected by pressure sores should be checked at frequent intervals so that they can be looked after immediately a sore develops.

Artificial sheepskin bootees relieve pressure on the heel.

Adapting your environment

First and foremost a home provides shelter and comfort, but it's also a private place where you can find self-expression and independence. As we grow older it is important that a home should be a place where we feel safe and secure so be security conscious. If you are a particularly nervous person have a burglar alarm and smoke alarm fitted throughout your house, put a spy-hole in your front door and perhaps even install an intercom. Feeling at ease means being able to relax.

Plan ahead so that you can make changes to your house gradually, over a period of several years, so that everything is in place and ready for use when most needed. Start by putting all electric sockets about 3ft (1m) from the floor so that they can be easily found and reached. Double points should have switches on the outside edge. Fit handles to plugs so that they have the switches on the outside edge. Always have two sets of lighting in every room, to provide better light, and a spare light source in case you blow a fuse. Always get an expert to do any gas and electricity repairs.

Have plenty of comfortable places around the house where you can have a break from daily chores. If necessary, lengthen or shorten chair and table legs and fit them with plastic or rubber tips to make them non slip. Hunt around for good chair designs, it's well worth investing in an electrically-operated elevating seat which helps you to sit down and get up.

Many accidents happen in our homes as we get older because our senses of smell become blunted as we age. Without a strong sense of smell, leaking gas can go undetected for long periods and this is a serious hazard. If you have the opportunity to plan well ahead, or if you are intending to purchase a retirement home, opt for the safety of electricity and all-electric appliances throughout your property.

Be on the look-out for whatever other labour-saving devices there are apart from those mentioned in this chapter. Planning your resources carefully means that you need not carry heavy cleaning equipment backwards and forwards. If you can afford it, keep two sets, one upstairs and one down.

PLANNING A KITCHEN

Preparing a kitchen for the time when you have stiffer joints and weaker muscles needs careful consideration. Everything used frequently should be close to hand, along two adjacent walls of the kitchen.

Work surfaces will be much more comfortable if they are lower than standard. A knee-hole under the sink will make life easier because you can sit while washing-up or preparing vegetables. A refrigerator and cooker should be at a height you can reach easily. Standard ovens with hobs can be difficult to manage so have a small, table-top toaster, oven or grill.

Kitchen aids

Cutlery and plates
Specially-made cutlery and kitchen tools are available which have thick, grooved handles that are easy to hold.

Mincer
This is useful to chop, shred or mix small amounts of food.

Trolley
A solidly-built trolley serves a dual purpose: it saves walking to and fro unnecessarily and it can be a useful walking aid.

Eye-level cooker

Transparent saucepans

Pull-out drawer for storing pans

Pan stabilizer

Reacher so that you don't have to stretch

Pull-out work surface

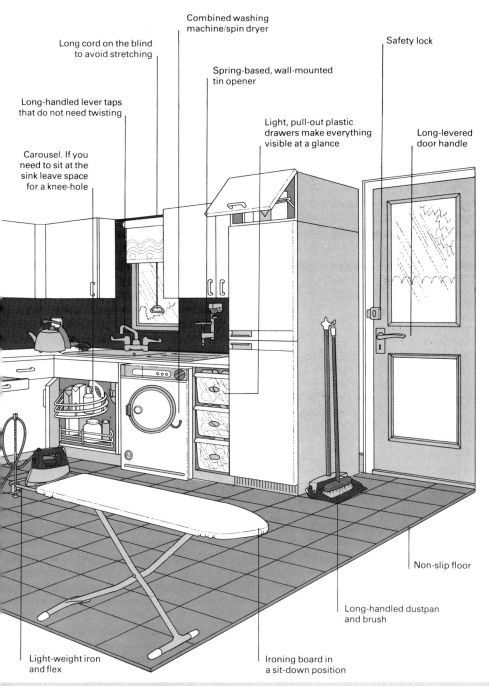

Long cord on the blind
to avoid stretching

Combined washing
machine/spin dryer

Safety lock

Spring-based, wall-mounted
tin opener

Long-handled lever taps
that do not need twisting

Light, pull-out plastic
drawers make everything
visible at a glance

Long-levered
door handle

Carousel. If you
need to sit at the
sink leave space
for a knee-hole

Non-slip floor

Long-handled dustpan
and brush

Light-weight iron
and flex

Ironing board in
a sit-down position

PLANNING A BATHROOM

I remember well the bathroom of my childhood: spartan and cold, freezing ice on the window. Now I prefer it to be warm and inviting.
A bidet is no longer a luxury. It's very comfortable, quick and easy to use. Don't use rugs, even rubber-backed ones slip and wrinkle at the edges. Fitted carpets are a good investment. When filling the bath put the cold water in first and then fill with hot water until you reach a comfortable temperature.

Bathroom safety aids

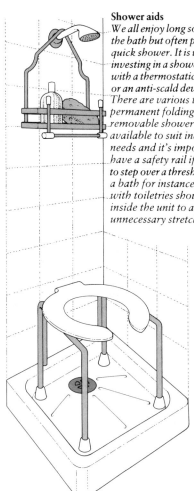

Shower aids
We all enjoy long soaks in the bath but often prefer a quick shower. It is worth investing in a shower unit with a thermostatic control or an anti-scald device. There are various types of permanent folding or removable shower seats available to suit individual needs and it's important to have a safety rail if you have to step over a threshold, into a bath for instance. A shelf with toiletries should be inside the unit to avoid unnecessary stretching.

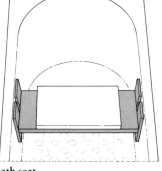

Bath seat
There are many types of bath seat on the market but one which fits inside the bath is usually stronger and much more secure than one which is suspended from the bath's rim.

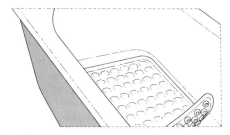

Bath mat
Non-slip or suction mats or adhesive-backed, rubber-silicone treads in your bath or shower are a vital precaution against slipping.

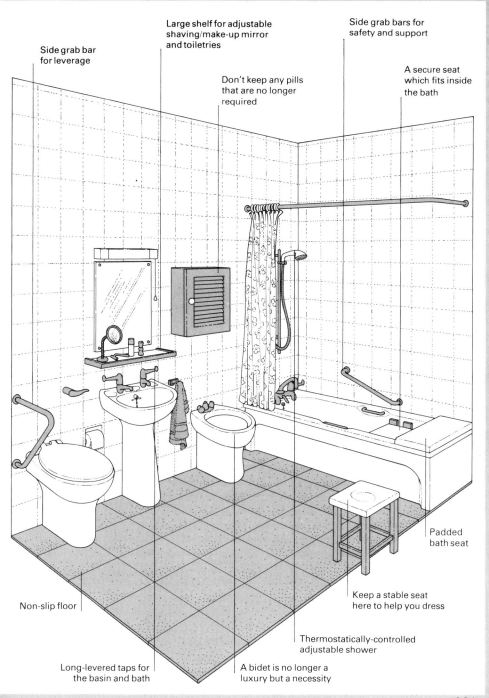

Side grab bar
for leverage

Large shelf for adjustable
shaving/make-up mirror
and toiletries

Side grab bars for
safety and support

Don't keep any pills
that are no longer
required

A secure seat
which fits inside
the bath

Padded
bath seat

Non-slip floor

Keep a stable seat
here to help you dress

Long-levered taps for
the basin and bath

A bidet is no longer a
luxury but a necessity

Thermostatically-controlled
adjustable shower

PLANNING A BEDROOM

As I get older I tend more and more to use my bedroom as a sitting room. This is where I keep a book-case of interesting books and magazines.

Now is the time to get that electric blanket that you have been promising yourself. Do follow all of the manufacturer's instructions and have it checked in the autumn ready for use through the winter.

Choosing the right bed is important. It must be easy to get in and out of and it might be useful to have a solid piece of furniture next to it for leverage.

Daily living aids

Dealing with shoes
A long-handled shoe-horn (left) saves bending down, as does this device (above) when it comes to taking shoes off.

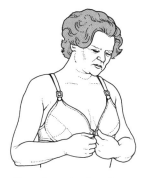

Front-fastening brassiere
This makes dressing simpler for weak and arthritic hands.

Extend-a-hand
Such an aid can be adjusted to reach any length as though it were tailor-made.

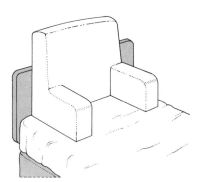

Bed rest
This is useful when reading or watching T.V. It's the same shape as the back and sides of a comfortable armchair.

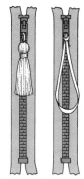

Zipper pulls
These make zippers easier to open and close. Wide loops can be made from spare material.

Always remember to switch off an electric blanket before you go to sleep

Only put things that you seldom use on high shelves

A two-way light switch near to the bed

T.V. remote control to save you getting up

Transparent pull-out drawers make clothes visible at a glance

A shelf will stop you accidentally resting against a hot radiator

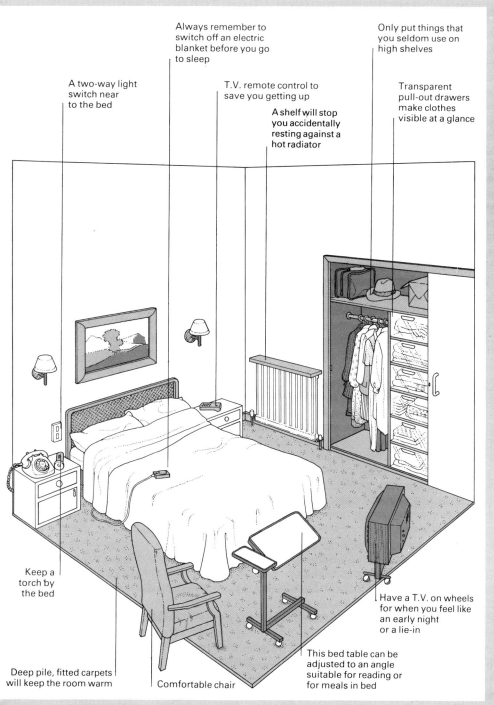

Keep a torch by the bed

Have a T.V. on wheels for when you feel like an early night or a lie-in

This bed table can be adjusted to an angle suitable for reading or for meals in bed

Deep pile, fitted carpets will keep the room warm

Comfortable chair

PLANNING A LIVING ROOM

This is a room which is going to be used more and more so it's worth taking the time and trouble to make it as comfortable as possible. Rooms facing north and south catch the sun, so they make ideal living rooms.

Everything used regularly needs to be close to hand: T.V. control, hi-fi, knitting, telephone and reading lamp. Make sure that there are no trailing wires to trip over and also that there are no sharp edges on the furniture. If you have an open fire make sure that the guard has a fine, spark-proof mesh. Finally, draught proof doors and windows.

Chairlifts

Most of us find climbing stairs a problem at some point in our lives but this needn't necessarily mean confinement to one floor.

Stairlifts are available which can be fitted unobtrusively to most shapes of staircases. The motor and control mechanisms are compactly housed under the seat so that they don't take up too great an area and don't hinder other stair users.

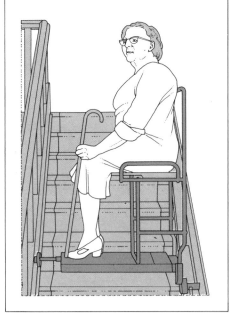

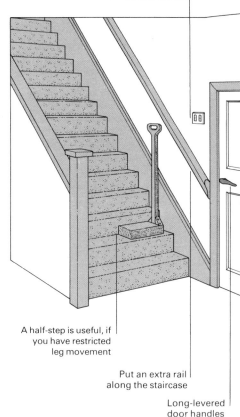

Two-way light switch

A half-step is useful, if you have restricted leg movement

Put an extra rail along the staircase

Long-levered door handles

Hallways

These should be well-lit and have two-way switches at the top and bottom of the stairs. If your hallway is narrow leave it clutter free, chairs and small tables are unnecessary.

Wooden extensions to chair arms provide support

Lightweight carpet sweeper

Security locks on all doors

A kitchen hatch will save carrying to and fro

Make sure you have sufficient lighting for reading

Have easy-to-manage indoor plants.

A comfortable, supportive cushion on a favourite chair

Comfortable rocking chair for a mid-afternoon snooze

Carpet must be well fastened

Non-slip mat

Have a volume control fitted to the telephone earpiece

PLANNING A GARDEN

Gardening is a very relaxing and creative hobby. If a garden is small enough to be manageable there will always be a corner that needs attention when you have some spare time. Some thought on the design of the garden, choosing the right tools and selecting flowers and plants that need little attention, all mean less effort in the long term. Flower beds should not be too wide, so that they can be tended from the path and lawns without flower beds or shrubs in the middle are easier to mow.

Staking plants and flowers can be difficult because it involves a lot of bending down and a good deal of balancing, so have self-supporting plants.

Light-weight tools with extra-thick handles are easy to hold with a weak grip and there are many plastic pots and trays and even light, peat-based compost available in gardening shops. Don't stay in one position for too long if it's uncomfortable, do a little at a time and do stop before getting tired!

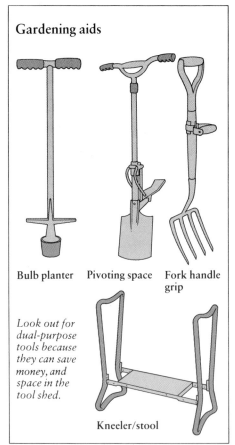

Gardening aids

Bulb planter   Pivoting space   Fork handle grip

Look out for dual-purpose tools because they can save money, and space in the tool shed.

Kneeler/stool

Have a seat somewhere on the raised flower bed

This is a tool for lifting leaves without bending

A well-balanced light-weight wheelbarrow is easy to pull and tip

Flower beds should be
well edged so that any
trailing, slippery plants do
not obstruct the path

Window boxes can be
tended from indoors

A small, well-drained
lawn is easy to
maintain

Front and back doors,
as well as windows,
should have strong
locks. A spy hole
is a good idea

Pathways should be wide
and made of non-slip slabs

OTHER USEFUL HOUSEHOLD AIDS

Furniture blocks
*If tables, chairs and beds are not at the most
convenient height they can be raised by fitting
wooden blocks to the legs. These need to be
hollow to a third down so that they securely
support the legs.*

Shopping trolley with a seat
*Here is something useful in
several ways: it has a built-in
seat; it is a useful walking aid
when being pushed along; and it
has ample storage space.*

Jar opener
*Fixed underneath a shelf, a jar
can be opened by twisting with
one hand.*

Dolly
*Such a labour-saving device
means less carrying. It's useful
for a pail or a hoover and can be
pushed along the floor by a foot
or a cane.*

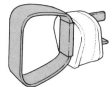

Leg support
*This needs to be securely
fastened before it can provide
adequate support.*

Plugs
*If you have handles fitted to
plugs they immediately become
easier to pull from their sockets.*

Tap turner
*This can be readily bought, made
in plastic or wood, to suit any tap
in the house.*

SAFETY TIPS

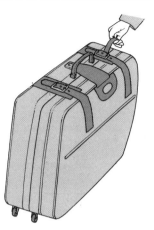

Suitcase on wheels
When you go on holiday, wheels and a towing handle make life easier.

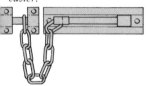

Security chain
This, with a spy-hole, means that you can check who your visitors are before opening the door.

Entry phone
This is not only useful for security, it saves walking flights of stairs to let visitors in.

More accidents occur in the home than anywhere else, most of which could have been prevented, and it is now especially important to take adequate safety precautions. Here is a list of useful household safety tips:

• Don't lean over the front two burners of the oven to get to pans cooking on the back two;

• When cooking in an open frying pan, keep a lid the same size nearby in case the fat catches fire. Cutting off the oxygen by putting the lid over the flames quickly extinguishes them. Don't forget to turn off the source of the heat immediately;

• Keep a fire extinguisher in the kitchen, but never attempt to tackle any fire which might get out of hand. Go for assistance immediately;

• Cook vegetables in a frying basket to avoid having to drain boiling water;

• Use oven gloves rather than pot holders when taking hot dishes out of the oven because they provide a much better grip;

• Use a ladle when transferring hot sauces from one pan to another to avoid spillage;

• A long barbecue utensil is ideal for turning food in the oven without having to get too close to the heat;

• Don't have deep shelves which make it necessary to stack utensils and fit narrow rims along the edges so that nothing can slip off accidentally;

• Don't overload electrical circuits;

• Make sure that no electrical cords are lying where they may be tripped over;

• Only use good quality plugs;

• Make sure all plugs are wired correctly;

• Check flexes and fittings regularly;

• Have your wiring circuit tested every five years;

• If you have a time-switched heater make sure it is well clear of curtains and furnishings;

• Switch off the television and hi-fi when not using them and remove the plugs from their sockets;

• Have all your household appliances serviced regularly by an expert;

• Be sure that all carpeting is well fixed to the floor, and especially to stairs;

• Tack down all loose rugs;

• Have a telephone extension in every room if you possibly can, and emergency numbers on pads nearby;

• If you live alone arrange for a neighbour to call round at least once a day.

Useful addresses

This section of useful addresses is relevant to the various chapters in the book. Hopefully, if you feel that you need advice and guidance on a specific problem, one of these organizations will be able to help you, or at the least, put you in touch with one that can.

UK

GROWING THROUGH LIFE

Centre for Policy on Ageing
Nuffield Lodge
London NW1 4RS

Equal Opportunities Commission
1 Bedford Street
London WC2A 8PS

Forty-plus Career Development Centre
High Holborn House
49–51 Bedford Row
London WC1V 6RL

Pre-retirement Association of Great Britain and Northern Ireland
19 Undine Street
London SW17 8PP

Pre-retirement Choice Magazine
Bedford Chambers
London WC2E 8HA

The Woman's Therapy Centre
6 Manor Gardens
London N7 6LA

KEEPING PHYSICALLY FIT

Action on Smoking and Health (ASH)
27–35 Mortimer Street
London W1N 7RH

Alcoholics Anonymous
PO Box 514
11 Redcliffe Gardens
London SW10 9BQ

Health Education Council
78 New Oxford Street
London WC1A 1AM

The Sports Council
15 Upper Woburn Place
London WC1H 0QP

KEEPING A TRANQUIL MIND

Age Concern England
Bernard Sunley House
60 Pitcairn Road
Mitcham

Cruse
29 Sheen Road
Richmond, TW9 1UR

Legal Advice Centres
(see telephone directories and local press for details)

National Association of Citizens Advice Bureaux
110 Drury Lane
London WC2 5SW

National Association for Mental Health (MIND)
22 Harley Street
London W1N 2EO

National Council for Voluntary Organizations
26 Bedford Square
London WC1B 3HM

Psychological Treatment Unit
The Maudsley Hospital
London SE5 8AZ

A LIFETIME OF LOVING

The Albany Trust
32 Shaftesbury Avenue
London W1V 8EP

Divorce Conciliation and Advisory service
38 Ebury Street
London SW1W 0LU

Marriage Guidance Council
76a New Cavendish Street
London W1M 7LB

Sexual and Personal Relationships of the Disabled
The Diorama
14 Peto Place
London NW1 4DT

CARING FOR A CHANGING BODY

Contour
2 Hans Road
London SW3 1RX

Mastectomy Association
25 Brighton Road
South Croydon CR2 6EA

Menopausal Clinics
(contact local health authority for addresses)

Royal National Institute for the Deaf
105 Gower Street
London WC1E 6AM

RETIREMENT

Adult Education
(Your library will give you details
on courses run locally)

*British Association of Retired
Persons*
14 Frederick Street
Edinburgh EH2 2HB

*Company Pensions Information
Centre*
7 Old Park Lane
London W1Y 3LJ

The Employment Fellowship
Drayton House
Gordon Street,
London WC1EH 0BE

Help the Aged
32 Dover Street
London W1A 2AP

Open University
The Admissions Office
Walton Hall
Milton Keynes MK7 6AA

*Saga (Senior Citizens') Holidays
Limited*
119 Sandgate Road
Folkstone, Kent CT20 2BN

The University of the Third Age
6 Parkside Gardens
London SW19 5EY

SPECIALIST HELP

British Dental Foundation
2B Ravensdale Avenue
London N12 9HS

General Dental Council
37 Wimpole Street
London W1M 8DQ

*The Women's League of Health
and Beauty*
Beaumont Cottage
Ditton Close
Thames Ditton
Surrey

SPECIAL MEDICAL PROBLEMS

British Diabetic Association
10 Queen Anne Street
London W1M 0BD

British Migraine Association
178A High Road
Byfleet
Weybridge, Surrey

BUPA Health Promotion Centre
Battle Bridge House
300 Gray's Inn Road
London WC1X 8DV

*The Chest, Heart and Stroke
Association*
Tavistock House North
Tavistock Square
London WC1H 9JE

The Colostomy Welfare Group
38–39 Ecclestone Square
London SW1V 1PB

*Disablement Income Group
Charitable Trust*
Attlee House
28 Commercial Street
London E1

Parkinson's Disease Society
36 Portland Place
London W1N 3DG

Private Patient's Plan
Tavistock House South
Tavistock Square
London WC1H 9JE

LIVING WITH LONG-TERM AILMENTS

*The Arthritis and Rheumatism
Council for Research*
41 Eagle Street
London WC1R 4AR

British Red Cross Society
Aids for the the Disabled
9 Grosvenor Crescent
London SW1X 7EJ

Cancer Aftercare
Lodge Cottage, Church Lane
Timsbury, Bath, Avon BA3 1LF

Disabled Living Foundation
346 Kensington High Street
London W14 8NS

*Marie Curie Memorial
Foundation (for the welfare of
those with cancer)*
124 Sloane Street
London SW1X 9BP

*National Society for Cancer
Relief*
Michael Sobell House
30 Dorset Square
London NW1 6QL

*Orthopaedic bedding advisory
service*
Brittania House
Dace Road
London E3

*PHAB (Physically Handicapped
and Able Bodies)*
42 Devonshire Street
London W1N 1LN

The following companies
manufacture aids to living.
Further addresses can be
obtained from the Disabled
Living Foundation

Aids for the Disabled
Homecraft Supplies (Fleet Street)
Ltd
27 Trinity Road
London SW17 7SF

Carters (J and A) Ltd
Alfred Street
Westbury, Wilts BA13 3DZ

Llewellyn Living Aids
Carlton Works
Carlton Street
Liverpool L3 7ED

311

ADAPTING YOUR ENVIRONMENT

Department of the Environment
2 Marsham Street
London SW1

National Association for Disability and Rehabilitation
25 Mortimer Street
London W1N 8AB

Royal Society for the Prevention of Accidents (ROSPA)
Cannon House
The Priory
Queensway, Birmingham B4 6BS

AUSTRALIA

AUSTRALIAN RETIRED PERSONS ASSOCIATION

26 College Street
Sydney NSW 2000

300 Little Lonsdale Street
Melbourne Vic 3000

5 Chesser Street
Adelaide SA 5000

69 Hay Street
Subiaco WA 6008

366 Queen Street
Brisbane Qld 4000

Maitland House
35 London Circuit
Canberra ACT 2600

69 Bastick Street
Rosney Tas 7018

CITIZENS ADVICE BUREAUX

NSW Council on the Ageing
34 Argyle Place
Sydney NSW 2000

Victorian Association of Citizens Advice Bureaux
176 Wellington Parade
East Melbourne Vic 3002

Citizens Advice Bureau
136 King William Street
Adelaide SA 5000

Citizens Advice Bureau
81 St George's Terrace
Perth WA 6000

Brisbane Citizens Advice Bureau
69 Ann Street
Brisbane Qld 4000

Citizens Advice Bureau
Griffin Centre
Bunda Street
Canberra ACT 2601

Citizens Advice Bureau
Eastlands Shopping Centre
Rosny Park Tas 7018

Northern Territory Council on the Ageing
PO Box 2476
Darwin NT 5794

COMBINED PENSIONERS ASSOCIATION

Combined Pensioners Association of Victoria
Cnr Lygon & Victoria Streets
Carlton Vic 3053

Combined Pensioners Group Inc
9 Thurso Road
Myaree WA 6154

Tasmanian Pensioners Union
154 Elizabeth Street
Hobart Tas 7000

DISABILITY

Australian Council for the Rehabilitation of Disabled (ACROD)
55 Charles Street
Ryde NSW 2112

Disability Resources Centre
127 Sydney Road
Brunswick Vic 3056

Disability Information and Resource Centre Inc
215 Hutt Street
Adelaide SA 5000

Disabled Advocate and Self Help Group (DASH)
Hakea House
55 Duncraig Road
Applecross WA 6153

Multiple Handicapped Association of Queensland
303 Padstow Road
Eight Mile Plains Qld 4123

Liaison Officer on Disabilities Issues
GPO Box 1507R
Hobart Tas 7001

Tasmanian Association of Disabled Persons
20 Greek Road
Lenah Valley Tas 7006

Disabled Persons Bureau
PO Box 1701
Darwin NT 5794

HOME HELP

Home Care Service
31 Macquarie Street
Parramatta NSW 2150

Victorian Council on the Ageing
1st Floor, 449 Swanston Street
Melbourne Vic 3000

Silver Chain Nursing Association
19 Wright Street
Perth WA 6000

Emergency Home Help Service
(Red Cross)
PO Box 161
Civic Square ACT 2608

Tasmanian Council on the Ageing
2 St Johns Avenue
New Town Tas 7008

*Rosebank Home Aid Service for
the Disabled*
Co-ordinator
Rosebank Centre
60 Central Avenue
Moonah Tas 7009

Australian Red Cross Society
NT Division, PO Box 81
Darwin NT 5794

STATE COUNCILS ON
THE AGEING

*New South Wales Council on the
Ageing*
34 Argyle Place
Sydney NSW 2000

Victorian Council on the Ageing
1st Floor, 449 Swanston Street
Melbourne Vic 3000

*Queensland Council on the
Ageing*
1st Floor, Hotel Canberra
Building
318 Edward Street
Brisbane Qld 4000

*South Australian Council on the
Ageing*
23 Coglin Street
Adelaide SA 5000

*Western Australian Council on
the Ageing*
11 Freedman Road
Mount Lawley WA 6050

*Tasmanian Council on the
Ageing*
2 St Johns Avenue
New Town Tas 7008

ACT Council on the Ageing
Hughes Community Centre
Hughes ACT 2605

*Northern Territory Council on
the Ageing*
PO Box 2476
Darwin NT 5794

UNIVERSITIES OF THE
THIRD AGE

Australian Council on the Ageing
1st Floor, 449 Swanston Street
Melbourne Vic 3000

NEW ZEALAND

*National Council of Adult
Education*
PO Box 12114
Wellington North

*National Marriage Guidance
Council*
Private Bag
Wellington

*NZ Association of Citizens
Advice Bureaux Inc*
PO Box 26039
Newlands
Wellington

NZ Senior Citizens Service
PO Box 197
Auckland

Old People's Welfare Council Inc
PO Box 27271
Wellington

*Retired Persons Association of
NZ Inc*
National Office
PO Box 5087
Wellington

All addresses were correct at the
time of going to press. It might be
a good idea to check local
telephone directories for changes.

Index

prevention, 81
signs, 221
Hypnosis 207
Hypoglycaemia 253
Hypotension 267-8
Hypothermia 235-6
Hysterectomy 259-61

I

Imagery training 28, 81
Immune system 131
Impotence 91, 107, 116, 172, 173
Inactivity-stress syndrome 34
Income 61, 75, 102-3
Incontinence 161, 164, 251, 291-4
aids 292
Indigestion 155, 175, 240
Injury 151, 154
Inquest 103
Insomnia 57, 58, 92, 101
during menopause, 168, 170
patterns during depression, 87, 88
Institutional care 280
Insulin 247, 253
Intelligence 76
Intercourse
frequency, 108, 113
painful, 168
see also **Sex**
Intertrigo 137-8
Intestines 156, 238-9
see also
Gastro-intestinal tract
Iodine treatment of thyroid 165
Iridectomy 245
Iron 19, 233
Isolation 86, 94-5

J

Jaundice 241
Jaw realignment 149
Jewellery 180
Jogging 49-51
Joints
in arthritis, 228-32
effects of exercise, 35
injuries to, 154

K

Kidneys 162
check-ups, 53
gout, 231-2
infection, 175
surgery, 262
Kinsey report 108, 109, 111
Kitchen, planning 298-9

L

Laxatives 243, 244
Learning ability 67
Legs 151
Leukaemia 212
Libido, loss of 91, 168, 173
Librium 65
Lifting 39
Lip-reading 147, 287
Lips, making-up 183
Liver 62, 241
Living-room, planning 304
Loneliness 94-6
Long-sightedness 143
Luncheon clubs 128-9, 280
Lungs 54-5, 159
see also **Chest, X-ray**

M

Make-up 135, 181-3
Mammography 54-5, 213
Marital relationships 72
Masculinity 73
Mastectomy 214
Masters and Johnson 109, 111, 112, 113, 114, 171, 173
Masturbation 110, 114
Mattress 36, 38, 58
Meat 19, 23, 24-5, 33
Meaning of life 9
'Medical' *see*
Check-ups
Memory 35, 67, 91, 169, 226
Ménière's disease 253-4
Menopause
age of onset, 167-8
female, 54, 86, 166-70
male, 170-3
Menstrual cycle 167-8
Mental agility 66-9
Metabolic rate 18, 157-8
Migraine 78, 81, 176
Milk in diet 20, 24, 32
Minerals 19, 132
Mitchell, Ross 99
Moisturizers 133, 135, 181
Monilia 241
Monoamine oxidase inhibitors 92
Monoplegia 222
Mood 62, 85, 90
Motivation 75-77
Mouth 148-50, 241
Muscles 152-5
effects of exercise, 35
flaccid, 225
spastic, 225

N

Nail care 152
Neck 138, 139
Neurosurgery 262
Nursing 283, 286-9
checklist for daily living, 289
Nutrition *see* **Diet**
Nystatin 241

O

Occupational therapy 234, 281
Oestrogen 167, 168, 215, 216-7
Old age, definition 14
Orgasm, female 107, 110, 111-2
Orgasm, male 107, 114
Osteoarthritis 228-30, 248, 277
Osteomalacia 232-3, 256
Osteoporosis 153, 159, 168, 232, 255-6
Otosclerosis 146
Ovaries, surgical removal of 259

Acknowledgments

Dorling Kindersley would like to thank the following for their help and assistance: Warren Mitchell and Gordon Dungate for their hard work on the typesetting and make-up; Jonathan Dean; Choice magazine for pre-retirement; Disabled Living Foundation; Les Greenyer; The Harrow Health Care Centre; Michael Sobell Day Centre; Pearl Posner; Rita Roberts; Saga Holidays plc; Dr John Schetrumpf; and all those who took the time and trouble to be models for reference shots and photographs. Hair by James of Vidal Sassoon for jacket photograph of Dr Stoppard.

Illustrators
David Baird
Andrew Farmer
Elaine Keenan
Edwina Keene
Patricia Ludlow
Coral Mula

Photographers
Maria Bartha
Geoff Dann
Nancy Durrell-McKenna
Peter Fisher
Paul Fletcher
Andrew de Lory

Picture Agencies
John Watney
Zefa UK Ltd

Typesetting
Rowland Phototypesetting (London) Ltd
Text Processing Ltd

Lithographic Reproduction
Repro Llovet, Barcelona